THE PASSION

THE STORIES BEHIND 125 YEARS OF CANTERBURY RUGBY

ISBN: 0-9582535-1-X

Set in Palatino Regular 11/13pt

Design by Tristan Brehaut for Willson Scott Publishing Limited
Email: design@willsonscott.biz

Printed in China by Everbest Printing Company
through Willson Scott Publishing Limited,
Christchurch, New Zealand
Email: publish@willsonscott.biz
www.willsonscott.biz

Distributed by Nationwide Book Distributors
info@nationwidebooks.co.nz

THE PASSION

THE STORIES BEHIND 125 YEARS OF CANTERBURY RUGBY

PHIL GIFFORD

willsonscott
PUBLISHING

This book is dedicated to my wife, Jan,
for staying patient when I got grumpy,
and to the large number of
Canterbury rugby players
who have managed
the very difficult feat of
staying decent human beings
when they became rugby heroes.

- Phil Gifford, August 2004

FOREWORD

To me, there will always be something special about Canterbury rugby. As someone who had the good fortune to wear the red and black jersey, you'd probably expect me to say that. But when you look back, as this book does, on the 125 years since the Canterbury Rugby Football Union was formed, how could you not feel warmly about the men who made the history?

Many of us love rugby because there's a place for all players, whatever the shape, size or speed. In Canterbury, our heroes have ranged from someone like Fergie McCormick, a ball of hard muscle from head to toe, to Andrew Mehrtens, with his skill and a rugby brain like a computer; from giants like Bob Duff and Tiny Hill to Graeme Bachop, mixing it with men head and shoulders taller than him.

What joins us all is a love of the game, and a determination to make sure that, if you play against Canterbury, you'll be facing a team where mates help each other out and surrender isn't an option.

It's been a great 125 years so far. Let's look forward with hope and great expectations to the next 125.

-Tane Norton, August 2004

CONTENTS

ILLUSTRATIONS

Willson Scott Publishing would like to thank
the following people and organisations. Each of whom have made
generous contributions towards the photographic content of this book.

Ken Baker
Tiny Hill
Dion Kerr
Geoff Sloan
Andrew Tizzard
Kerry Walker

Canterbury Rugby Football Union
Christchurch Star
New Zealand Rugby Museum

Richie McCaw, from sweeping the flat to sweeping up field.

CHAPTER ONE

GAME DAY

It's big-game day for Crusaders flanker Richie McCaw. At 7.35p.m. a Super 12 semifinal between the Crusaders and the Hurricanes will kick off at Jade Stadium. With nine hours to go, he's cleaning the Riccarton house he shares with Nigel Hall, Marcus Gargiulo, and fellow All Black, Ben Blair.

'I gave the floor a sweep and the carpet a vacuum. I had nothing else to do, so I thought I might as well do something constructive.'

It's not that McCaw is a tidiness freak; just that, like most professional players, he finds the long hours that drag through to a night game a dull burden. He hadn't set the alarm in his bedroom on this occasion, and didn't wake until nine o'clock.

'That's quite a big sleep-in for me. I actually don't like sleeping in, but you're trying to fill up the day as much as you can.

'There was an opportunity to stay in the team hotel, and some guys do, but I find it's better to be in your own bed, and with a long day it's better to stay at home.

'We don't get together until 2.30 in the afternoon, so the whole morning's free. It's probably the most boring time you have during the week.

'You can't go and do anything because you've got your mind on other things. In the past I've tried watching footy – gone to see my little cousin playing – but I feel distracted.

'I have my normal breakfast, some cereal and toast. No different to any other day. I find that if you start doing other stuff your body's not used to it.

'I sleep pretty easy usually. They do reckon that two nights before a game is when you need the big sleep but, to be honest, before this game the nervousness wasn't quite as much as it could have been.

'I always make myself toasties at about midday. I throw in the old favourite ham, cheese, onion and tomato. I pop down to the local service station and got a bottle of Powerade and some water.

'I spend about half an hour sipping through that, to fill the time in, really. Then I'll go for a walk just to do something different from sitting around. I wander through some back streets where nobody recognised me.'

Tom Matthews, running on five Weet-Bix, not 21.

In Merivale 11-year-old Tom Matthews wakes early and immediately thinks ahead to the pre-season game his St Andrew's College under-12 team will be playing against Medbury School.

Initially he forgets that his parents, Hugh and Sonya, are away for the day, but then remembers he'll go to his game, just down the road at St Andrew's, with his grandfather, Ron Cox.

He decides an All Black-sized helping of Weet-Bix is ideal preparation for the game, so he piles up 21 before his grandmother insists he limits himself to five, with cold milk, followed by some toast.

He changes into his blue St Andrew's jersey and white rugby shorts. The extra touch is a pair of gloves as first worn by the Highlanders in the Super 12. 'I only use them if the ball might be slippery,' says Tom. 'They're the Rugby Tec brand. I got them this year for about $10.'

As long as he can remember he's always played in boots, which is pretty handy when there's still frost on the ground at ten o'clock. 'I can remember one game where the mud had frozen into ridges. There were little tiny cuts on my legs from the ground. I like it best when it's muddy. You're all black from mud on one side, then when you turn round you're all white on the other side.

'I've also played tennis and athletics. I do a bit of sprinting, some running in cross-country.'

An hour before the eleven o'clock kick-off he asks his grandfather to come to the school with him so he can have some kicks with his friends.

'Tom,' asks Ron Cox, 'what do you expect me to do? Stand round in the wet grass for an hour?'

By 10a.m. Ron is standing in wet grass for an hour on a crisp Christchurch morning as Tom and his mates boot a ball back and forth.

Dion Kerr, sandwiched by two Old Boys players, is never happier than when he's playing in the dark red and blue of his Sydenham club.

At Dion and Cath Kerr's home in Hoon Hay, there's a bit of a sleep-in until 8.30a.m. for the former Canterbury and New Zealand Maori player, now turning out in senior club play for Sydenham.

Their sons, nine-year-old Thomas and six-year-old James, have their sports gear laid out from the night before. Four-year-old Olivia will be on the sideline at Thomas's game.

'I generally eat a lot the day before, more than on game day,' says Dion. 'So I just had some porridge with the kids, and then I took Thomas to soccer, to play for Cashmere, and Cath took James to rugby, to play for Sydenham Red, he's Cantablack. They chose what sport they wanted to play.

'Thomas played at Summerfield Park, where they drew one-all, and James' team lost by two tries. The soccer game was at 10.30, and they play for a good 40 minutes. Thomas tried really hard the whole game, and after the game I told him how proud I was that he'd given his all.

'Olivia asked me what I was proud of her for. I said, "Aw, you only moaned for half the game." She was actually really pleased about that.'

The family gets together at the Kerrs' business, Reptiles, on the Main South Road in Sockburn, which they started in 2001. They import ceramic tiles and sell to the trade and the public. On most Saturdays, when his club has a 2.30p.m. game, Dion will be there until one o'clock.

So it is on this day. 'We were all at work for about an hour or so, helping out the other staff. Then we came home. Cath bought some ham rolls for lunch, and we went down to Cashmere playground. I got a couple of coffees at Coffee Culture, we had some lunch and the kids played. Cath and I just talked.'

Richie McCaw is still whiling away the hours. He absently watches the Discovery channel, but his mind is not really on the habits of African birds of prey.

At last it's time to get into his green Ford Falcon, supplied as part of his All Black contract, and drive to Jade Stadium for a 2.30p.m. check-in.

He picks up his shorts and socks waiting for him at the ground, and leaves his No. 1 formal gear – Canterbury blazer, white shirt, tie, grey trousers and dress shoes – in the team's changing shed under the new west stand. It's a legend in the Canterbury side that Norm Maxwell once forgot his shoes and attended an after-match function in collar and tie wearing football boots with the studs screwed out.

But at 2.30p.m. on game day McCaw is still in a tracksuit and trainers. 'We go out on the field, run through a few moves together, run the ball through the hands, and do a few lineouts, for 20 to 30 minutes, just to get the feel of things and in the right frame of mind.

'From then we start to build towards the game. Before then I try to not think about it as much as possible. By three o'clock we're finished.'

Now comes the drive back to the Cotswold Hotel in Papanui Road. This is the first real contest of the day for the players, all of whom have gone to Jade Stadium in their own cars. The limited number of parking spaces at the hotel mean that on game afternoon there's a premium on not missing green lights.

There are rooms for the units of players inside the team, so McCaw shares his thoughts with the loose forwards, captain Reuben Thorne, Scott Robertson and Sam Broomhall.

At 3.30p.m. there's a meal, dictated by sports nutrition experts. This is definitely fuel, not haute cuisine. 'It's usually pretty boring, mashed spuds, chicken, spaghetti, things like that. I used to struggle eating at that time and would run out of puff during a game. I had to learn to eat enough to keep me going. Normally I have a good piece of chicken and a bit of potato.

'There's a match programme sitting on the table for the game, so I have a flick through that while I'm eating.'

The profile on McCaw in the programme gives the bare details, born on the very last day of 1980 in Oamaru, 1.88 metres tall, weighing 105 kilograms, first a Canterbury rep in 2000, an All Black since 2001.

What it won't say is that he's already regarded by good judges as the best openside flanker the country has produced since Michael Jones emerged at the 1987 World Cup. That team-mates in the Crusaders reckon he sometimes gets penalised by referees because his ability is so great the refs can't believe it's possible for him to make a tackle, and bounce back to his feet so quickly that he can then legitimately steal the ball.

Todd Blackadder's verdict on Richie McCaw: "The guy's got everything."

It won't mention that at Lincoln University his studies were so outstanding that a senior staff member swears that if McCaw wasn't already committed to professional rugby he would be almost guaranteed a Rhodes Scholarship. 'He's not just an A student,' explains the academic, 'he's an A+.'

It won't mention that he's managed to keep himself sane and level as adoration levels among the public soar. The son of a farming couple, he's travelled the world but still slips the odd 'crickey' into conversation when he's amazed by something.

And it won't mention that after just one training session his captain, Todd Blackadder, was privately praising him to the skies. 'This guy's got everything,' said Blackadder at the time. 'He's strong, he's skilled, he's fearless and I reckon he could be as good as any loose forward Canterbury has ever had.'

Dion Kerr and his boys drive to Sydenham's home ground, Sommerfield Park, where the seniors will be playing Christchurch, who shape as formidable opponents. He takes just his boots and socks. The jersey and shorts will be in the changing shed.

For James and Thomas this is familiar territory. There's a playground there, and they usually act as ball boys. The team co-coach Alan Edge's little boy, Oliver, is always there as well.

'Our boys have been part of that team from the time they could walk,' says Dion. It's the second round of the town competition, and the teams are all eight games in. Sydenham are battling, getting frustratingly close but not quite winning the nailbiters.

That Kerr is still playing senior rugby in 2003 is almost an accident. He's been a committed Sydenham man since he was a child, turning out for the under-10s, alongside another club stalwart, future Canterbury and Crusaders halfback Aaron Flynn.

After playing at halfback for the Xavier College First XV, Kerr was called into the Sydenham seniors as an 18-year-old first five in 1988.

A self-described 'chirpy chap', he needed resilience to keep enthused during a career that saw him play for the New Zealand Colts and New Zealand Maori, and appear in two All Black trials, but struggle to seal a Canterbury spot.

At first it was Greg Coffey, a classy player with great goal-kicking skills, who prevented him being a regular starter, and then, as Coffey was about to leave the scene, 'along came a guy called Mehrtens.' Dion did manage 27 games for Canterbury, including a Ranfurly Shield challenge and a game against Ireland, but would end his NPC career as an import player for Nelson-Bays in 1997 and Marlborough in 1998–99.

Through it all his devotion to Sydenham never wavered. 'It's a club with a wonderful culture, and this extends right through the grades. Everyone is part of the club. People do things for the right reasons, not self-interest. Players don't leave Sydenham unless there's a very good reason. That tells you a lot.'

The glory days for Kerr and Sydenham came with four successive titles from 1996.

'When we won in '96 it was wonderful for Sydenham. Finally it had happened (the last time Sydenham had been champions was in 1948). In '97 it was special, because in the final we beat an old rival, Marist-Albion, and the way we played the second half on that freezing day was unbelievable.

'The third win, in '98, didn't have quite the same impact, perhaps because we did no more than what was expected of us. But in '99 the support and enthusiasm was back again.

'That was probably because, after seeming unbeatable for so long, we struck a bad patch and only just sneaked into the final. I will never forget that game, mainly because our whole season came down to the last five or six minutes, when Old Boys were on a roll and throwing everything at us.

'It was a character test and we came through. That's what made it special. It was a team effort, no-one panicked. All the hours of training and team talks had prepared us for this and we held together. In many ways it was the most satisfying of the four championships.'

Kerr himself was the stand-out performer of the 1999 season for Sydenham. John Durning would write in Red and Black, his annual round-up of Canterbury rugby, that 'Kerr was the side's dominant figure and playmaker. A yard slower in pace, but more composed than in earlier years, his generalship was the key to the team's wonderful record.'

By the start of 2003 Dion Kerr was playing fifth grade for Sydenham. 'I hadn't played seniors for a couple of years. When we started our business I had a couple of years when I wasn't that interested in playing. I helped coach our division-two side in 2002.

'Then we were out early this year with some friends, and I just thought, 'It'd be quite nice to play again.' My brother plays with the Sydenham Cavaliers team in the fifth grade, so there was no choice which team I was going to play for.

'I had a couple of pre-season games with the Cavaliers, and then the senior team started having a lot of injuries. [Coaches] Bob Kerr and Alan Edge rang me up and said, 'Would you mind reserving for one game?' I haven't played for the Cavaliers since.

'One week I played first five, then I played fullback because the regular guy was injured. So I've been filling in, and I haven't really filled out.

'Every week Edgy rings me, or I ring him, to find out if I'm going back to the Cavs. I've been lucky enough to have the nice days when we've won, so I like helping out with the guys that haven't had that good fortune.'

Tom Matthews has been playing rugby for five years. Like his older brother James and younger brother Chris, he started playing age-grade footy for the Christchurch Club.

'Some of my friends from then are going to other schools, but we've stayed friends.'

In Tom's first year at St Andrew's, in 2003, year seven, the equivalent of the old form one, there were trials for the under-12s and all the players were asked to nominate two positions they would like to play. Tom picked second five or centre.

He was picked at centre, a big change from his previous year for Christchurch Club and Elmwood School, where he'd been at No. 8 or the side of the scrum.

Rugby runs on both sides of the family. Maternal grandfather, Ron Cox, played senior rugby for Belfast and grade rugby for Canterbury. Paternal grandfather, Norman Matthews, was a Southern club man and had a couple of games for Otago.

Go further back into the family tree and you find an All Black, great-great-uncle Don Cameron, a tiny but very fast winger from Taranaki.

Never weighing more than 10 stone 6 pounds (66 kilograms) at any time during his career, he was eighteen when he first played for his province in 1906. When the Taranaki team was assembling for a southern tour Cameron was standing on the platform at the Hawera railway station with Taranaki selector, Dan Malone, waiting for the southern train to pull in.

The 1905–06 All Blacks Originals forward, Jimmy O'Sullivan, disembarked and started chatting to Malone. 'I say, Dan, who's the nipper?' he was reported in a local newspaper as asking. When the nipper was revealed as a new team-mate, an embarrassed O'Sullivan apologised profusely. He explained, 'I thought maybe he was the mascot.'

In 1908, still only twenty, Cameron played all three tests against the Anglo-Welsh

When Tom Matthews and his team from St Andrew's College play there's a lot of chasing.

team in New Zealand, scoring a try in each of the two tests the All Blacks won. He was twice offered places in All Black teams touring Australia, in 1907 and 1910, but turned both chances down because he had to work.

Tom Matthews, his father notes, is more a doer than a watcher, which means it may be some years before he pursues more history on Don 'Racecourse' Cameron, as his great-great-uncle was known.

Tom's rugby heroes play for Canterbury. 'Leon MacDonald is really good, and I like Justin Marshall a lot. I've got a poster of Andrew Mehrtens up on my wall.'

Three hours away from the first whistle and Richie McCaw gets into a settled routine.

'About 4.30 I go and have a shower, then at five o'clock I go down and have my thumbs and my back strapped by the physio, John Roach.

For Richie McCaw emptying the tank in a game is a motto he lives by.

'We all amble in at that time, and by 5.15 I've got time to kill again before the team meeting just after six.'

McCaw impressed playing rugby at Otago Boys' High School before moving to Christchurch to attend Lincoln University.

The Canterbury rugby system picked up on him very quickly. He was brought into the provincial squad in 2000, but that year in the NPC, and again in the 2001 Super 12, injury prevented McCaw from showing his range of abilities.

However, at the end of 2001 NPC coach, Steve Hansen, moved All Black Scott Robertson from the open side to the back of the scrum to accommodate McCaw.

'We all knew Richie had the attributes a good openside flanker needs,' Hansen told Rugby World magazine. 'He is very brave on the ball, he is a strong tackler, and he is intelligent. He has a remarkable sense of where to be out there. A remarkable sense of timing.'

As six o'clock draws near, time at last starts to move quickly for McCaw. 'I write down a few things I want to achieve during a game. Some of what I write has been a focus all season. But for this game the first one is to make my tackles. I fell into a trap at times of looking for the ball before I finished my tackle off.

'Another focus was to get an effective clean-out. To link with the backs and give them support. Another one's to empty the tank, to beat the guy I'm marking to the ball everywhere I go. That's my goal there. The last one is to enjoy it.

'They change a little bit each week. I don't read it, but I think about it while I'm writing it down, to get the old mind ticking.

'At six o'clock I usually go and throw my bag on the bus. At 6.10 there's a team meeting where the chairs are lined up in a circle. We go in there and by now the guys are pretty quiet.

'The coaches [Robbie Deans and Don Hayes] come in and say their last bit. They talk about the set pieces. There's a quote that's new each week. Something along the lines of what you bring to the moment is what makes the moment. At the time it sinks in, but the next day I often can't remember what was said. It's what happens during the week that makes the difference.

'The team talk only takes a few minutes and we're on the bus quite quickly. It's quiet there too. Some guys have headphones, but that's not really my scene.

'I sit beside Joe Maddock. Everyone has their set seats. It isn't worked out, it just happens to be the way it is.

'As you get older you move further back. I'm still near the front of the bus. The bus always goes the same way to the ground, into Bealey Ave, down Barbadoes Street, into Fitzgerald Ave.

'You get a few people waving, a few horns tooting. By about half-past six we're at the ground. I'm one of the first to get into the shed, where all the jerseys are laid out for us. My bag has a couple of pairs of boots in it.

'I usually go outside in my T-shirt and tracksuit for a wee look round. At 6.40 I come back in and do a bit of extra strapping on my wrist and fingers.

'Ten minutes later I have all my gear on apart from the jersey, and go to a big room we use for a warm-up. I have a jog, chuck the ball around.

'At seven I do fifteen minutes on my own for a warm-up. I do the same every week, some stretching, a bit of a run. It's repetitive but at the end of it you feel you're ready to go.

'At 7.15 we come together for a team warm-up, which involves four different drills: handling, clean-outs, some lineouts and scrums, then a D (defence) drill.

'Eight minutes before kick off we pop back into the shed, I get my jersey and headgear on and then, with about two minutes to go, we all come into a huddle, Reuben says a few words, and out we go.'

Tom Matthews played touch rugby in the summer and says he loves intercepting the ball. 'That's really fun. I like to run with the ball. A real big tackle, if someone has made a break and you just tackle him, that's good too.'

In the St Andrew's midfield on this morning, there aren't many chances to run. At this level there's a lot of individual effort and a lot of chasing. Just before the end of the first half, with his team trailing, Tom punts the ball 30 metres downfield, there's a scramble on the Medbury line, and a St Andrew's player scores a try. There are seemly scenes of congratulations all round.

At full time, however, Medbury have won 19–14. Tom returns to his home with his grandfather. He and his bothers have all played rugby that morning, and they refuel with pizza and chips, cooked by their grandmother. Tom feels today's game was 'all right.'

The Sydenham seniors know they're up against it when they play Christchurch. 'They've only lost three times in the last three years,' notes Dion Kerr.

Trailing 19–14 late in the game, Sydenham tries everything to bridge the gap. From a move in the Christchurch 22, Kerr finds the dancing feet of old, slipping past tacklers and diving in between the posts for what looks like a try that, with an easy conversion, will win the game.

Just as team-mates race in to hug him and slap his back, the referee's whistle blows for an earlier infringement. The try is disallowed. The match is lost.

'It was so disappointing,' says Kerr. 'We got so close and just a couple of things let us down. The real heartbreak was when I went in under the posts, but that's the way it goes.

'What was disappointing was that we've been trying so, so hard. This is the hardest that a team's ever tried in any outfit I've ever been involved with.

'The level of training on a Tuesday and Thursday, the level of spirit and commitment, and all the great things about rugby haven't diminished in any way. There have been more bad times with results than there have been good things, but the spirit has stayed the same.

Dion Kerr and his son Thomas. The Kerr family are all regulars at Sydenham during the season. For Dion it's a commitment that started when he was at primary school.

For that reason I've been enjoying it.

'They're not really bad losses. We're only just missing out.'

Club rugby at senior level for Dion and his team-mates is played purely for the love of the game.

'There's no money for the players. Six or seven years ago there were some players in Christchurch who went to clubs for money, but that doesn't happen at Sydenham.

'The club will try to get the boys jobs, but we don't pay any money to individual players.'

After the game many players stop and chat to friends and family before heading to the changing shed.

'They encourage everybody to eat, things like bananas and bread, and lemonade, sometimes a few beers.

'We all sat around after the Christchurch game for an hour or more just gassing, which is good stuff. No different from anyone else I guess. That's what club rugby is about.'

The Hurricanes have come to Jade Stadium with some hopes of making the final. They have stars in Tana Umaga, Christian Cullen and Jerry Collins, and have produced some of their best rugby ever in Super 12. It is also a fact that, in the previous three or four years, Wellington and Hurricanes teams had posed more problems to Canterbury and Crusaders sides than more highly fancied outfits.

'A lot depends on whether the Hurricanes really come to play,' former All Black and television commentator, Murray Mexted, had said before the game. 'If they do, it'll be a fascinating contest.'

It's soon obvious that the Hurricanes have come to play. But the Crusaders have come to win. Before half-time the Crusaders have shunted the Hurricanes pack back, tipped them over and walked over the top of them.

For Richie McCaw, it was a defining moment in the game. 'When we walked over the top of them their heads dropped and it felt like we had it over them after that. We put a bit of pressure on their lineouts too, and we picked off a few takes.

'Just before half-time we had a crack at the corner and, though we didn't actually score, we felt we were really getting on top of them.

'At the break we talked about how they'd come out knowing they only had one crack at it, and that first ten minutes after half-time they'd have to lift up a level.

'They did, scored a try and got back to six points. We had to grind them back down again, but once we got the last try she was all over.

'In the second half I got cracked on the eyebrow and had to go into the blood bin. I went straight into the changing room to get it fixed. The doctor put in three or four stitches and the adrenalin was pumping. I'm a bit rude to the doc at those times. I started saying, 'Get in there, get in there.' There's a TV set in the changing shed, and it's quite strange watching a game going on that you're playing in.'

The brief time out seemed to work for McCaw. Within a minute of being back on the field he plunged over for a try.

A place in the final sewn up, the Crusaders can relax after the game. 'We took over an hour to shower, get changed and cool down a bit. We had some music on. I'm in charge of the music committee, with Caleb Ralph. We usually do a couple of team songs, and always sing 'The Search for the Holy Grail.'

'After a game you've won it's easy to get the boys going. It's harder when you lose.' McCaw laughs. 'A couple of times we've had no music.

'After we've been in the shed we have a couple of awards, then change into our No. 1s and go to the official after-match function with partners, wives, girlfriends, parents. We also pop into the Supporters' Club.

'At about 11.30 we get on the bus and go to the Holy Grail (the Crusaders' official bar in Worcester Street) for a feed in a bar up the top of the building. We have a few beers together and then you're free to do what you want.'

"When we walked over the top of them their heads dropped."

Rugby had a fertile nursery at Christ's College in the 19th century, and that tradition is still strong today.

CHAPTER TWO

BEGINNINGS

Let us now praise famous Canterbury rugby men and begin with the first captain of a New Zealand team, William Victor Millton.

His life story reads like a Victorian melodrama, filled with youthful achievement, local and national leadership, heroism, and a tragically early death.

It is also entwined with rugby and the first steps for the game, both in Canterbury and New Zealand. Millton was born in Christchurch on 10 February 1858 and attended Christ's College, where several staff members were former English public schoolboys who enjoyed a game that had its origins at Rugby School.

A plaque is now displayed at Rugby, stating that a boy called William Webb Ellis, 'with a fine disregard for the rules of football as played in his time, caught a football and ran forward with it, thus originating the distinctive feature of the rugby game. A.D. 1823.'

Rugby historians have argued for many years over whether Ellis was really the first Rugby School pupil to run forward with the ball, or just a damned good spin doctor. But while the legend may be questioned, it will certainly never die, not while Ellis's grave in Menton in France is cared for and treated like a shrine by French rugby people, and while the official title of the World Cup is the Webb Ellis Cup.

What can be stated with certainly is that rugby, if not quite as we know it, had a fertile nursery at Christ's College. By 1862 the school had its own rules for football, with a game played on a field 150 yards long and 76 wide. Most games had no limit on the number of players, and a goal was scored when the ball was kicked or thrown between the goal posts.

Christ's College did not have a monopoly on the game in the colonial city of Christchurch. Our local hero William Millton grew up in a town where football, of various kinds, had been played virtually since the arrival of the Four Ships, with 800 settlers, in 1850. Possibly, considering that the Deans brothers, William and John, the forebears of Robbie and Bruce, settled on the Canterbury Plains in 1843, football might have been played even earlier.

While Christchurch grew as a settlement, the rules of rugby were loose and in dispute.

William Victor Millton, a hero of shipwreck and rugby ground.

Despite this, interest bloomed in the sport, both in the town and in the rest of the Canterbury province.

When the Christchurch Football Club, the first rugby club in New Zealand, was formed in 1863, a founder, R. J. S. Harman, was an old boy of Rugby, so you might have expected that school's rules to be adopted.

But the Christchurch Club's game actually sounds more like a variation of Aussie Rules, with the ball having to be bounced every four yards. 'Arguments over the rules were commonplace,' it would be written later, 'and sometimes play would be held up for several minutes while a point was being settled.'

By 1876 the arguments were finally stilled at the Christchurch Club. They agreed with Harman, who would be club president for 36 years, that the laws as defined by the Rugby Football Union of England in 1871 would be officially adopted.

But, a year earlier, the South Canterbury Football Club had formed in Timaru, and on 24 May 1875, Queen Victoria's Birthday, South Canterbury played a North Canterbury team, composed largely of players from the Christchurch Club, in Ashburton.

The previous afternoon the South Canterbury players set out on a Cobb and Co. stagecoach from Timaru, stayed the night at the Waihi Crossing, and finally reached Ashburton by rail truck at 11.30 a.m., just half an hour before the planned kick off.

The players then had a 3km walk to the ground, a paddock on the Wakanui farm of John Holt, which fell away from one goal line to the other.

South Canterbury's captain, a lawyer called Alfred St George Hamersley, was on a visit to New Zealand after being an English international for the previous four years, and England's skipper in 1873. As a 68-year-old he would later command British Heavy Artillery in the First World War. In the campaign of Wakanui farm he needed all his leadership skills when, after he lost the toss, his men played the first half not only against the wind but battling uphill.

Despite the problems for South Canterbury, they held on for a draw and, with only enough time left for manly handshakes with their opponents, raced away so they could ford the Rangitata River before night fell. Late that night, in pouring rain, they arrived back in Timaru. They all agreed, said a report of the time, that it had been 'a wonderful occasion.'

But the gutsy effort wasn't enough for the *Timaru Herald*. Rugby might have arrived, but so had media criticism. 'The strength of the Southern team was all forward,' grumped the paper's rugby writer, 'the backs having little to do, and not doing that little well.'

Exactly four months later, on 24 September 1875, came the first-ever visit to Christchurch by a visiting team. Fittingly, it was a squad from Auckland. Seventeen touring players arrived in the city by sea from Dunedin at 11a.m. for a game that afternoon against the Christchurch Club. Earlier in the tour, for Auckland's games against the Wellington Club and Dunedin's combined clubs, it had been the same pattern of playing just a couple of hours after arriving.

On game day, shops and offices in Christchurch closed for the afternoon and three thousand people, about a quarter of the town's population, ringed the field at Cranmer Square to watch a one-sided victory, Christchurch winning 9½ to nil. (At the time a try was worth two points, a conversion four points, and touching down the ball behind your own line conceded half a point to the opposition.)

The Aucklanders weren't big men by today's standards, 11 of the party weighing in under 70kg. However, *The Press* reported that 'the heavier weight of the (Auckland) forwards told against our lighter players, but owing to the deficiency of back players the advantage they had gained was thrown away.'

Did the Aucklanders cop anything untoward in Canterbury? Not on the field. According to the *Lyttelton Times*: 'The whole match was beautifully played. The greatest fairness and good humour prevailed, and though many a heavy tumble occurred in the course of the afternoon, not the slightest ill-will was evinced.'

Certainly not from the crowd. Judge for yourself from *The Press* report: 'We were glad to see the friendly way the game was conducted, and every piece of good play, especially on the part of Auckland, was loudly cheered.'

No jeering from the reporter over the loss either: 'Although Auckland did not score a point, yet it must not be forgotten that they had only just landed from a sea voyage, and had very little time to recover.'

Meanwhile our fresh-faced champion, 18-year-old William Millton, still at Christ's College, played in a trial game and gained selection in a Canterbury team for a northern tour in 1876.

The Press reported that 'as the time for sailing [to Auckland] approached, some of our best players who had promised found that business prevented their going at the time appointed. However, although the selection committee has met with these disappointments, they have selected a team that will fairly represent the province.'

Eventually three fullbacks, three halfbacks and twelve forwards set off for Auckland, most from the Christchurch Club; some, as in Millton's case, from Christ's College; and others from North Canterbury, Kaiapoi and Temuka.

Here's something that may not be a surprise. The Auckland media started bagging the Canterbury team before the squad had even arrived. Eighteen days before the game the *New Zealand Herald* claimed that 'we have heard that one of the Christchurch team arrived by the Hawea yesterday, and will, no doubt, try to find out the weak points in our team, and report thereon for the benefit of his friends.'

The game itself, on 31 August, attracted a crowd of a thousand people to Graham's Gardens in Ellerslie, despite heavy rain. There was a half-hour delay because the local officials had forgotten to bring a ball, but eventually, on a muddy field, the first clash of the provincial titans was won 7–3 by Auckland.

'The play of the Canterbury forwards was superb,' it was reported in Auckland, 'but although many of the Auckland team played well, there was a lot of loafing outside the scrummages, as is often the case nowadays.'

After the Auckland game, the Canterbury team reboarded the *Hawea* and sailed for New Plymouth, where a game with Taranaki was scheduled. But the weather was too rough for the ship to berth and so the Canterbury men sailed on to Nelson, where they beat a local selection 12–0, and then to Wellington for an 18½–1 victory over a combined Wellington-Wairarapa team.

In 1877 it was time to start the rivalry with Otago. A team representing the Dunedin and Dunedin Union clubs set out to play a six-game tour of New Zealand, which it would eventually finish undefeated.

This hadn't been a good year for the game in the north, after a fatal accident involving an Auckland club player who broke his neck in a tackle. The district coroner, Dr T. M. Philson, in his findings, suggested that 'the game of football was only worthy of savages.'

But for the game in Christchurch, where the Dunedin clubs would face a combined club team, enthusiasm was high. Five thousand people thronged Cranmer Square on 8 August, and the fans were astounded by the way the men from the deep south played the game.

Dunedin based its game on passing rushes, whereas Christchurch preferred the old ways of dribbling the ball and driving in the forwards. By the time it was over the innovative southerners had won 4–0.

That loss bit deep. The following year, instead of traditional Christchurch-Merivale and South Canterbury-Temuka club games, there were trial matches and new clubs such as North Canterbury, based in Rangiora and Kaiapoi, were invited to join the trials.

It all paid off when, on 28 August 1878, what is regarded as the first game between representative teams from Canterbury and Otago was played at the Caledonian Ground in Dunedin.

Heavy rain made the ground wet and slippery, and play was mostly a forward slog. At the time, the match was promoted as the unofficial championship of New Zealand, and the arm wrestle ended in a scoreless draw.

All of these games had been played without the benefit of a Canterbury Rugby Union. It took a visit by an Australian Rules team to force the issue.

A Rules side from Victoria came to Christchurch in 1879, and the popularity of the games they played galvanised local rugby men, most notably Montague Lewin, who had emigrated from England in 1873.

A small man, even by the standards of the time, Lewin sported a waxed moustache that twirled out past his cheeks. He was a gamecock too on the playing field, flinging his small frame into action without any concern for his own personal safety.

He joined the Christchurch Club and in 1875 tried to get the rules of the English Rugby Union adopted. That attempt failed, as did his efforts to get rugby played with a round ball, to help dribbling skills. But Lewin was well-liked and he was a good boardroom politician. In 1876, working in conjunction with Christchurch Club president, R. J. S.

Harman, the decision to play England's rules in Canterbury clubs was unanimous.

On 26 July 1879, after a game between the South Canterbury and North Canterbury Clubs in Timaru, a meeting was held at the Grosvenor Hotel with representatives from South Canterbury, Christchurch, Temuka and Ashburton.

Picture the scene in that smoky room. Most of the men were young enough to have played that afternoon, and above their starched collars and woollen suits, bruises and abrasions marked faces that became more flushed as the evening wore on. Churchgoing was a huge part of life then, but men of the day weren't necessarily wowsers. There were already half a dozen breweries flourishing in Canterbury, and the average settler drank three gallons of spirits a year.

There would have been a mixture of accents. Lewin, who in later years was never seen without a monocle, had a voice that would not have been out of place at Eton. As the night wore on, others would speak in less genteel tones, using phrases that were then considered more American than English, like 'no fear' instead of 'certainly not' and calling a stream a creek.

Lewin was elected to the chair, and he wasn't thinking small. He proposed calling the organisation the New Zealand Rugby Union and to invite other clubs in what was then a colony to join in.

In the course of the meeting it was agreed that perhaps that was just a tad ambitious. Eventually it was agreed to form the Canterbury Rugby Football Union, the first in New Zealand. Later in the year a union was formed in Wellington, followed by Otago in 1881, Auckland in 1883, and Hawke's Bay in 1884. The English Union had been founded in 1871, but the Canterbury Rugby Football Union is actually older than the Welsh Union (1880) and the Irish Union (1881).

The clubs that made up the first Canterbury Rugby Football Union were Christchurch, Christ's College, Temuka, North Canterbury, South Canterbury, Eastern, Ashburton and Southbridge.

There was little division between officials and players. Lewin was still playing for Canterbury at the time he was elected union secretary. Treasurer, William Millton, was 21 when the Union was formed.

A year earlier, in 1878, Millton had shown that his bravery wasn't limited to the rugby field. He would be noted for his heroic role in the shipwreck of the *Melrose* off Timaru. A local report says that 'the dauntless fashion in which he plunged again and again into the boiling surf full of broken spars and wreckage to save life was not more marked than the perfect silence which he afterwards kept of his share in the day's events. To him it seemed he had not done anything out of the ordinary.'

Millton was described by his contemporaries as someone with a 'gift to be able to mix with the roughest and most thoughtless of lads and men and yet always remain in the side of the good. He managed to maintain a spotless character without acquiring the fatal reputation of being a saint. There are few young men who can honestly do this. He did it.'

Photographs of the time reveal him as a fit-looking, open-faced man with deep-set eyes, who continued to play rugby and cricket as he studied to qualify as a barrister.

He was a talented cricketer too and, in the summer of 1883–84, travelled around

New Zealand captaining the Canterbury cricket team. However, Millton toured with an ambitious plan that had nothing to do with cricket.

In 1882, a New South Wales rugby team had toured New Zealand, and the fourth of the seven games was against a Canterbury team captained by Millton. New South Wales won 7–2, but it was even closer than the score suggests, the local referee disallowing three tries after Canterbury men had crossed the line.

The visitors, the first overseas team to visit New Zealand, were well-liked. At the intervals, with most games played in four 30-minute quarters, they shared cold drinks and chatted with the opposing team. By the end of the tour, when they issued an invitation for a return visit by a New Zealand side, Millton and a Dunedin businessman, Samuel Sleigh, decided to put a team together.

Remember that at the time the formation of the New Zealand Rugby Union was still eight years away, so during his cricket travels in the summer Millton was very much the entrepreneur as he negotiated with rugby officials in Auckland and Wellington. It wasn't just a grand adventure he was suggesting, it was also an expensive one.

But he was a persuasive man and, by May 1884, nineteen players, from as far south as Invercargill to as far north as Auckland, were confirmed to travel to Australia.

There were no trials, no announcement at NZRU headquarters (because there wasn't one), but the team is now universally recognised as our first national side.

It wasn't easy getting the squad away. Auckland three-quarter Bob Whiteside wanted expenses to tour and, when that was declined, withdrew. Some other first-choice players, including the originally selected captain, George Campbell from Wellington, had to withdraw because of work commitments.

There were other hiccups. Aucklander Joe Warbrick, who four years later would organise the famous Natives tour to Britain, missed the steamer from Auckland to Wellington to assemble, and had to travel directly to Sydney on his own.

Southlander James O'Donnell was arrested on a fugitive warrant in Clinton, while on a train north, and was returned by police to Invercargill to face tradespeople he owed money to. For reasons lost in time his creditors failed to turn up when he appeared in court, so he was able to join the side for a practice game against a Wellington team. (When the tour was over O'Donnell chose to stay and live in Sydney.)

It was still a strong team which assembled in Wellington, where the players voted to decide on a captain. Millton, whose younger brother Edward was also in the squad, was elected.

The *Hauroto* was held up at the wharf so Millton and his men could finish a warm-up match against Wellington. The game duly won 9–0 by the tourists, they washed off the mud from a slushy Newtown Park and set off for Sydney on the afternoon of 21 May 1884.

Four days later they arrived in Sydney, signalling their intentions by running a football up the masthead of the ship.

These pioneering tourists were not, strictly speaking, the All Blacks. They played in a dark blue jersey with a gold fern. The black jersey and silver fern would first be worn nine years later.

Millton played and captained the side in seven of the eight games in New South Wales. In the only game he didn't play, he acted as one of two umpires (there was no referee) when New Zealand played a Combined Suburbs team. He started the tour at fullback but after the first game played in the forwards.

Team manager, Samuel Sleigh, described Millton as 'the right man in the right place. A steady dribbling forward, always near the leather. His good-natured, unselfish play tended in no small degree to make the games pleasant and at the same time successful.'

The team was certainly successful, going through the tour unbeaten and winning what amounted to the three tests against New South Wales, 11–0, 21–2 and 16–0.

The games were played in two halves of 45 minutes, with a try worth two points, a converted try five points, and a goal from the field four points. Millton top scored on tour, with 35 points, from four tries and nine conversions.

The *Sydney Sportsman* said that the New Zealanders were 'a fine body of men, well-built, and with their muscular powers fully developed, although their dark uniforms made them appear thinner than they really were. By their side the New South Wales men appeared very light. From the first they were over-matched by the visitors from Maoriland.'

Feted by rugby officials and Sydney politicians, the players were farewelled with praise for their modesty, their 'refusal to cavil at umpires' decisions' and playing with good nature and forbearance.

The tourists were welcomed back to Wellington by festooned boats, and Millton would continue the gentlemanly talk at a banquet hosted by Governor Sir William Jervois. If ever a team didn't need a captain, said Millton, it was this one, as every member played a most unselfish game, and their whole desire was to return with a good record.

As well as his rugby, Millton continued with his cricket, captaining Canterbury against a touring England team in 1886.

His remarkable life ended on 22 June 1887 when, just 29 years old, he died of typhoid in Christchurch.

Before the turn of the century, the rules of rugby would have been largely recognised by today's players, but the style was quite different.

The measure of a rugby man then was how well he could shove in a scrum. A future Prime Minister, George Forbes, played for the East Christchurch Club, which would be gone by 1887, largely absorbed by Linwood. East Christchurch had the gun team of the day in the late 1880s but can't have been much fun to watch. Forbes, a halfback, said years later that a good match was one that contained almost nothing but scrums, varied by the odd dropped goal. In one game at Lancaster Park in 1886, East Christchurch beat Merivale 20–4 by five dropped goals to one.

Teddy Francis kicked three of East's droppies and would recall that 'we would play two halves, three three-quarters, and a fullback. The plan was for the halves, when they were in the opponent's quarter, to get the ball and whip it to the centre three-quarter, with the object of giving him a shot at goal.'

The first game between two officially formed New Zealand provincial rugby unions took place on 27 August 1881, when the new Otago Union sent a team north to face

Canterbury at Christ's College. They slugged it out for four 25-minute spells, with Otago scoring a goal and a try to beat a scoreless Canterbury.

Rugby first came to Lancaster Park on Easter Monday 1882, when sports fans had a double treat. A cricket match between Canterbury and Wellington was played, and in the lunch interval a rugby match between East Christchurch and South Canterbury was contested, East winning by three goals to a try.

Games were also played at Hagley Park, but the flocks of sheep which still grazed there made the fields unattractive for players who didn't want the whiff of manure on them when the game ended. There was another trick too. In an 1887 match, an East Christchurch player, F. Fuller, dived across for what he believed was a winning try but he had actually grounded the ball over what proved to be a well-worn sheep track.

Representative fixtures were a novelty, not a regular feature, but there was certainly a demand for them from the public. In 1885 Canterbury beat Wellington 6–0 at Lancaster Park, in a game played in heavy fog on a muddy surface. W. Bean kicked the dropped goal that won the match. How excited were his team-mates? The game stopped while they hoisted him on their shoulders and marched him round the field to the wild applause of the crowd.

When Canterbury had beaten Otago the previous year in Dunedin, six thousand people packed the Caledonian Ground to see Teddy Francis pot the goal that secured Canterbury a 4–1 victory.

By the end of the 1880s, most referees were using a whistle to control play, but it was a Canterbury man, W. H. Atack, who was the first to do so. He would later say, 'the referee had to use his voice to stop the game, and when both sides were appealing the voice had to be exercised loudly, and I found it exhausting. Thinking it over one day my fingers strayed into a waistcoat pocket, where they encountered a dog whistle. The inspiration came to me that it would be a fine thing to use the whistle to stop the game. The next time I refereed I called the teams together and they agreed to play to the whistle. It was a great success, and was speedily adopted all over the country.'

So now we've got to rep games, playing at Lancaster Park, and referees whistling rather than shouting. All that was required now was the chance to play a full international team.

That milestone arrived in Canterbury in the shape of the 1888 Great Britain tourists. The game with Canterbury on 5 May (there were no test matches on the tour) drew a new record crowd to Lancaster Park of six thousand people. Great Britain won 14–6, and just four days later won again, 4–0. Between the rugby games, the Great Britain side played a Canterbury cricket team and won that match too.

By the end of May, the British were on their way to Australia, where 15 games were played. In August, the first of several personal tragedies struck the team when its captain, Bob Seddon, drowned while sculling on the Hunter River.

Despite the shocking loss of Seddon, the tourists continued, returning to New Zealand for ten more games, including a third encounter with Canterbury, which they won 8–0.

All three games with Canterbury were refereed by the Reverend John Hoatson from the Trinity Congregational Church in Manchester Street. Nothing too unusual about that, except for the fact that Hoatson was also a Canterbury selector. Apparently he took his religious beliefs seriously, records of the day showing that, while not everybody agreed with his selections, he was a fair and impartial referee.

The British tour, while approved by the England Rugby Union, was privately organised, and you can see why some thought it was jinxed. The loss of a small fortune on the tour by promoter Arthur Shrewsbury would be followed by his suicide less than five years later. Andrew Stoddart, the star player who took over the captaincy when Seddon died, would also commit suicide, shooting himself at his home in London in 1915.

If ill fortune followed the tour for the British, what Canterbury rugby people got from the visitors were new ideas in the game, most notably the dummy pass in the backline and, as hard it might be to believe now, the concept of rucking. Until Great Britain toured, it was considered by New Zealanders that the act of the forwards heeling the ball back for the backs to play with it made the forwards offside.

The next eye-opener came not from an international side, but from the Alhambra Club of Dunedin, who visited Christchurch on 16 August 1890 for a match at the old A&P Showgrounds (later Sydenham Park) against Merivale.

At the time, Merivale was the powerhouse of Christchurch club play, with men like the brilliantly named 'Tiddly' White, 'Baldy' Lang, and 'Dutchy' Evans overwhelming most opposing teams. Evans bemused tacklers with his special trick of flicking the ball from one hand to the other on the run.

But the southerners stunned Merivale and two thousand spectators by passing the ball and then, to local astonishment, backing up and handling again in one movement. Their forwards also regarded the main job as getting the ball to their backs rather than holding possession themselves until the backs had a chance to kick for goal. As part of that plan, Alhambra also had a player who stood between the halfback and the three-quarters, and controlled most of the game.

Until then most teams played with two halfbacks, and then the three-quarters. What should they call the new position? A Merivale player, F. Childs (apparently without a nickname) reckoned five-eighths would do the job, and thereby invented a new phrase in the sport.

The passions aroused by club footy were high. As well as Merivale, Linwood and then Kaiapoi had potent combinations. But it was the fans at a game between East Christchurch and Sydenham in 1891 who made headlines. East won 7–2, but when the game was over referee T. L. Smith had no time to hang around for a discussion of finer points of law.

He was chased from the Sydenham ground up Colombo Street all the way to Moorhouse Ave by a mob who threw clods of dirt and stones at him. Smith later blamed the Sydenham team members for not protecting him. Yes, he conceded, there were rumours that he'd taken bets on the game, but he emphatically denied this.

Such behaviour was 'inexcusable' thundered the *Lyttelton Times*, and a special meeting of the Rugby Union banned one Sydenham player for a year, and another until the end of the season, for using obscene language and questioning the referee's decisions.

The committee also warned Sydenham that if another referee was chased off the park, there would be no more games at the Club's ground. Sydenham initially picked up the ball and went home, resigning from the Union, but after several meetings they agreed to stay.

On-the-field lessons learnt from Alhambra in 1890 came back to haunt Otago in 1892. Canterbury prepared by travelling to Auckland and whipping the blue and whites 24–0 at Potters Paddock, now the Alexandra Park trotting track. Then the team headed south.

South Canterbury was spanked 44–0, and in Dunedin the first victory over Otago for seven years was achieved, 7–4. Even the traditionally frantic Christchurch welcome that has greeted the Crusaders and Canterbury Ranfurly Shield teams in recent years was probably topped by the fans of 1892.

When the steam train from Dunedin arrived the day after the game, a massive crowd was at the station to welcome the footballing heroes. The Canterbury players climbed onto a horse-drawn dray ready to be taken to the Commercial Hotel for celebrations. That wasn't quite good enough for the supporters, a horde of whom unharnessed the horses and pulled the dray to the Commercial, the procession made even more festive by a hundred bandsmen blowing cornets and banging bass drums.

When Otago returned the next year there were two thousand people to meet them at the station, and six thousand lined the streets to the Clarendon Hotel. On the field Canterbury again prevailed, 5–2.

Canterbury and Otago needed each other at this time because they were estranged from virtually every other provincial union in New Zealand. In 1891 the first meeting to try to form a New Zealand rugby union was held in Wellington. A draft constitution, including the resolution that the new national union would 'discourage lavish expenditure in the entertainment of visiting teams in the form of dinners of smoke concerts', was written.

But the following year, when the time came for provincial unions to commit, Canterbury, along with Otago and Southland, expressed strong opposition to the idea of a national union. The man promoting the NZRU, journalist Ernest Hoben, was surprised by Canterbury's stance. In the summer of 1891 he had met Canterbury's management committee, which voted 7–2 in favour of joining the New Zealand union. 'In doing so they misled the promoter [Hoben], as they did not represent the views of the Canterbury players,' it was reported. All seven men who had voted to join the union lost office when Canterbury's annual general meeting was held early in 1892.

The stumbling block for Canterbury was something that didn't change for the next 94 years. Until 1986, living in Wellington was a prerequisite to be on the NZRU's executive committee. In words that would be echoed for the next nine decades whenever rugby officials were unhappy with NZRU decisions, the 1892 Canterbury Union said that a New Zealand union would put 'the whole of the management in the hands of Wellington men.'

Hoben was angry. If Canterbury and Otago wanted to stay away, 'it was their loss.' He was disappointed to hear threats that Canterbury and Otago would not play with unions affiliated to the proposed national union. If the southern unions' officials had so thoroughly misunderstood and misread the suggested constitution, 'I am not surprised at them deciding not to join the new union. I have done all in my power to bring Canterbury and Otago in, but if they will not come others will not stand still on their account.'

The New Zealand Rugby Union was officially formed on 16 April 1892. Hoben was elected secretary, and the meeting, which had started at 7.30p.m., was declared closed at midnight.

The ill feeling continued through 1893, when Canterbury refused to play against South Canterbury, which had joined the NZRU, and Canterbury, Otago and Southland players were not considered for the 1893 New Zealand team to Australia, the first to play in black a jersey with a silver fern.

It took another year for the tide to turn. When the East Christchurch Club sent a telegram to Hoben wishing the New Zealand team to tour Australia every success, the NZRU secretary wired back that he regretted the lack of the province's players in the side. Canterbury's general meeting was now divided on the issue.

In 1894 the change of heart was complete. Canterbury joined the NZRU, followed soon by Otago and Southland.

Goodwill between Canterbury and Otago was strained in 1896 when 'Dutchy' Evans, by now a referee, disallowed a try to Otago, with Canterbury winning 6–5. The southerners appealed, first to the New Zealand Union, and then, when that was unsuccessful, displayed colonial cringe by appealing to the English Rugby Union. That worked and the game result was altered to give Otago an officially recorded victory of 8–6.

In club rugby the characters who make rugby so fascinating kept emerging. In 1896 Ngai Tu Ahuriri, a team based on the Maori pa near Woodend, produced W. Uru, a 100kg winger. The average weight of a forward then was just over 80kg, and the heaviest forward in the 1905–06 All Black team to Britain was 95kg.

Yet here was a wrestling and tug-of-war champion, flying down the wing, whose party trick was the ability to kick goals with a heavy leather ball in his bare feet.

You didn't mess with referees then, either. After a heavy defeat at the hands of Canterbury College, a Merivale player said, 'I don't think much of the referee.' His remark was overheard and he was cited, then banned for the rest of the season.

But overall the love of rugby in Canterbury was heating up as the turn of the century neared. When a Canterbury team in 1898 toured the North Island, beating Hawke's Bay, Wellington, Wairarapa and Wanganui, and losing only to Auckland, the welcome home was ecstatic. The players marched single file into the rooms of the Chamber of Commerce for an official welcome, while the Fox Brothers String Band played 'See the Conquering Heroes Come'.

Joining the NZRU had again given Canterbury players the opportunity to wear the New Zealand jersey. When New South Wales toured in 1894, there were three Cantabrians in black when the only intercolonial game was played, at Lancaster Park.

William Balch, who would later be the headmaster of Shirley School, was a three-quarter; Alf Cooke, who would die just six years later in a hunting accident at Lake Ellesmere, was the halfback; and George Humphreys, who had emigrated to Christchurch from Wolverhampton in 1887, was a loose forward. The first New Zealand team to play at Lancaster Park lost 8–6.

In 1905 there was the unusual situation, repeated just once more, 52 years later, of a New Zealand team playing at Lancaster Park, not against a touring side but against Canterbury.

Preparations for the first All Blacks tour to Britain at the end of 1905 had begun in 1904, when a group of 53 players from whom the touring team would be selected was named by the NZRU.

In July 1905, a squad of 26 players was named for a three-match tour of Australia, preceded by a game against Auckland and followed by games against Otago-Southland, Canterbury and Wellington Province.

The touring team was unbeaten after five matches when it faced Canterbury midweek on 27 July 1905. It wasn't a sparkling display, although New Zealand won 21–3, and on the Saturday, against Wellington, New Zealand lost 3–0.

Because the game in Wellington was played on a ground as slippery as a skating rink, hopes were still high when, on Sunday morning, 30 July 1905, the first New Zealand team that would be called the All Blacks, sailed on the *Rimutaka* for their journey to England.

In that team, which would play 35 games in Britain, France and the United States, five Canterbury men initially got the selectors' nod.

One, halfback Peter Harvey, had to withdraw before the tour. He was a lip-reading teacher at the Sumner School for the Deaf and was refused leave. His case went all the way to Parliament, where Prime Minister Richard Seddon announced that Harvey could not be spared as he was the only man teaching lip-reading in the whole country.

Those who did travel were George Gillett, fullback in four of the tests on tour, who would later play league and establish the code in Wellington; Eric Harper, a national 880 yards champion in 1902 with a time of 2 minutes 2 seconds, who played one test on the wing against France, scoring two tries; Fred 'Fatty' Newton, a railways fitter, who locked against England and Wales and was on the side of the scrum against France; and Bob Deans.

Deans would be the central figure in one of the great legends of the New Zealand game – 'the try that never was' – in the test against Wales.

The great-uncle of Robbie and Bruce Deans, Bob was the baby of the Originals, just 21-years-old, but his character reflected a man much older than his years. Every Sunday morning, like clockwork, he would be off to church, making sure he had gathered a group to go with him. His kindness was remarkable. Team-mates would recall later how those who were short of money would find a five-pound note pressed in their hand.

His attitude is best summed up by a practical joke that Bill Stead, the vice-captain, played on him. Stead took Deans' gold watch from his room and waited for his reaction. For a couple of days nothing was said. Finally Stead could wait no more. He approached Deans and asked if he'd noticed something missing and why hadn't he mentioned it.

Deans replied that the only people who could have stolen the watch were his team-mates, whom he knew would never do it, and the two chambermaids, and they 'had honest faces.'

Bob Deans' character becomes important to the story because, with no moving or still cameras to record the occasion, it was only eyewitnesses who could vouch for what happened when the All Blacks played Wales at Cardiff Arms Park.

What can be stated with certainty is that, with his team down 3–0, Deans raced to the Welsh line, where he was tackled by a Welshman. (Most reports say the player was Teddy Morgan, but some say it was Rhys Gage.) The referee, a 27-year-old from Scotland, John Dallas, disallowed the try. It was the only game the All Blacks lost on tour.

But should the try have been awarded?

Deans' version of what happened was stated clearly and briefly in a cable on 17 December 1905, the day after the test, to the *Daily Mail* newspaper in London: 'Grounded ball 6 inches over line. Some of Welsh players admit try. Hunter and Glasgow can confirm was pulled back by Welshmen before referee arrived. Deans.'

Hunter was Jimmy Hunter, the All Black midfielder; Glasgow was Fred Glasgow, a loose forward.

On the other hand, when he arrived back in Edinburgh, referee Dallas would report, 'On the Monday morning I was astonished to read in the papers that Deans had scored a try I had disallowed. When the ball went back on its way to Deans, I kept going hard ahead and when Deans was tackled he was grounded six to twelve inches short of the goal-line. At that moment he could neither pass nor play the ball and I blew my whistle shrill and loud. It is true that when I got to the spot to order a scrum the ball was over the goal-line, but without hesitation I ordered a scrum at the place where the ball was grounded. I never blew my whistle at the spot. It was gone before. No try was scored by Deans.'

In the years after the incident, Welshman Teddy Morgan would confirm that Deans had scored, and so would, without exception, the All Blacks who were there, especially Billy Wallace. In many ways the legend grew greater because there can never be a definitive verdict.

For Bob Deans there would be only three more years playing for Canterbury and the All Blacks. He led Canterbury to a 13–8 victory against the Anglo-Welsh team in 1908, and his last test was against the Anglo-Welsh in Auckland, where he scored a try. Two months later he would die at the family's Homebush property in Colgate from an attack of pneumonia following an appendix operation.

The start of the twentieth century saw the first of many great Canterbury inside-back combinations emerge. Halfback Paddy Burns, first five Doddy Gray and second five Joe Weston all played for Albion and their combination for club and province was described as being 'near to wizardry.'

Burns was a Lyttelton boilermaker, so fast that on the 1910 All Black tour to Australia he played one test on the wing and two at centre. Gray was regarded as one of the greatest first fives to ever play for New Zealand, a runner and passer but rarely a kicker. A stocky timberyard worker, he was described by a rugby writer as 'keen witted, never flurried, and a constant source of anxiety to the opposition, every ready to spring something unorthodox.' Weston would never play for New Zealand but, in 1909, was good enough to join Gray and Burns in the South Island team that beat the North Island 19–11 in Wellington.

You might have thought that at some point Canterbury would have taken aim at the Ranfurly Shield, which was presented at half-time in the 1902 inter-island game in Wellington to the Auckland Union by the then Governor of New Zealand, Lord Ranfurly.

The talent was certainly there. Canterbury had stars in the backline, and it had tough forwards too. Men like blacksmith Bernie Fanning, who started his rugby with Kaiapoi and, at age 20, made the Canterbury side when he moved to town and played for Linwood.

Described then as the best forward in the All Blacks, he played 56 games for Canterbury between 1895 and 1904 as a powerful, ruthless lock who was said to hold the scrum together like a vice. His younger brother, Leo, wrote that Bernie 'wasn't exactly a born footballer, but he started with a splendid quantity of raw material, bone and sinew tempered in a blacksmith's forge.'

So there were class players, and there was passion. In 1909, after Canterbury lost 3–0 at home to Auckland, the *Lyttelton Times* reported that 'a small section of the spectators hooted the Auckland team as they left the ground in their drag.' (Drag then, by the way, was a horse drawn cart, not women's clothes.)

Talent, passion, eager to beat Auckland? Sounds like a recipe for a swag of Ranfurly Shield challenges. Actually, no. The Shield wasn't the magnet it would later become. The major reason was simple: the money it cost to challenge. Normal provincial games in the early 1900s saw the host union spilt the gate proceeds with the visitor. But the Log had its own rules: all the cash stayed with the host union.

No wonder that from the time the first Ranfurly Shield game was played in 1904 (Auckland losing the shield to Wellington), Canterbury, after losing the first challenge to new holders Wellington 6–3 the same year, challenged Auckland in 1906, were beaten 29–6 at Alexandra Park, and didn't bother to challenge again until 1910. In fact, in 1909 Auckland played just one challenge game.

That year the Auckland Union's president, disturbed at what he saw as the shield's adverse effect on club rugby, said that it might be a good thing if someone took the shield and lost it on the way to Wellington. If that wasn't possible, Aucklanders wondered if the shield could go in the cupboard at the NZRU and not be competed for until five years had passed.

The Ranfurly Shield, in fact all rugby, became a minor issue in 1914, with the outbreak of the First World War. Patriotism swept the country and, by 1916, the senior competition in Christchurch was abandoned, with the top grade restricted to players aged under 20, to make sure, Union officials said, that 'shirkers' from the war effort would not be able to play.

In 1917 and 1918 no play at all was possible on Lancaster Park, as the ground had been dug up and planted in potatoes. Some of the proceeds went to assist the troops, and some to help meet costs at the ground, where no major games meant no gate takings.

If the very young men still playing club footy became over-enthusiastic, they were quickly reminded of where that energy should be aimed. A Marist v. Linwood game which ended in a scoreless draw was, said the *Christchurch Star*, 'an appalling travesty labelled rugby football, showing to what depths of degradation a noble sport may be dragged. Too many players disregarded all sportsmanlike feelings, and played the man not the ball with a ferocity that would have been more appropriately employed against the ravagers of Belgium.'

Another scoreless draw, between Marist and Merivale at the Hospital Corner ground, saw police swarm over the sideline crowds, checking that men attending all had military certificates that forgave them service.

In July 1919, with peace restored, a huge crowd turned up at Lancaster Park to see a Returned Soldiers team play Canterbury. The rugby was hard and entertaining, and the occasion was festive. At half-time players and officials were treated to afternoon tea by the old Merivale star, now the former president of the NZRU, 'Dutchy' Evans and his wife. Going into the second half, the well-fed soldiers, who had been ahead 9–0 at the break, started to struggle and Canterbury led 10–9 into the last minutes of the game.

Up stepped Harry Davis, a Linwood man just back from service in France with the 1st New Zealand Expeditionary Force. His last-minute penalty goal won the day for the soldiers, 12–11.

Davis had to retire from rugby with a chronic knee injury in 1923, when just 27 years old, but he was already a Canterbury selector, and by 1924 was a South Island and New Zealand selector. He was part of a seven-man panel in 1924 that picked 19-year-old George Nepia to be the only fullback for what would be the All Blacks' unbeaten tour of Great Britain and France. Many years later, at his beloved Linwood club, he would help develop another rugged, fearless fullback, Fergie McCormick, who would be a pallbearer when Davis died in 1977.

By the time the Invincibles were selected, Canterbury rugby was in the middle of a golden decade, the 1920s, when the province beat South Africa, won the Ranfurly Shield for the first time, produced 25 All Blacks, and 13,665 people (an attendance record for a club game that stands to this day) flocked to Lancaster Park for a club final to see Marist beat Merivale 6–3.

The 1921 South Africans, the first Springboks to tour New Zealand, arrived in Christchurch undefeated and were quickly the toast of the town. They were granted honorary membership of the Christchurch RSA and the Liberal Club, and the giants of the team, 'Baby' Michau and 'Royal' Morkel, both over 17 stone (110kg), posed for a photograph at Riccarton racecourse with an apprentice jockey who has the haunted, rigid look of a lamb asked to relax for the camera while standing between two hungry lions.

The welcome wasn't so warm at Lancaster Park. Rain pelted down on the day of the match, and by the afternoon the surface was greasy and muddy.

Spotting 12kg a man in the forwards, Canterbury struggled to compete at set plays, but in the loose it was a different story, as the local pack, led by the team's sole All Black, Bill Cummings, and captain Cecil Murray, rushed from breakdown to breakdown.

Second five Colin Deans, the younger brother of Bob, was a key man in both Canterbury tries. A Deans' kick to the wing set Albion's G. R. Wilson free for a try in the first half. Although a dropped goal, then worth four points, saw the 'Boks lead 4–3 at half-time, two minutes after the break Deans kicked ahead and bustled South Africa fullback, Gerhard Morkel, into a weak clearing kick. The ball was grabbed by the other Canterbury wing,

Merivale's Jockey Ford, who crashed over in the corner. Canterbury won 6–4.

The home forwards were chaired off the ground by spectators, who might fairly have hoisted Canterbury coach 'Nuts' Hasell as well.

'The gallant Canterbury forwards,' reported the *Christchurch Sun*, 'battled untiringly against a much heavier mass of brawn.'

Hasell would later tell journalist Larry Saunders how he devised the tactics for the game: 'I knew the South Africans were good at picking up the ball, but our fellows were good dribblers, and the ball was slippery. So I said to our forwards, "Don't try to pick the ball up. Just skid it along the ground, not too far at a time, and keep on chasing it."'

The first successful Ranfurly Shield challenge came in 1927, at the Showgrounds in Palmerston North against Manuwhenua, a hybrid union formed when Manawatu and Horowhenua combined in 1925.

By now Canterbury had a host of All Blacks. The entire backline had either already played for, or inside the next year would play for, New Zealand.

Fullback Jack Harris, who would die in 1944 fighting in Italy during the Second World War, had played for the All Blacks against New South Wales in 1925. Winger Alan Robilliard, an Ashburton flier, was in both the 1924 All Blacks and the 1928 All Blacks to South Africa, while the other wing, Jack Steel, a professional sprinter from the West Coast, was the top try scorer on the 1924 tour with 21 tries. Centre Syd Carleton was a rugged tackler, but his forte was setting up his wings with slick passes, a talent that saw him play three tests on the 1928 tour of South Africa, and three tests in Australia the following year. Second five Herb Lilburne was playing senior rugby for Albion as a 16-year-old, and in 1929, when just 21 and 112 days old, became the youngest-ever captain of the All Blacks when he led the side against Australia. Canterbury's captain and first five-eighths, Neil McGregor, toured in 1924 and again in 1928, and was famous for his courage under fire. One of the country's greatest coaches, Norman McKenzie from Hawke's Bay, claimed that McGregor would 'stop a train, or try to.' Halfback Bill Dalley, a stock agent from Leeston, was with Robilliard and McGregor in Britain and South Africa, and on the latter tour he was one of the stars, a powerful, quick runner with the ball and a scrapper on defence.

In the pack front-rower Jim Burrows toured South Africa in 1928, and his leadership qualities would be demonstrated in the Second World War when he commanded the 20th Battalion of the 2nd RNZEF and then the 4th and 5th Brigades, winning the DSO and Bar. Fellow front-row foward Frank Clark played all three games for the All Blacks against New South Wales in 1928. Lock Geoff Alley, the brother of Rewi Alley, who would become a legend for his work in China, was a giant of his day and toured South Africa in 1928. Loose forward 'Son' White had toured in 1924, when he was described as 'the team's best forward in the loose, the most perfect player in control of the ball, follows up fast and is a demon on defence and attack.' Wing forward George Scrimshaw would beat Cliff Porter, captain of the Invincibles, for a place in the 1928 tour to Africa.

As might have been expected with all that talent, Canterbury beat Manuwhenua 17–6, Robilliard scoring two tries and Dalley one. Dalley kicked a goal from a mark, Lilburne a conversion and Carleton a penalty goal.

By the time the shield season of 1928 arrived, Canterbury was short of eight players, on tour in South Africa with the All Blacks. Despite this, the shield holder easily disposed of the first challenge from South Canterbury, 29–9, but the next, a Wednesday game against Wairarapa, was always going to be tougher.

The challengers were led by Bert Cooke, a midfield back so gifted that the great George Nepia would say he sometimes 'had to really concentrate during a game when I was at fullback [for the All Blacks], because I'd find myself just watching the man with my mouth dropping open.' It wasn't just Nepia who was impressed. The Prince of Wales, later King Edward VIII, described Cooke, at a 1924 London luncheon for the All Blacks as 'the little rat.' Cooke asked the prince, who said he had watched eleven games the team had played, why he called him that. 'The way you dart at a hole,' Edward replied. 'You are quicker than a rat.'

His Royal Highness had one thing right: Cooke was little. When he was weighed for the 1924 tour he was 8½ stone (54kg). Worried that selectors would see such a lightweight as too small for test rugby, Cooke later claimed that he persuaded the doctors at the weigh-in to list his weight as a still-less-than-dreadnought 9 stone 12 pounds.

Size was never an issue on the field. Quicker than professional sprinter Jack Steel over 50 metres, Cooke was also an impeccable tackler ('they can't run with their knees jammed together'), a great handler, with a superb sidestep, and a trick of kicking the ball ahead, then gathering it and racing away without a hand laid on him.

He brought all his gifts to Lancaster Park in 1928, but a crowd of 20,000 red and black fans must have thought the Log was safe when, late in the game Canterbury led 7–3. Rugby historian, Arthur Carmen, described what happened next. 'With time running out Cooke seemed to divine [Wairarapa first five] Cundy's purpose to kick, and sped up to gather the ball almost off Cundy's boot, beat his opponent in a twinkly run to the line, and then touched down midway between the uprights. Not trusting anyone else he sent a low kick over the bar to win the match and the shield.'

As Cooke left the field, a woman he later claimed was the mayoress of Christchurch confronted him and growled, 'You little cheat.'

You little genius might have been a fairer call. *The Press* reported the following day: 'It wasn't Wairarapa who took the Ranfurly Shield from Canterbury. It was Cooke. Cooke is the player of the century.'

If it was the mayoress who berated Cooke, she might have felt better had she known that better times with the shield for Canterbury were close at hand. The successes of the 1920s were just a taste of what was to come.

When the manager of the 1930 Great Britian team, James 'Bim' Baxter, was asked why his side wore clashing dark blue jerseys he replied 'Because dark blue is the colour of Great Britian's rugby representatives,' end of discussion. The All Blacks played all three tests in white.

CHAPTER THREE

BATTLES

Times were tough in the 1930s. The Wall Street crash of 1929 had started the Great Depression, and life in New Zealand soon included, in the words of historian Keith Sinclair, 'the ragged army of men on the dole; architects, teachers and carpenters chipping weeds on the footpaths; malnutrition in the schools, and children stealing lunches; ex–servicemen begging outside a pub; and the queue at a soup kitchen.'

Christchurch suffered with the rest of the country. In 1927, as the city's population neared 100,000 people, £846,461 was spent on new buildings. By 1933 that figure had plummeted to £130,045.

The Canterbury Rugby Football Union offered free passes to relief workers, the men the government paid to cut trees, to dig drains, to do any job that needed little capital but a lot of labour. The pittance these workers received made paying even threepence to see club rugby beyond their means.

Yet the decade in rugby began with huge promise. First, there was the game against the 1930 Great Britain team (not yet called the Lions), which drew a crowd of 25,000 spectators to Lancaster Park.

This was the second-to-last year that the 2–3–2 scrum was used in international play in New Zealand. While the British, South Africans and Australians were using a front row with three men, in New Zealand a two-man front row was employed in a seven-man pack, with the eighth designated forward called the wing forward.

At scrum time he stood with the backs on defence, and the manager of the 1930 Great Britain team, James 'Bim' Baxter, a silver-medal-winning rower for England at the 1908 Olympics, was determined to stamp out the use of the wing forward.

To give an idea of the sort of man Baxter was, the first question he was asked in New Zealand was why his team wore dark blue jerseys when earlier sides touring from Britain had not worn jerseys that would clash with the All Blacks. 'Because dark blue is the colour of Great Britain's rugby representatives,' replied Baxter. End of discussion. The All Blacks played all three tests in white.

On a tour of Auckland, the rugby league ground, Carlaw Park, was pointed out to

Baxter. 'I suppose every town must have its sewer,' he drawled.

Baxter was unequivocal on the issue of wing forwards: they were, he proclaimed, 'nothing less than cheats.' Baxter had been a member of the International Rugby Board since 1927, and in those colonial times New Zealand didn't even have a seat at the board table. By 1932, the two-man front row and the wingforward were outlawed.

But those issues were still well away from the minds of the 25,000 who came to Lancaster Park on 7 June 1930, when halfback Bill Dalley led out a Canterbury side which included thirteen men who were, or would become, All Blacks.

At fullback, Albion's Herb Lilburne would quickly show his class in a game where he was lauded as Canterbury's outstanding player. He could also play in the inside backs, being good enough to keep the great Mark Nicholls out of the All Black first five-eighths position for the first test against Great Britain in 1930.

Another outstanding Canterbury player, Charlie Oliver, was at second five. Like Lilburne, he started his senior club career at the age of 16, playing for Merivale while working as an apprentice carpenter for New Zealand Railways. Oliver was a hugely gifted sportsman, such a good batsman that he toured Australia in the summer of 1925–26 with the New Zealand cricket team, and missed the rugby season of 1927 because he was in England playing cricket for New Zealand.

There were, as always, some tough, hard men at the centre of the Canterbury pack, critics of the time singling out Jim Burrows and Ron Stewart for their play against Great Britain.

Hooker Burrows was playing his last game for Canterbury, a leg injury sustained in a pupils versus masters game at Boys' High a couple of days later forcing the then school teacher out of rugby as a player, although he continued to represent his province at cricket as a medium-pace bowler, and would soon be Canterbury's rugby coach.

Burrows would be decorated for bravery three times during the Second World War, then rejoin the army in 1950 and command New Zealand's K-Force in Korea in 1954. While in command of the 20th Battalion in 1941, already known by his troops as 'Gentleman Jim', he sent a justifiably famous memo to headquarters after Jack Hinton was awarded the Victoria Cross exactly one week after Charles Upham had been awarded his first VC: 'It would be a convenience if in future the names of the members of the Twentieth Battalion who win Victoria Crosses were published in one list, and not on different days, as appears to be the present practice. Signed, J. T. Burrows, Lieut.-Colonel.'

Stewart, a big, fast loose forward or wing forward, was playing his only season in Canterbury, finishing his career with the red and backs after earlier making the All Blacks from South Canterbury and playing an amazing 18 of the 22 games the All Blacks played in South Africa in 1928, including all four tests.

It was Stewart who set up the first Canterbury try, 25 minutes into the game, with a powerful run, fending off two tacklers before setting a up a ruck that allowed George Scrimshaw, who had been a surprise selection ahead of Cliff Porter for the 1928 All Black tour to South Africa, to plunge over for the try.

A penalty by centre Syd Carleton, who had also toured in 1928, replacing Bert Cooke (who withdrew to be with his ailing wife and newborn son), sent Canterbury to the break 6–0 up.

After half-time Britain rallied and the pressure by their much bigger pack saw a South African Rhodes scholar, Brian Black, who chose to play for England and seven years later would be a world bobsleigh champion, score a try and then, unusually for a middle-row forward, convert it himself. When English flanker Harry Wilkinson scored with 15 minutes to go, Canterbury was down 8–6.

The home team now dug very deep. A long throw to the lineout was delivered straight to second five Gordon Innes, a 1922 All Black against Australia, who streaked upfield. He then passed inside to forward Rex King, backing up from the lineout, who was crossed for the try. When Lilburne converted, Canterbury was back in front, 11–8. Minutes from time, the fullback added a penalty and the match was won by six points.

British manager Baxter scraped up a smile for the official dinner at Warners, saying he 'would like to pay a tribute to the Canterbury team for the magnificent way in which it played the game.' Just to seal the goodwill, the tourists visited Tuahiwi Pa the following day, then made a trip out to Amberley for a hare drive.

The good news for Canterbury continued in 1931, when, after losing 17–14 to Hawke's Bay in Hastings, the province went to Wellington to play for the Ranfurly Shield, which had been secured from Southland in the last challenge of 1930.

Canterbury's second five Gordon Innes scored a try in the first half. Innes was to be an All Black the following year and he might have had a long career in the black jersey. But in 1933 he signed to play league for Wigan and went to England, where he won a unique place in sporting history as the only All Black to ever represent Great Britain at league.

Despite Innes's try, Wellington led 6–3 with just fifteen minutes left on the clock.

Tom Mullan, a former St Bede's boarder who retained as an adult not only the small frame of a schoolboy but also the pluck and liveliness, was at halfback for Canterbury, and he flung the ball clear of a ruck to first five Gordon Day. All afternoon Day had been shovelling the ball on to Innes because the man opposing Day, Mark Nicholls, was considered not just a good but a great All Black, whose special gift was an ability to read an opposing attack and deal with it.

This time Day held the ball, ran straight and hard at Nicholls, and jabbed out a fend that left the great man on the deck as the Cantabrian ran on to score. Years later Frank Kilby, Wellington's halfback that day, recalled how behind the posts Nicholls had stormed up and down the ranks 'explaining everything' as Alby Roberts converted to give the challengers an 8–6 win and the shield.

An outstanding loose forward for Canterbury was Alan Andrews, who would play three times for the South Island, and was selected for the 1934 All Blacks to tour Australia. However, he had university exams coming up, so chose not to go. The chance to play for New Zealand would never come his way again although, after rising through army ranks to become a colonel in the war, he would manage the fabled Kiwi rugby team through Britain and in New Zealand.

On 29 August, a week after winning the Log, Canterbury added to the trophy cabinet the scalp of the touring Australians, a team which included two famous figures in the sport across the Tasman, centre Herbie Towers and forward 'Wild Bill' Cerutti. Once again, this was a close game to the final whistle, fullback Alby Roberts kicking the penalty that sealed the game for Canterbury, 17–14.

The only defence of the shield in 1931 was against Otago, a game won 17–6, and marked by one of the great Canterbury tries.

It was started by loose forward Jack Manchester, who burst away from a maul just a metre from Canterbury's line. He thundered to the 25, where he passed to Gordon Day. Five more men handled before Norm Dunshea crossed for the try.

It was, in many ways, Manchester's bad luck that his reputation as a captain would be damaged by being made leader of the 1935–36 All Blacks, who followed in the wake of the unbeaten Invincibles and suffered what was then the worst-ever test loss by an All Black side, a 13–0 defeat at the hands of England.

Manchester's manager-coach, Auckland lawyer Vincent Meredith, though known to be a brilliant tactician in provincial rugby, was apparently swept into the social whirl of British rugby to the degree that the players were basically running their own show.

In a book on the tour by team members Eric Tindill and Charlie Oliver, the latter was careful to say that Meredith was 'like a father to us.' Sixty years later another member of the side, Jack Griffiths, would tell writer Paul Verdon that the coach, who insisted all players address him as Mr Meredith, was 'so involved with official matters the team did not often benefit from his knowledge at training sessions. Tactics were left to discussion by team members.'

The other burden for Manchester was having to move from loose forward to lock, as the All Blacks grappled with changing to the 3-4-1 scrum. 'In New Zealand,' wrote Tindill and Oliver, '[Manchester] had been always been an outstanding loose forward, but he had to change his style of play by becoming a scrimmaging forward. He led his forwards well towards the end of the tour, but lacked the necessary experience to be a great leader.'

However, in 1932 and 1933, as Canterbury successfully turned away fourteen challenges, leadership wasn't an issue for Manchester. The side was captained by 'Beau' Cottrell from the front row.

Jim Burrows, who had just retired from playing, coached Canterbury during those two seasons and had strong views on what sport did for a young man. 'I've got an old-fashioned idea,' he said in 1966, 'that the team game is important for a young chap. Fourteen other footballers, or ten other cricketers will soon cut him down to size. A boy can play individual sports by all means, but if he misses out on team sport, life will be a little harder. If you haven't got team spirit you've got a packet of trouble, in the army or anywhere else.'

It's high praise for Cottrell, a Christ's College boy who became a barrister, that Burrows called him a 'natural leader, both on and off the field. He was one of the best captains I have ever known.'

Cottrell played eleven consecutive tests for the All Blacks, from 1929 to 1932. In the process he was a hooker in the two-man front rows until 1932, when he propped against Australia in the first three-man front row fielded by New Zealand. He was tough and unyielding, qualities that served him well when, now Captain Cottrell of the 2nd NZEF, he was captured at El Alamein in 1942, lying wounded with half his foot shot away. He would spend the last years of the War in prisoner-of-war camps.

The toughest challenge Cottrell's Canterbury team faced in 1932 came not from Wellington, although it was just beaten, 9–8; not from Auckland, despatched 14–0; and not from Waikato, beaten 17–6; but from West Coast.

It was a golden time for Coast rugby and, when the challengers came to Lancaster Park on 27 August, their team included fullback Mike Gilbert, who would tour Britain with the 1935 All Blacks, and lock Ron King, who would captain New Zealand against the 1937 Springboks.

King was a goldminer, shy and retiring off the field, but fierce on it. He was surrounded by similar blue-collar battlers who lashed into Canterbury. Although Cottrell led the way with a try, converted by Alby Roberts, the defenders led by just 5–3 with five minutes to play.

The Coasters were hard on attack on the Canterbury line when local referee Ernie Empson blew his whistle, not for a scrum or a penalty, but for full time. All around the ground there was consternation. Every other clock there showed at least four, probably five, minutes still to play. The mistake was soon admitted, but not quickly enough for the game to restart. Canterbury officials did what they could to make amends, offering a charity game to be played in Christchurch at the end of the season, with all proceeds to go to the relief of the unemployed on the West Coast.

It's a measure of the Coasters that not only was the offer accepted, but, at the special request of the West Coast Union, Empson refereed a 6–6 draw watched by a crowd of 10,000 people on 1 October.

Leading into the 1933 shield season, the Canterbury team set off on a northern tour that we will never see the like of again. The manager was CRFU vice-president, Irish lawyer, Jack Moloney who, in a 1954 history of the Union, would say that he 'decided to show what could be done in the way of planning a tour in which football would be serious, yet full of fun. We had all the fun in the world.'

The touring team lost 14–6 to Wellington, and then 11–8 to Manawhenua in Palmerston North. 'I was persuaded by mine host at the hotel in Palmerston North,' said Moloney, 'that my charges were jaded, and a drop of champagne would work wonders at the interval. The lads were, frankly, suspicious of the contents, so I sampled it. It was a vintage wine, Heidseck '27, which sat well on the palate.'

The last game on the northern trip, against Wairarapa, was lost too, 11–9, but Moloney said his team 'did achieve a great measure of dash and fire. In these days, when all sport, especially rugby, is in the hands of the cost accountants, this was a wonderful adventure. We arrived home full of confidence to await the onslaught of Southland.'

Sure enough, just as Moloney had hoped, the challengers were well beaten, 21–3, in front of 25,000 people, the biggest crowd of this shield era. The following week, in a much tighter game, the true grit in the Canterbury side saw it come back from being down 5–0 against Otago to win 8–5.

But the real thriller of the 1933 season came in the sixth challenge, from Taranaki.

With less than ten minutes to go, Jack Moloney was asked by the CRFU president to leave the stand and go to the office to get the shield. Taranaki was ahead 15–11 and the game seemed lost.

As Moloney mournfully set off on his task, time on the field agonisingly ticked by. With just two minutes to go, the ball went to Canterbury's first five Ray 'Buck' Hazelhurst, a member of that year's champion Sydenham team, which was led by Hazelhurst's five-eighths partner, Gordon Innes.

In 1932, a dropped goal was worth four points, and would not be reduced to three until 1948. Hazelhurst was almost 40 metres out when he steadied himself, took aim and dropped the goal that tied up the game 15–15 and kept the Log in Canterbury.

That night, to complete a perfect rugby day, Hazelhurst was named in the South Island team. But on the Sunday night his rugby dreams were shattered when he was seriously injured in a motorbike accident. Although he did recover, when he was well enough to play football again, he switched, as many players did in those cash-strapped days, to league.

Fifteen successful defences was the record Canterbury carried into the first challenge of the 1934 season, from Hawke's Bay, but the total would not be increased.

Colin LeQuesne, in the 1960s a hugely successful coach for the Bay, was an astute first five in 1934, operating behind a grinding pack and with a backline featuring Charlie Smith, whose bullocking runs on the wing made it forever a mystery why he was never an All Black.

On a heavy ground Smith scored one of the Hawke's Bay's three tries and the match was lost 9–0. The Bay didn't hold the shield long, though, losing to Auckland, 18–14, in the last shield game of 1934.

It was a huge surprise to rugby fans when the Log was brought back to Christchurch after the second challenge of the next season.

Why the surprise? Firstly, history was against Canterbury. By 1935 the province had gone 43 years without a victory over Auckland in Auckland. Secondly, while Auckland had lost seven players to the 1935 All Black tour to Britain, and the challengers had lost just three, the Canterbury selectors had picked a team that was, reported the *Auckland Star*, 'a mystery team of unknown players.'

The most unknown, outside Canterbury, was the captain, Geoff Parsons, a 22-year-old second five who was playing not just his first shield game but his first game for Canterbury. Parsons scored what proved to be the winning try when he sidestepped through the defence to dot down between the posts. He and his team had to endure a nerve-racking finish when Auckland's former All Black fullback, Ron Bush, lined up a penalty wide out on the 25. The kick was high and long, but just missed the uprights and Canterbury celebrated a 16–13 victory.

The *Auckland Star* summed up: 'Outstarred, outplayed and outgeneralled all the way through the first spell, Auckland, in patches in the second half, played the bright, open and devastating way that is traditional, but the whole side on the way was committed to a dreadful chain of errors, and they certainly did not deserve to win.'

This time the Log did not stay long in Christchurch. There was brief controversy off the field when the Canterbury Union rejected five requests for midweek challenges. On the paddock the fourth match of the season, against South Canterbury, was saved with a last-minute try that left the challengers, as future All Black and national coach, Tom Morrison, would carefully phrase it, 'very hot at the time.'

South Canterbury was down 11–9 when fullback George Gaffaney kicked the ball out metres from his own line. It was snapped up by Canterbury winger Ray Brown, who took a quick throw-in to his Sydenham team-mate, Ock Hattersley, who dived across for the try. Canterbury 12, South Canterbury 11.

So far, so good. But the South Canterbury players to a man, believed that Hattersley was no more than three metres from the sideline when he took the ball.

The referee was Dick Blazey, one of a trio of brothers who would be leading sports administrators. Ces was the chairman of the NZRU from 1977 to 1981; Harry was NZRU president in 1966; and Dick was not only a referee but, with Ces and Harry, made history when all three were Canterbury delegates to the annual meeting of the NZRU in 1957.

There was no charity game to soothe feelings for South Canterbury as there was for West Coast and, in the next challenge, the Log was lost to Otago, 15–6, the first time that province had held the Ranfurly Shield. It would be fifteen years before it returned to Christchurch.

With no shield rugby, the highlight of 1936 was a victory over the touring Australians, where the excitement started before kick off when the team's mascot, a live wallaby, escaped while the teams lined up, as was the custom then, to have a photograph taken together. The feisty beast got away to the south ground before being recaptured by an Australian reserve.

Canterbury roared away to a 19–3 lead soon after half-time, but the Australians recovered and in the last 20 minutes got to within a point, finally losing 19–18.

This was the last game for Canterbury's most dangerous back, George Hart, and, because of the Wallabies' close marking in the midfield, it was a quiet one for the flying winger.

Hart was the 1931 New Zealand sprint champion, clocking 10.4 seconds for 100 yards on a grass track and, with a subtle but devastating swerve on the rugby field, he was a sensational try scorer. In eight years of club rugby he scored 80 tries; in 40 games for Canterbury, 42; and in 35 games for New Zealand, another 28.

His vice-captain on the 1935 tour to Britain, Charlie Oliver, described a try Hart scored against Leicester: 'he controlled the wet ball with his feet for half the length of the field, gathered it on the bounce when reaching the fullback, punted it over his opponent's head, and regained possession to score under the posts.'

Hart was followed into retirement a week later by his 1935 tour captain, Jack Manchester, and Charlie Oliver gave up the game at the end of the season.

So when the 1937 Springboks, the team so good that they were called the greatest side to ever leave New Zealand, arrived in Christchurch for a 21 August clash with Canterbury, there was a very different look from the province's teams which had won and defended the shield earlier in the decade.

Canterbury was still to be treated with respect, though, especially in the forwards, where the pack was anchored by two men who would become All Blacks the following year, Harold Milliken and Claude Williams.

Williams, a civil engineer, played flanker for the All Blacks in Australia in 1938 but locked the Canterbury scrum with Milliken, who would move to Papakura to farm, switch to league and become one of the unfortunate 1939 Kiwis whose tour to Britain lasted just two games before war broke out.

One of Milliken's clubmates from Sunnyside (which would become the Suburbs Club in 1962) was on the side of the scrum for Canterbury. Cyril Pablecheque was a local legend, an extremely strong, champion axeman whose party tricks included lifting up a man in a sling with his teeth and chewing beer glasses.

Jack Hooper, another Sunnyside man, who would play all three tests for the All Blacks in 1937, was a shrewd and talented second five, while 'Nip' McAuliffe, the leader of a hugely talented University Club side in the late 1930s, was Canterbury's captain.

Behind a massive forward pack the 'Boks had an ace in first five Tony Harris, whom they had foolishly left out of their first test side, when they suffered the only loss on tour. Harris, who also represented South Africa as a cricketer, was almost impossible to pin down on the footy field, slick and nippy to a frustrating degree if you were an opposing flanker.

Canterbury's wood-chopping champion, Pablecheque, was marked by South Africa's hard man, the wonderfully named Ebbo Bastard, a hatchet-faced Natal farmer who would die in a 1949 gunfight with a neighbouring farmer, but not before he had shot the other man to death.

South Africa was ahead 20–0 shortly after half-time and, despite gutsy play from the home team late in the game, the result was inevitable, the 'Boks winning by 23–8.

Ten Canterbury players were at the All Black trials held in 1939 for a proposed tour to South Africa in 1940. We will never know how many may have gone on that abandoned trip, but McAuliffe, the goal-kicking halfback who led Canterbury against South Africa, was the captain of a selection called The Rest who beat the New Zealand team 23–3 in the final trial.

Two others who starred in that match were Jim Cartwright and Ag Hunter. The great radio commentator, Winston McCarthy, said this pair from the Canterbury University Club were the wingers who caught his eye. 'Hunter had a slashing match in the fourth trial, scoring two tries, and looking every inch an All Black. He could run at great pace and swerved intelligently. Cartwright was a lovely mover, fast and clever, a grand player.'

Hunter was the nephew of Jimmy Hunter, the leading try scorer of the 1905–06 All Blacks, and carried many of his illustrious uncle's rugby genes. Cartwright was just 20 years old in 1939, still at teachers' training college and in his first year of senior rugby.

Neither would play for New Zealand and both served in the Second World War, during which Hunter was severely wounded and Cartwright killed.

The war claimed, or scarred, the lives of far too many young New Zealanders, and rugby players were no exception. Canterbury rugby followers grieved for the loss of men like Cartwright, Gus Hart, Don Cobden (an All Black against the 1937 Springboks), Jack Harris (a 1925 All Black) and hundreds more who died in combat.

Rugby continued, after a fashion, during the war, although there were no internationals, no Ranfurly Shield games and very few provincial games from the winter of 1940 until the winter of 1946.

Servicemen did play club rugby, and in 1942 an RNZAF team, based at Wigram and usually captained by a rangy lock, Ernie Todd, from Wellington (who would later manage the 1972–73 All Blacks to Britain and send Keith Murdoch home), played the Canterbury Regiment in the club final. The Regiment team was actually from just one battalion made up of 800 men based at Stewart's Gully. The army men were fit and fully trained, but virtually all were under 21.

Leave restrictions were eased for the 3 October final, and many of the six thousand spectators were clad in the blue of the air force, or the khaki of the army. The match lived up to all expectations, with the Regiment ahead 6–3 with ten minutes to go, until a late rush from the Air Force saw it through to a 16–6 victory.

When the war finally ended, the first great celebration at Lancaster Park was in the form of a 27 July 1946 game between the 2 NZEF team (the Kiwis) and Canterbury.

The Kiwi team was the brainchild of Lieutenant-General Sir Bernard Freyberg, VC, who persuaded the New Zealand government to give him £7000 so soldiers serving in Italy and Egypt could compete for 29 places in a team to tour Britain and Europe. They weren't the All Blacks but, as British rugby journalist O. L. Owens wrote, 'they played rugby of which any fully representative team could have been proud.'

After losing just two games on a 33-match tour of Britain, France and Germany, and beating Wales, England and France in the process, the Kiwis returned to New Zealand to play five games, the third of which was against Canterbury.

Of many great players to emerge from that team, including Fred Allen, J. B. Smith and Johnny Simpson, perhaps the greatest was Bob Scott, the first All Black fullback fit to compare with George Nepia.

It was the luck of Lancaster Park fans to see Scott in the Kiwis' game with Canterbury at his very best. The way the match was played suited Scott, with such open, accurate running and passing that the first set scrum, according to the *Christchurch Star*, was not set until the 23rd minute.

Scott was famous for kicking goals during half-time exhibitions from halfway with his bare feet, but it was his electric responses that were on show during the Canterbury game. 40 metres from the Canterbury line he shaped to drop a goal off his right boot. Charged by a rushing defender, he sidestepped and switched to his left foot. When the ball struck another defender, Scott grabbed it on the rebound, threw a dummy and sprinted away for one of the Kiwis' eight tries in their 36–11 romp.

The first Ranfurly Shield challenge since 1939 was played by Canterbury in 1946, travelling to Invercargill to play Southland. That game was lost 11–3, but the following Saturday, back at Lancaster Park, victory was achieved over Australia.

Leading the home side was Pat Rhind, a powerful prop who had been considered a certainty for the abandoned 1940 tour to South Africa. After time spent as a prisoner of war, Rhind was a member of the Kiwis and would play both tests against the Wallabies in 1946. Another Kiwi and a 1949 All Black, Garth Bond, was Rhind's fellow prop, while Bob Duff, a fresh-faced Christchurch forward who had just celebrated his 21st birthday, was at lock.

The star of the Canterbury team, though, was Linwood's Wally Argus, a potent try scorer on the wing or at centre, with a fend that stopped tacklers in their tracks.

But Canterbury was still several years away from the great teams of the 1950s, and, to be honest, this wasn't a very good Australian side. Still, the 20–11 win was something to cherish compared with what would follow.

The nadir probably came in 1948. More provincial games were lost than won, and the Ranfurly Shield challenge against what had become a superb Otago team was a horror show.

To be fair to Canterbury, eleven of the Otago players in 1948 would be in the All Black team that toured South Africa the following year, and the Otago coach, Vic Cavanagh, must surely be the unluckiest man to never coach the All Blacks. A brilliant reader of the game, he was a tutor to coaches ranging from Dick Everest, who coached Waikato to victory over South Africa in 1956, to 1995 World Cup coach Laurie Mains. Fred Allen, the only unbeaten All Black coach, flew Cavanagh from Dunedin to give a team talk to his Auckland 1960s Ranfurly Shield side.

All of which would be little consolation to the Canterbury team, sent packing 31–0 and able to get just one player, halfback Larry Savage, into the squad of 30 for South Africa in 1949. 'And even Savage,' despaired a Christchurch writer, 'had been brought up in Nelson.'

The year had been a dismal one for Canterbury, with 68 players used in fourteen games, 27 dropped after just one appearance for the province, and some training runs attended by only seven or eight players.

It was time for a big change, and it came with the appointment of a two-man selection panel comprising Jack Rankin (of whom we will learn a lot more in the next chapter) and 1928 All Black, Lance Johnson, who had played in the great Hawke's Bay teams of the 1920s.

In 1950 there were two big targets for Canterbury. The first was a match against the British Isles, the first team to be called the Lions. The second was a Ranfurly Shield challenge against Otago, although after 1948 that prospect looked as attractive as walking barefoot in gorse.

Canterbury faced the Lions first, on 7 June , two games after the first test in Dunedin had been drawn 9–9. Despite fielding a team with ten of their test players from Dunedin, including the masterful Irish flyhalf, Jackie Kyle, the Lions fumbled through a largely mediocre perfomance but still managed a comfortable 16–5 victory.

It was no great surprise, then, that Otago fans stayed away from a midweek shield challenge in August. Just 12,000 spectators were at Carisbrook on a wet, chilly Wednesday, and what happened on the field was regarded with disbelief when the final whistle blew. As Iain Gallaway, later a great rugby and cricket commentator, would say, 'Throughout the match I waited for Otago to come back, almost as a matter of right.'

Canterbury was led by 32-year-old flanker Doug Herman, a man so durable he would play nineteen seasons of senior rugby and set a record of 90 games for Canterbury by the end of 1950, his last season of provincial play. Herman was an inspiring leader, extremely fast around the field and capable of kicking goals from halfway. 'He must rank,' wrote veteran Christchurch journalist, Larry Saunders, in 1979,' as one of the unluckiest players in New Zealand to never be an All Black.'

The game against Otago was Herman's 100th first-class match and the occasion could hardly have been more perfect. The first try of the game came from a blindside move in the second half, a favourite tactic of selector Lance Johnson, that saw halfback Pat Vincent set first five Peter Kearney, captain of the champion Marist Club team, across the line.

Canterbury's second try, scored by Tom Lynch, a nuggety midfielder who would play for the All Blacks in 1951 and then move to England to play league for five years, would seal the game for Canterbury, 8–0.

Hundreds turned out to welcome the team home, with one sign reading 'Herman for Mayor.' But the excitement that year would be short-lived. In the very first challenge, just seventeen days later, the Log was gone, lost to a Wairarapa team captained by Alan Blake. This former Kiwi and All Black was a terrific forward who also captained the New Zealand Maori team. He would be front-page news again in 2003 when he admitted he was actually of Afro-American descent and had not a drop of Maori blood in his veins.

With no score in the game at Lancaster Park towards the end of the first half, a stray clearing kick went into the arms of the burly Wairarapa fullback, Andy Mahupuka, near halfway. Without hesitating he belted over a dropped goal to snatch the shield 3–0.

Coach Rankin would later tell author, Lindsay Knight, that losing the shield then was not actually a bad thing for Canterbury. 'We weren't, at that stage, good enough to hold it.'

It would not be long before Canterbury was not only quite good enough to win the shield, but also more than good enough to hold it. The first great shield era in Canterbury rugby was on the horizon, and it would produce one of most charismatic characters to ever wear the red and black jersey.

Pat Vincent (left), a true one off, leads Canterbury out against South Canterbury, with time to exchange pleasantries with Des Grant.

CHAPTER FOUR

PAT

It's nine o'clock on a 1955 Saturday night in Christchurch. They're packed into the Riviera Cabaret, the old Union Rowing Club building on the Avon Loop, the air heavy with the scent of Blue Grass perfume, Palmolive hair oil and Capstan cork-tipped cigarette smoke.

On the stage the vocalist looks sharp. His reddish hair is slicked down, his hand-painted tie set against a crisp white shirt, his suit coat draped open as he steps to the microphone.

He taps a highly polished shoe, picking up the tempo set by drummer Basil Carroll and bassist Dave Easterbrook. In a voice with a hint of Sinatra the singer croons 'I'd like to get you, on a slow boat to China, all to myself alone.'

A stranger in the crowd might wonder why the singer, so urbane in every other respect, down to his liking for a between-sets crème de menthe, has what looks like a graze across his forehead and just the hint of a black eye.

The local dancers know. The man at the mike is Pat Vincent, and when he's not singing at Saturday dances, he's captaining the great Canterbury Ranfurly Shield team.

That's right, the 1950s Canterbury rugby captain is also a dancehall singer and recording artist. Think of Todd Blackadder mixing turntables as a dance-party DJ after a Super 12 game and you have a very fair idea of how unusual Vincent's mix of talents was in his day.

But Pat Vincent was never your run-of-the-mill footy player. Vincent, who in 1956 would lead the All Blacks in the first two tests of the famous series against the Springboks, was not just one of the great Canterbury players. He was something of a renaissance man, a gifted schoolteacher and an aficionado of American culture, which would eventually lead him to the States, where he was a pioneer of rugby in San Francisco.

'He was an amazing, interesting man,' says team-mate Dennis Young, an All Black hooker. 'He had a slight American touch about him. He had a drawl when he spoke. American history was something he was very serious about. When he went to America it came as no surprise to any of us. He had what amounted to a cult following in Christchurch, which went beyond the rugby. I've never known anyone quite like Pat. He was a true one-off.'

Vincent the player was a halfback, a man with all the quick wit needed in the position. After one lack-lustre performance by his forward pack, he murmured to one of the better-known Canterbury forwards, 'I'd have to say I thought that scrum you pushed in was a vital one.'

Young says that 'to break up the monotony [Vincent] would stand on his head in the changing room and say he was practising his yoga. As a halfback he was unusual in that he didn't bark at his forwards, he talked to them. About the most aggressive he ever became was one day when he was getting a lot of tap ball, bad stuff in those days, with the opposition players screaming through at him. After about 20 minutes of this he threw up his hands and said, "This is appalling." All of us stopped and looked at him and thought, "Hell, it must be bad."

'We played Fiji when he was teacher at Boys' High and this bloody great Fijian was chasing a high ball, and Pat stepped aside and let the ball bounce. On the Monday a smart kid said to him, "Please, sir. Is it true you stepped aside from a high ball on Saturday?" Pat thundered at him, "That's a lie. I ran away."'

Stories abound concerning Vincent's wit. When a toast was proposed to the refereeing of Mr Barron after an unhappy game against Southland, the Canterbury captain muttered to his team-mates, 'What a pity his mother wasn't.'

When his Old Boys club side trooped into the changing shed at half-time after a poor performance up front, the players waited for the rockets to fly from their captain. Instead, Vincent leaned on the door jam, thoughtfully sucking an orange as the minutes ticked by. At last the referee blew his whistle to get the teams onto the field. Vincent opened the door to go out, paused, and then quietly broke his silence: 'You forwards were awful.' In the second half the team was on fire and emerged with a victory.

Pat Vincent was the man in control on the paddock during most of the first big Canterbury Ranfurly Shield era, from 1953 to 1956, when a record 24 challengers came to Lancaster Park and left empty-handed.

A great shield team, they say, needs three things: a great captain, a great coach and great players in key areas. Step up Vincent, the leader; Jack Rankin, the coach; and players who would become stars in this era, such as hooker Young, lock Bob Duff, ferocious forward toiler 'Tiny' Hill, lethal attackers Morrie Dixon and Alan Elsom, and goal-kicking midfielder 'Buddy' Henderson.

Vincent wasn't famous for his passing skills, although they were better than he was given credit for by northern critics. Rankin was so incensed with the bagging Vincent took over his pass that in the 1954 season he took a stopwatch to every game and checked how long it took the ball to move from the moment it touched a halfback's hands to when it reached the hands of his first five. The range for Vincent was 0.7 to 0.9 seconds. Other All Blacks opposing Canterbury that season were Auckland's Keith Davis (1.1–1.3 seconds), Otago's Lindsay Townsend (1.1–1.4) and Waikato's Ponty Read (1.2–1.4).

Once a dancer, always a dancer. Dennis Young (right) relives his childhood days with his rugby playing son Mark, as a joke for a Christchurch radio station.

Critics remained unconvinced. If there are lies, damned lies and statistics, the variables in a rugby game do make the best efforts with a stopwatch of arguable value. What everybody did agree on about Vincent was that he was strong, fast and, when he needed to make a break, he could outstrip wingers in a race to the line.

On the field he was the man the red and blacks looked to for something different, something sensational. He provided it when Canterbury took the Ranfurly Shield from Wellington in 1953.

Picking up the ball one-handed at halfway on Athletic Park, he loped 50 metres for a try without a hand laid on him. Great Christchurch writer, Dick Brittenden, would say, 'how did Pat Vincent, travelling at an apparent jog-trot, manage to race from halfway and score under the posts? He started with that characteristic loping stride of his, and spectators instinctively looked around for Wellington's breakaway forwards to close in on him, or for the ever–menacing Ron Jarden with his terrific speed. They were not there. Cover-defenders began to hurry across the paddock, but Vincent started to go faster. "Over the last 20 yards he simply cleared out," said a team member. What is the explanation? It must be that Vincent's loping stride is deceptive, very deceptive. He must be covering a lot of ground with every stride, and covering it with the speed of a crack sprinter.'

Dennis Young recalls that 'when Pat ran he had a Groucho Marx loping run, usually with his tongue hanging out of the side of his mouth. People would get a hell of a shock at how he ran.'

Vincent was a West Coaster, born the baby of a family of nine, six boys and three girls, on 6 January 1926 in the house his parents had built on a Whataroa farm. His father had turned to farming after giving up his work as a ferryman south of the Fox Glacier.

It was soon discovered that Pat suffered from asthma attacks and to protect his health the family moved across the Alps in 1928, to Francis Ave in St Albans.

He played hockey at Shirley Intermediate but, when he became a pupil at Christchurch Boys' High School, he started to flourish as a cricketer and then as a rugby player.

On every occasion he could talk his way through any situation. In his last year at school, in 1943, he persuaded the only woman teacher, Joy Hadfield, that it would be a disaster to make her history class, which included five 1st XV players, sit a test on the day of the annual game with Christ's College. Instead, he was allowed to take over the blackboard and show her how rugby worked, the better for her to enjoy the afternoon's game. Then, as the teacher told Alan V. Barley in his book *The Five Faces of Pat Vincent*, he 'went into a huddle with the other boys in the team, and said he had their permission to divulge the team's tactics to me. As they were known only to the players, and their coach, Henry Dyer, I must put my hand on my heart, and swear not to tell a soul.' Desks were pushed back, moves were demonstrated and that afternoon CBHS emerged victors.

If Vincent was a charmer at school, he quickly demonstrated how competitive he was too when he moved into senior rugby with High School Old Boys.

In a game against arch rival Marist, the Old Boys team was struggling. Vincent bent to pick up the ball at the base of a ruck just as Marist forward, George Lindstrom, swung a big boot at it. Vincent grabbed his face, staggered back and sank to the ground. Old Boys' supporters in the crowd of eight thousand screamed for Lindstrom to be sent off. But the referee just warned him and awarded Old Boys a penalty.

After the game Lindstrom sought Vincent out to apologise. 'I'm sorry, Pat, I didn't even feel my foot connect with anything.' Vincent couldn't conceal a grin. 'You dirty rotten bastard, Vincent,' said Lindstrom. 'The crowd was baying for my blood and the ref was ready to send me off.' Replied Vincent, 'I had to do something, George. We were in trouble.'

Vincent's time in Canterbury colours coincided with the careers of several superb players and one superb coach.

The coach was Jack Rankin, who had been a lightweight loose forward for Canterbury and for the All Blacks, including one test against the 1937 Springboks, where he had harassed the great halfback, Danie Craven, until a massive 'Bok forward knocked him out. He became a provincial selector in 1948 and brought an intensity and a decency to the coaching role for Canterbury that would bring some big results, very quickly.

Twenty years after his coaching days, Rankin told Christchurch journalist Larry Saunders that the aim he and his fellow selectors had 'was to train players to think for themselves, to play as a team, and to adjust tactics according to the game. It was their game, and if they enjoyed it, so did the public.'

The selection policy was straightforward. Players were told that if their first game for Canterbury was bad, they were forgiven. If their second was bad, the selectors would be suspicious, but they would still get a third game. If that was a shocker, they were axed.

'Jack Rankin was totally enthusiastic,' says Dennis Young. 'He wasn't a scone-doer in any way. He had a very personal approach to every player, and that was something he didn't just restrict to rugby. He was a really decent sort of man.'

The big chance for Canterbury to prove its worth as one of the powerhouses of provincial rugby came on a beautiful spring afternoon, Saturday 19 September 1953, at Athletic Park, when Wellington put the Ranfurly Shield on the line against the red and blacks.

In some ways it was a strange time to be playing a challenge. The All Blacks to tour Great Britain and France had been announced just four days earlier, with seven Wellington and six Canterbury players in the squad of 30.

Men who would soon be joining forces in the black jersey were now lining up against each other, and it was quickly obvious that Canterbury, led by the newly minted All Black captain, Bob Stuart, was there to win.

In a touch typical of the Rankin style, the coach gave handwritten letters to every player. 'He wrote personal letters to everyone,' recalls Dennis Young, 'which were given out on the way to the ground. Brief letters saying what he expected, a final personal touch to each player.'

Stuart had decided at the start of the 1953 season that it would be his last, and Terry McLean would write at the time that his main reason for playing that year at all, at the age of 32, was in the hope of seeing his brother, the gutsy fullback Kevin, in the All Blacks.

Kevin didn't make the squad, although he would appear in an All Black jersey at last in 1955, but Bob, in McLean's book on the 1953–54 tour, is credited with 'personally reviving great captaincy in New Zealand rugby, and when every other aspect of this tour has been forgotten this service to the game should be remembered.'

Recalls Young, 'Bob Stuart was a very serious man. He was demanding, and expected you to do the job, and if you didn't he let you know. He was a good man. He was a blindside flanker, a really hard grafter.'

In the Canterbury shield team, Stuart was joined in the forwards by some tough, worldly, gallant players.

A fellow veteran was Nelson Dalzell, a hugely powerful Culverden sheep farmer who, it was claimed, could lift a 44-gallon drum of oil from the ground to the tray of a truck. By rights he probably shouldn't have even been playing rugby. Serving in the Pacific during the Second World War, he was severely wounded by a bomb blast and carried splinters of shrapnel in his legs and back, with army doctors talking seriously of amputation. The wounds, and imbedded shrapnel, gave him some problems but not enough to keep him away from rugby.

Dalzell's great moment in international rugby was the winning of the test at Twickenham against England. Passed the ball ten metres from the line, he was confronted by the English winger John Woodward, a 15-stone butcher, who was only a few pounds lighter than Dalzell. 'Down went Dalzell's head,' wrote Terry McLean, 'and he bunted forward as violently as an enraged bull. Woodward, struck on the chest, fell all ends up and Dalzell hurtled forward to score.'

Dalzell locked the Canterbury scrum with Bob Duff, who would have himself been a first choice for the 1953 All Black tour if he had not decided to concentrate on his work as a young accountant in Lyttelton. There was nothing fancy about Duff as a footballer, but he was technically impeccable, strong and utterly reliable. His association with Pat Vincent was long and warm. They'd played together in the 1943 CBHS 1st XV and made their Canterbury debut in the same game in 1945, against Ashburton County.

On the side of the scrum was 'Tiny' Hill, an army staff sergeant who had come to Canterbury after growing up in Taranaki, and then serving with the occupation forces in Japan after the war.

In Canterbury, he was based with the 11th Coast Regiment at Godley Head, and his training regime when he started playing for the Christchurch Club was rigorous. 'I'd get a ride into the city with the leave truck, and train with Christchurch at Hagley Park. That would be followed by a meal at the pie cart, and then I'd take the tram car to Sumner, get off and run over the hills to Godley Head. It was eight miles by road, so probably about five miles over the top.'

How tough was Hill on the field? Let me quote a story Colin Meads tells at rugby clubs. In 1957 Meads was a brand-new All Black, playing as a loose forward in a test against Australia in Sydney.

Chasing a long kick, he found himself confronting the strapping Aussie fullback Terry Curley, whom he grabbed in a ball-and-all tackle. From behind he heard a voice yelling, 'Put him down. Put him on the ground.'

Curley was stronger than Meads expected and the two men ended up in a wrestling, staggering dance. The voice, which Meads realised belonged to Hill, got louder. 'Put him down!'

Meads wrestled some more. The parade-ground voice was now almost in his ear. 'PUT HIM DOWN!'

Then there was a massive smack in Meads' short ribs. He and Curley crashed to the ground with Hill looming above them, his face like thunder. He snarled at Meads, 'When I say put him down, bloody put him down!'

In the 1950s flankers could follow the ball through the scrum and then launch themselves at a halfback.

'Tiny was a sight to be seen when he came round the side of a scrum,' says Dennis Young. 'His nostrils used to flare and he looked like an American Indian on the warpath. He put the fear of God into a large number of halfbacks.

'Tiny was always a very dominant figure. He asked me to go out and speak in the sergeant's mess at Burnham. It's a fair drag from Woolston to Burnham, and I was five minutes late. He was standing at the gate, and the first thing he said was, 'You're late and you need a haircut."

For all that Hill and some others in the Canterbury forwards were fierce, Young insists they weren't dirty. 'At the top level there was no really foul play. I don't remember anyone being kicked in the head. You were walked on and would end a game with a lot of sprig marks, but I don't remember anything that you'd call out-and-out foul play. But if you went down on the ball, you were walked on. You expected it, and you got it.'

In the Canterbury front row with Young were props Ewen Hern and Peter Eastgate. Hern was a toiler, a man who 'gave his soul' in a team-mate's words, while Eastgate was yet another All Black, a rugged deerstalker whose business interests were in scrapmetal.

Young was soon to become an All Black as well, in 1956, and would stay in the hooker's jersey for New Zealand from 1960 until the end of 1964, when he was 34 years old. The only questions ever raised about Young were about his size, or lack of it. At 5 feet 8 inches (1.73 metres) he was shorter than Byron Kelleher, but what statistics don't show is how much strength he packed into that frame, and how big the heart was inside the chest.

Winning their own scrum ball was the paramount requirement for hookers then, and Young, calm under pressure and with lightning-fast size-seven feet, was a master of his craft.

Two of the great characters (in a team not short of these) in the Canterbury backline were Alan Elsom and Morrie Dixon.

As with Nelson Dalzell, it was almost a miracle that Elsom was playing rugby at all in 1953. Six years earlier, in a game for his Albion club, he had broken his neck. He spent most of a year lying in a hospital bed, and it was 1951 before he ventured onto a rugby field again. What was remarkable was that he was never troubled by neck problems again, despite becoming a fearsome tackler.

They weren't clubmates, but Elsom and Sydenham's Dixon were quickly firm friends in the Canterbury team and then the All Blacks.

Dixon played his footy like an early version of the Energiser bunny. As a child he had been a tap-dancer, often performing a double act with Dennis Young, winning competitions, talent quests and, the ultimate accolade at the time, working together on John Maybury's nationwide radio programmes.

Morrie Dixon, who played his rugby like an early version of the Energiser bunny.

As you might expect from a former dancer whose show stopper was a somersault to finish a routine, Dixon was quick and nimble on the rugby field, and a constant pain to whoever was unlucky enough to be marking him. His special target was Ron Jarden, a former sprint champion who played on the left wing for Wellington. Dixon's response to his opponent's speed off the mark was to never give Jarden a sliver of daylight. He would stick closer than paint when both were chasing after the ball.

Jarden, later to be a world yachting champion, rebutted some rumours in his 1961 book, *Rugby on Attack*: 'Because of the incidents that often accompanied our meetings, our relationship became the subject of widespread comment, and it was frequently stated that we were violent enemies both on and off the field. This was completely erroneous.

'Maurice and I certainly had our moments on the field, but have always been good friends off it. While he rarely made it possible for me to get close enough to the ball to score tries, I made sure that a large proportion of his blocking and obstruction did not go unnoticed. Sometimes it meant chasing him several yards to do it.'

There was one occasion when Jarden freely conceded that Dixon had got the better of him. 'During the North-South match of 1954 the ball had been grubber kicked through the South Island backs by Jim Fitzgerald, and Morrie ran, according to my interpretation, right across my path. In a moment of fury, I flung myself upon him, and the two of us rolled to the ground, with the ball 25 yards away. His fans, 30,000 of them, rose to a man and in the uproar the referee penalised me for playing the man without the ball. One up to Morrie.'

Dennis Young recalls that 'Dixon and Elsom worked as a combination, especially when they were up against Ron Jarden. They'd psyche him out of the game. Ron was a pretty highly strung sort of guy. Jarden didn't really want any conversation, but Dixon wouldn't leave him. Once, at the start of a game, he said, "It's your lucky day, Ron." Eventually Jarden couldn't help himself and he had to say, "What do you mean?" "They've got the stretcher on your side of the paddock," explained Dixon.'

When the shield challenge arrived in 1953, the biggest surprise to everyone, including the Canterbury players, was how easily the Log was lifted.

Bob Stuart won the toss and chose to play into the brisk wind. Despite that handicap, Canterbury was ahead 9–3 at half-time, with tries to Elsom and future All Black wing, Ross Smith, and a penalty kicked by fullback Kevin Stuart.

In the second half Canterbury just raced away, with Vincent's great solo try adding to those scored by Dixon and Bob Stuart, all three converted by the fullback.

Years later, Wellington players would suggest that the timing of the challenge was unfortunate, coming so soon after the naming of the team for the All Blacks' tour of Britain, which was then a once-in-a-decade event.

Wellington coach, Clarrie Gibbons, told writer Lindsay Knight that 'it may have only been subconsciously, but I felt some of the fellows who were in the All Blacks were looking after themselves.'

From the Canterbury side of the fence, it might have been noted that what was supposed to be the last big training run of the week before the challenge was called off, and a couple of beers were enjoyed instead. So many Canterbury players were at the All Black trials that only eight were left in Christchurch during the week.

There were actually a couple of beers the night before the game in Wellington too. The local fans were delighted, believing the Canterbury team wasn't taking the challenge seriously, but it was actually nothing more than what had become a tradition before games in Christchurch. Two or three small beers, and then an early night, had worked in the past, and it worked again in Wellington.

If the victory at Athletic Park left the local supporters stunned, the frenzy it created in Canterbury was soon apparent. The new shield holders caught the overnight ferry

Tiny Hill is about to embrace the ball.
The Aucklanders opposing him will try to steal it at their peril.

to Lyttelton, as did a horde of Canterbury fans. The ferry was held up for an hour as the players and supporters surged across the wharf to get on board.

Tiny Hill didn't enjoy the melee. He'd hurt his shoulder making a tackling and 'it was still sore that night, when we had to board the steamer. There was an enormous crowd of people, and we had to fight to get up the gangway. People kept belting me on the back to offer congratulations. It was agony.'

Dennis Young didn't get away scot-free either. 'I went through the whole match without a bruise, and then, trying to get on the boat to get home, I got a cut that just about needed stitches. We were met by 10,000 people and the Lyttelton brass band when we arrived the next morning, followed by a triumphant train journey back to the Christchurch railway station.'

It was somehow appropriate that the players found themselves jammed onto the ferry with their admirers right from the start. There was no hint of six degrees of separation in the 1950s between those watching in the grandstands and on the bank, and the men on the field.

'In those times we really were the players of the people,' says Young. 'We all had jobs. I was a cabinetmaker. It wasn't a manufactured relationship between the players and the public. I'm not being critical, but with professional rugby now you have to manufacture times and situations for the public to have some contact with the players. This was the real thing. You were out there, listening to everything that people had to say about you. I'd go to play in a club game and my boss at work would be on the bank yelling out, "Rattle your dags." On the Monday he'd ask if I'd heard him. I certainly did.

'For a game we'd go straight from home to the ground. At no stage did we go to a hotel the night before. A few times we met for lunch at a hotel, but that was it. When you start winning shield defences, you don't change from what you did before. I would park my car in a spot that was often well away from the ground, and would then walk down the same side of the road. I'd sit in the dressing room in the same place, go onto the ground behind the same person. If something happened that made you change, you worried like hell about it.'

Amid the streams of people coming down Ferry Road or jostling into Stevens Street, some would be carrying small kitbags. They were the players. There was no inching into the park on a bus, stopping at a guarded gate, then vanishing into the depths of the stand.

Instead, there were two strands. One group in overcoats and hats headed towards the bank or the stands. The men with the bags, containing boots, a towel and a jockstrap, were the players.

'We'd emerge out of the crowd,' says Young, 'where there were people asking, "How do you think you'll go?" and wishing you good luck as you headed into the park.'

They were big crowds that our local heroes came from, too. By the time of the first challenge of 1954 against Southland, Bob Stuart was retired and Pat Vincent led out Canterbury in front of a crowd of 37,000 people, including a thousand who had travelled on a special train from Invercargill.

The visitors opened in spectacular fashion. Within minutes the Southland first five, 1951 All Black Len Wilson, had burst through for a try and after ten minutes Southland was ahead 10–0.

This was the game remembered not only for the recovery by Canterbury but for the one-man war waged in the forwards by Peter Eastgate, who crashed through the Southland forwards time and again, and for the potent tackling by Elsom and 'Bing' McPherson, a rugged second five. Together they soon made sure Wilson was no longer a threat to the Canterbury defence.

'Alan [Elsom] used to run right through the man he tackled,' says Young. 'He was rangy and quick, and he'd throw it all at them when he tackled. People shuddered to a halt.'

A football train arrived again a fortnight later, this time echoing to the sound of cowbells as Waikato, who had enjoyed its own shield reign early in the 1950s, arrived with a team that included the goal-kicking icon, Don Clarke.

Clarke was still to be an All Black, but he was already quite capable of kicking goals from his own half of the field and in fact, as a 17-year-old, he had kicked the two penalties that won Waikato the Log from Northland in 1951. By 1954 he was a challenger for the All Black fullback spot, but despite kicking two penalty goals, he had a rugged afternoon, being peppered with up-and-unders chased down by Elsom and company.

Canterbury managed a try from Vincent and a penalty from their own fullback, Kevin Stuart, in reply, which today would have brought a two-point win, but in 1954 produced a 6–6 draw, still enough to keep the shield.

West Coast was next up and, at a time when rugby on the Coast could still call on a bunch of tough, hard-edged coalminers, the game was scoreless until late in the second half when Canterbury pulled away for an 8–0 victory.

Crowds were big, excitement was high, but in the Canterbury camp things went on as usual.

'We would train twice during the week, and then on Sundays,' says Dennis Young. 'We'd often have a midweek game on a Wednesday too. The various levels of rugby didn't overlap much. Club rugby would get under way early in April, and we'd go through almost all of those games before the provincial season kicked off. So training runs of club and provincial sides didn't clash too much. The Sunday run was not usually a heavy run and would normally end up in a social function at the Dominion Hotel.'

The style of rugby being played, recalls Young, was based on simpler concepts than today: 'We wanted to move the ball wide, but that was the job of the backs. Basically, the role of the forwards was to get to where the ball was and provide it for the backs. A lot of the forwards could all get around and run with the ball too. We had some good runners in the forwards, but the ball came to them, rather than them going to look for it.

'If you had a ruck or a maul, you'd hear it from the backs if they didn't get the ball quickly. The worse criticism you could hear was that you were a seagull. As an example, a lineout would usually develop into a maul and, as the hooker, I'd hang off to cover the blindside defence. If you were on the bank side, you got it from the crowd yelling at you to get your butt into the action.'

All that had gone before was leading into the epic game with Otago, a contest that rates as one of the greatest ever played for the Log.

The Otago team, some suggested, wasn't the machine it had been under the coaching of the great Vic Cavanagh in the 1940s. However, the southerners could still call on the great rugby brain of Charlie Saxton.

Saxton had captained the Kiwi Army team which toured Britain at the end of the Second World War, a side that lived by his edict that 'the object of rugby is for fourteen men to give the 15th a start of half a yard.' It was Saxton who first articulated the three Ps of rugby: possession, position and pace.

To help win possession in the 1954 challenge, he had a pack anchored by Kevin Skinner, the man who would stare down the Springbok forwards in the famous 1956 series. Steering the team to field position were Lindsay Townsend and Robin Archer, the halfback and first five who would both later become All Blacks. And marshalling the pace of the three-quarters was Don Grant, a South Island representative at centre.

You do have to conclude that the Canterbury fans thought there wasn't much chance of an Otago victory in the 18 September clash. There were only 30,000 people at Lancaster Park for the Otago match, just a thousand more than the crowd who would watch Buller's challenge a week later.

Nevertheless, the day produced a perfect Canterbury spring afternoon, and the teams warmed up to the strains of the St Andrew's College pipe band.

There was quickly a need for a lament, as Canterbury's fullback, Kevin Stuart, was staggering and in enormous pain. Stuart waved away an ambulance man treating him on the sideline and tried to return to the field when Otago launched an attack. His arm flapped at his side and courage alone was not enough. His arm was broken.

Enter Derek Mayo, a 23-year-old playing in his very first shield game. It was about as tough an introduction to the big time as you could get.

Billy Wilson, the Otago fullback whose son Bevan would be an All Black fullback in the late 1970s, kicked an early penalty, and then another. Nine minutes before half-time Grant was given just enough space to get to the Canterbury line and plunged over in the tackle of Mayo. Wilson lined up the kick from near the touchline and there were gasps from the crowd as the ball hit a post and ricocheted away, so Otago was ahead 9–0 going into the second half.

The revival started, as it would end, with Mayo. After a couple of misses in the first half he kicked for goal ten minutes into the half and, almost typically in this most melodramatic of games, the ball hit a post but careened over the bar for three points.

After twenty minutes in the second spell Canterbury, now revved up and storming at a tiring Otago team, narrowed the gap again. Bing MacPherson, the powerhouse second five from Southbridge, cross-kicked to the left wing and the ball bounced in the Otago in-goal area. Wilson and Canterbury wing, Ross Smith, scrambled for possession. Smith wasn't the fastest wing in the country, but he would win an All Black jersey because he was strong, brave, determined and had a shrewd rugby brain. In the frantic race for the ball on this occasion, he just sneaked ahead of Wilson and dived for the try just a metre from the dead-ball line. Mayo missed the conversion: Otago 9, Canterbury 6.

These were desperate, desperate moments. Canterbury kept hammering away and Vincent moved into overdrive. 'With three minutes on the clock,' vice-captain Tiny Hill recalls, 'we were driving forward up front, slogging it out, but they had the measure of us. I talked with Pat and asked, "What'll we do?" Pat said, "Let's open it up and toss the ball around a bit." That's how it started.'

Time was up on the clock when Otago kicked the ball downfield. It looked as if it would go out and Auckland referee, Doug Graham, would blow for full time. But Hill managed to grasp the ball and set off downfield. 'I thought to myself, "I'm going to score a ruddy try here." I took off and headed back over halfway.'

When Hill saw a group of Canterbury players backing up on the inside, he flung a long pass infield. The ball was snapped up and taken forward into a ruck, with Vincent at the heels of his forwards. To his left, on the blind, were Elsom and first five Doug Wilson. But the halfback heard a voice screaming even louder than the hysterical crowd. 'Right! RIGHT!'

He fired the pass to the right, where it was taken by, of all people, prop Ewen Hern. He quickly passed the ball on to McPherson. Flying into the line outside him was

"You're late,"
Tiny Hill (above) said to Dennis Young,
"and you need a haircut."

Mayo, the newcomer, tasting for the very first time the thrills and tension of shield rugby. All Mayo saw now was the ball, safely gathered, and then the chalked line ahead. He dived across in triumph to score the try that ensured the Log would remain in Canterbury hands.

What followed was glorious chaos. On the press benches, people stared in amazement at Tom Fleming, the 65-year-old sports editor of the *Christchurch Star-Sun*, whose decorum usually befitted a man so experienced that in 1921 he became the first journalist to provide a running commentary by telephone back to his office of the Canterbury v. South Africa game. His hat was flung in the air and he leapt to his feet, yelling, 'Come on, Canterbury!'

On the field, as the *Star-Sun* reported, 'Within seconds the Canterbury players disappeared under a sea of jubilant supporters. When they reappeared, they were being carried shoulder high towards the pavilion. In no time, the playing area was packed with cheering thousands, many of them dancing in their delight. The referee had no possible hope of clearing the field for the kick at goal. It did not matter anyway.'

Reflecting on the 9–9 draw, Vincent managed a characteristically dead-pan response: 'We couldn't leave our run any later than that.'

Elsom would later suggest the score actually should have been 11–9 to Canterbury, as later in the night he and some mates had taken a ball out and Elsom had kicked a conversion. 'After a few beers,' he reckoned, 'you can do anything.'

Tiny Hill and a fellow soldier were driving back to Burnham that night when they picked up two young women hitchhiking back to Dunedin. Naturally the talk turned to the rugby that afternoon.

'I could kill that Tiny Hill,' said one of the women. 'If it wasn't for him we'd have the Ranfurly Shield now.' When the hitch-hikers were let out at the entrance to the Burnham Camp, Hill's mate informed them, 'By the way, my friend here is Tiny Hill.'

For Dennis Young, 'the Otago game would be at the very top of my fond memories, along with the actual winning of the shield from Wellington. You have your own personal highlights, but overall in comes down to those two games, and the one that left you with the warmest feeling would be the Otago game, because success came so late.'

Challenges from Wanganui and Buller were successfully turned aside and then, at the end of the 1954 season, Rankin, who had been a Canterbury selector since 1948, decided it was time to step down.

Two new selectors, Neil McPhail and Jack Morton, took over the coaching. Morton, as a player, had represented five unions, Canterbury, Wellington, Otago, Manawatu and Nelson, while McPhail would go on to coach the All Blacks, his greatest success being the 1963–64 tour of Britain and France, when the side was captained by Wilson Whineray.

To this day, Whineray speaks glowingly of McPhail, a man so modest he refused to wear an All Black tie on the British tour because, while a leading prop for Canterbury before the war, and considered by many a certainty for the abandoned 1940 All Black tour to South Africa, he had never played for the All Blacks.

Captured by the Germans in the Western Desert in 1941, McPhail spent years in prisoner-of-war camps in Germany and Italy, and was then a leading figure in the Kiwi Army team when the war was over.

Terry McLean wrote of how McPhail was a perfectionist, to the point that a lively argument developed between the two men after a South Island team coached by McPhail beat the North Island in Christchurch in 1962.

The problem for McPhail was that the winning of the match came down to a try scored by South's first five, Neil McAra. He had been loitering out on the wing late in the game when a clearing kick from the in-goal by North's Ross Brown failed to find touch. McAra trapped the ball with his foot and then scampered in for a try.

'He shouldn't have been there,' said McPhail. 'He was out of position, he should have been nearer his forwards.' Would you rather he hadn't got the ball and scored the try and given the South the win, asked an unbelieving McLean. 'Certainly,' snapped McPhail. 'That's barmy,' replied McLean.

Maybe, but the integrity displayed by McPhail's attitude sat easily with men used to the way Rankin had gone about his task.

Not that the 1955 season began promisingly. Early games were lost to Buller, 11–6, in the mud of Victoria Square in Westport, and South Canterbury, 12–8, in Timaru. But a northern tour saw the side unbeaten and, by playing Wairarapa on a Friday, the squad was able to get to Wellington to cheer on Kevin Stuart and Ross Smith as they played against Australia for the All Blacks in what would be their first and only tests.

In the first shield challenge of 1955, from Auckland, Stuart, whose courage was a byword, was knocked cold waiting for a high ball to land. Outraged, the Canterbury players were ferocious for the rest of the match, and emerged 12–6 winners.

But the big challenge for the season came on 7 September when Wellington arrived, complete with a supporters' group carrying a coffin for the body of Canterbury rugby.

This was a game that had a background of bitterness. At the after-match function when the Log was won in 1953, the president of the Canterbury Union, former All

Black Bill Dalley, had thrilled the crowd under the stand at Athletic Park by saying the traditional Canterbury v. Wellington game early in July the following year would be for the Log.

Keep in mind that the NPC was still more than twenty years away. There were no divisions, with guaranteed home and away games, and most fixtures were decided annually at what was known as the 'wool sale' at the New Zealand Rugby Union. Provincial union delegates negotiated normal games, and Ranfurly Shield challenges were very much at the discretion of the holder.

Dalley, it soon transpired, had been carried away by the moment in Wellington. In April 1954 the CRFU decided at an in-committee meeting that the July match would not be for the Log because the Union wanted to complete its club games before the shield games started.

Despite some peace meetings between officials from both unions, toys were thrown out of the Wellington cot to the extent that no game at all was played in 1954 between the two strongest teams in the country.

There wasn't universal backing for the Canterbury stand, either. *The Press* thundered in an editorial written by Dick Brittenden, 'Rugby football enthusiasts will regret that the Canterbury Rugby Football Union has neglected an opportunity to strengthen the spirit of sportsmanship that has grown up around the Ranfurly Shield in the last year or two. The Wellington Rugby Union has every right to expect its match with Canterbury to be a shield game. This is a "regular" fixture, the first of the usual home and away matches between the two unions. There would be no question of altering the arrangement if the trophy was not involved. There is ample precedent for shield matches in July.

'It is to be hoped the Canterbury Union will reconsider its present attitude. It cannot afford to give the appearances of trying to juggle its representative programme in order to preserve its hold on a trophy.

'The Ranfurly Shield has been a mixed blessing to New Zealand rugby. It has bred a good deal of cupidity as well as inspiring a higher standard of play.'

When the dust finally settled, the most anticipated challenge of 1955 was played, of all things, on a Wednesday, 7 September, to accommodate a game against the touring Wallabies three days later.

Did the midweek date keep the crowd down for the shield game? In fact, work in the city largely came to a standstill as 35,000 people crammed into Lancaster Park for the kick off. It was suggested at the time that never have so many grandmothers' funerals begun at exactly the same time in the afternoon.

Naturally the occasion wound up the Canterbury players. 'As defenders you did feel the pressure,' says Dennis Young. 'In the '53–56 era, when you started to build a team, you realised you were defending not only the shield but a record that kept improving each week.'

Wellington's style then was to fling the ball across a backline that featured an All Black on each wing, Ron Jarden and Tom Katene, a big, bullocking man originally from the King Country.

Jarden, as always, copped it hard and strong from the bank. 'I know that when the All Blacks played the 'Boks here in '56,' says Young, 'Morrie [Dixon] and Alan [Elsom] had to take Ron aside and tell him the crowd wouldn't be on his back the way they were when he was playing for Wellington.'

If Jarden suffered verbally, the Wellington centre, Maurice Palmer, suffered physically at the hands of Elsom, who crash-tackled his opponent again and again, as the Wellington inside backs shovelled the ball hopefully towards the wings.

Elsom featured on attack too, running in two tries, which, with the goal-kicking skills of the newcomer at second five, Buddy Henderson, saw Canterbury lead 19–0 at half-time, and go on to win 30–11.

Jarden called Canterbury the best provincial team he had ever played against, while Fred Boshier, the veteran sports editor of Wellington's *Evening Post*, claimed, 'the experience was almost as humiliating for Wellington as that of 29 years ago, when Hawke's Bay won by 50 points at Napier.'

Less memorable was the Canterbury performance three days later against Australia, a side good enough to beat the All Blacks in the third game of a three-test series.

It is claimed that laughter was actually heard during the Canterbury team's Thursday training run, but not much after the game, which the Wallabies won 19–8 in front of a crowd seven thousand people smaller than watched the Wellington match.

The fourth and last year of the 1950s shield era was dominated by even bigger rugby events: the tour matches of South Africa.

Canterbury faced the Springboks in the twelfth game of their tour on 21 July, a month before Ranfurly Shield matches began. There was just one warm-up game, against a combined South Canterbury-Mid Canterbury-North Otago side, won 25–6.

In their first game in New Zealand, the 'Boks had been stunned by a rampant Waikato side, which beat them 14–10, and the first test was lost 10–6. There was a feverish mood in New Zealand that year and Canterbury, as shield holders, was tipped to be the second provincial team to beat South Africa.

At Lancaster Park people slept outside the ground to make sure they found a prime spot on the terraces, and 90 minutes before kick off the gates were closed on police orders. At that stage the crowd was 45,000 people, but fans were so desperate to get in that they climbed fences and pushed down a gate, although the three thousand who packed in that way found they couldn't see the action: the crowd on the bank was so dense that most spectators couldn't even move their arms. All the latecomers could do was try to judge the game from the roars of the people in front of them.

The game itself was largely a battle between two potent forward packs. Terry McLean wrote at the time, 'Eight red Canterbury devils surged wherever the ball went. Friend and enemy were mown down like ripe wheat, a relentless, exhilarating attack was made upon the South African goal, and all was fire and spirit and manliness and unquenchable courage. You may have your 300-yard drive at golf, your sensational backhand at tennis, and your four minute mile in athletics, but there is nothing in all of sport, so I maintain, to compare with the sight of eight rugby forwards who are really moving forward who are resolved and relentless.

'So, at the end, one will always remember the tall, gaunt men, Bob Duff and Tiny Hill, the fresh newcomer Wilson Whineray (who had his sleeves rolled up so tight he might have been a butcher making a killing), the chunky hooker Dennis Young, the loose forwards John Buxton, Hugh Burry and Neil Roberts, and last, and perhaps the finest of them all, the prop Ewen Hern, who had reached the stage of his career where he could be called, with accuracy, a veteran who looked young, or a youngster who looked a veteran.'

After a blindside try by Buxton in the third minute, the game was tied up two minutes later when Jeremy Nel kicked a penalty for the 'Boks. At 18 minutes Henderson kicked a penalty, but the teams went to the break at 6–6, when South African halfback, Popeye Strydom, scored after Nel had sparked a sweeping back attack.

By half-time the local crowd flinched whenever the ball neared fullback Kevin Stuart. In 1956 no replacements were permitted in international games. If you were injured, you stayed on or you left on a stretcher.

After thirteen minutes Stuart had dislocated his right shoulder, repeating an injury he had suffered two months earlier in the inter-island game. It took some minutes for Dr David Dickson to push the shoulder back into place, and then, trying to relieve the intense pain, fashion a sling for Stuart to wear when he returned to the field.

Later in the game, the fullback dislocated the same shoulder while making a tackle. It was again pushed back into the socket, and he was still on the field at the final whistle. It was Stuart's last game in the red and black jersey. After scoring 383 points in 79 games, the man called 'the old Rock of Gibraltar' left the sport, with the Christchurch *Press* suggesting that 'in football skills he had few peers; in courage, none.'

Eight minutes from time, with the score still locked at 6–6, there was a ruck twenty metres from the South African line. The Hawke's Bay referee, Hugh McNeill, allowed it to run, and run. Some claimed he put the whistle to his mouth twice, or even three times, to signal a scrum before Daan Retief was penalised for backing into the ruck from an offside position.

Henderson wasn't fazed by the tension of the moment, asking Whineray on his way to the spot if he'd like to take the kick. There was no mistake with Henderson's effort, and the game was won for Canterbury, 9–6.

The coach of the Springboks was Danie Craven, who for the next 34 years would be the president of the South African Rugby Board. A former Springbok captain, he was having the tour from hell, and his response to the loss to Canterbury was immediate and extreme. He fired off an official complaint to the NZRU on the standard of the refereeing, and that night he gave an explosive interview to Terry McLean.

As McLean told Warwick Roger in his book *Old Heroes*, it was obvious 'in the bus on the way back to the United Service Hotel, that the Springboks were very upset, and justifiably. I went to my room, gave it a bit of thought, then went upstairs to the top floor and knocked on Danie's door. His opening words were, "I am not a happy man tonight," and he told me the story.'

Craven said, 'I do not begrudge Canterbury their victory, but I feel we should not have been defeated by an easy penalty. The refereeing in the North Island was excellent, but down south the standard seems quite different. We have long felt disposed to put in a complaint, but the referee in the Canterbury game was the straw that broke the camel's back. I am sorry there has been such a fuss. It's a pity, but there it is.'

At the time nobody asked Craven why he thought referees down south were bad when it was a Hawke's Bay man he was so steamed up about, but the official protest went nowhere and the result, as it always does when losing teams turn on referees, stayed the same.

From the dramas of the Springbok game, the shield challenges in 1956 came and went with the efficient dispatching of Mid-Canterbury, Hawke's Bay, Wanganui, West Coast, South Canterbury and Southland, before the 22 September visit by Wellington.

The lead-up to the game had its share of intrigue and giddiness. In the giddy file put the decision by Canterbury supporters who had pinched the Wellington coffin from the 1955 challenge, to keep it in hiding, then fill it with a stuffed dummy in Wellington colours and drop it into the visiting team's hotel lounge.

For intrigue, mark down the last Wellington training run, in Christchurch, where the ball was spun along the backline in the way that had been so notably unsuccessful the year before.

Only the Wellington squad knew that in a three-hour session in Timaru the day before, all the Wellington players had done was work on countering the kicks they expected their fullback to face from Canterbury, and the kicking game they would actually use themselves at Lancaster Park.

The match itself was dour, with Wellington's loose forwards Bill and Lindsay Clark (no relation) often leaving the forwards to thicken up the backline defence in order to frustrate Canterbury attacks.

This cunning plan, hatched not by Wellington's coach, Clarrie Gibbons, but by one of his selectors, Vince Paino, worked almost to the letter. Wellington won 8–0, and Bill Clark, an All Black loose forward, called it 'the most satisfying game I ever played in.'

It wasn't altogether an unhappy occasion for the Canterbury players. Tiny Hill would tell author Bob Howitt in 1975 that 'the boys, frankly, were pleased to see it go. Playing for the shield all the time creates terrific tension. Our players were singing in the changing room after Wellington's win.'

It was the last game of the season, and the last game for Pat Vincent, the first man to play a hundred games for Canterbury.

Footnote: Vincent's time as All Black captain was brief but dramatic. He was appointed leader for the first test against the 1956 Springboks, a series that took on mythical status even at the time.

Seven years earlier, the All Blacks had been beaten 4–0 in South Africa and, despite first playing against the 'Boks in 1921, the New Zealand had never won a series.

There was a great deal of bitterness after the 1949 debacle. In three of the four tests, the All Blacks scored more tries than South Africa, but the goal-kicking of the prop Okey Geffin, at a time when neutral referees were not used, was decisive.

As a 30-year-old, Vincent was a controversial choice outside Canterbury, but so popular in

Pat Vincent, wearing No.7, as halfbacks did in 1956, flings out a pass in the game at Lancaster Park with the Springboks, won 9-6 by Canterbury.

Christchurch that The Press reported that a publican shouted everyone in a crowded bar when the words 'P. B. Vincent, Canterbury, captain' emerged from the radio.

But when the All Blacks won the first test in Dunedin, 10–6, even one of Vincent's most trenchant northern critics, Terry McLean, was moved to commend him as a 'cool and resourceful halfback.'

What Vincent could not survive was the 8–3 loss in the second test in Wellington. He was, said McLean in his book on the tour, 'belaboured by Springbok forwards breaking upon him, whereas the South African halfback, Tommy Gentles, was protected by a human barricade through and over which the All Black forwards could do no more than peer with an agonized intensity of expression.'

Newsreels of the second test show in agonising slow motion a scrum where new prop, Frank McAtamney, is buckled, then pushed like a human staple into the air. 'If we'd applied pressure,' All Black lock Tiny White would say years later, 'he could have broken his back.'

The country wanted changes and Vincent was gone, replaced as captain by his Christchurch Boys' High School 1st XV friend, Bob Duff. There was some irony in the appointment, given that from schooldays Vincent had been the skipper.

Vincent agreed to deliver a speech on the night before the third test, at Lancaster Park, which the All Blacks would win, 17–10, before finishing off a series victory. After a long burst of sympathetic applause, Vincent's first words when he spoke were: 'You know that I'm only here through the courtesy of the New Zealand selectors.'

In the summer, while the country celebrated the first series win over South Africa, Vincent, who told friends he felt fit enough to play until he was 40, decided it was more sensible to retire.

In 1957 his passion for the United States was rewarded with a scholarship to the University of California at Berkeley to complete a Masters degree in American history.

Vincent plunged into not only his academic studies but American rugby too, playing for the university and joining in the 'beer busts', where a keg, a jazz band, and 'ruggerettes', girls from the varsity, would see what Vincent described in a letter to a friend as 'a buzzing jovial time. There is little rugby talk, as we know it, because very few know enough to be able to talk about it. I sometimes wish such was the case in New Zealand.'

His degree completed, Vincent returned to Christchurch to teach again at Boys' High. From 1959 to 1962 he was the coach of the Canterbury team, when his quirky approach saw the players visiting the Theatre Royal to learn stretching exercises from ballet dancers.

But America was always in his dreams, and in late 1967, without a job arranged, he left Christchurch permanently, to live initially in San Francisco, which had just seen the famous 'summer of love.'

Vincent plunged into life there, buying a Mustang car, working first as a cook and waiter, then managing an apartment block, before finding his true calling as a counsellor and rugby coach at Saint Mary's College in the Moraga Valley, 30 kilometres inland from San Francisco.

In rugby he was again an achiever. The number of teams at St Mary's grew from one to six, and in 1971 Vincent was able to unite bitter factions in Northern and Southern California to form the Grizzlies, a Californian rep team he managed on a nine-match New Zealand tour in 1972. He would also become a prime mover in the formation of the first United States Rugby Union in 1975.

In 1983 Vincent, then aged 57, took a Saint Mary's side on a tour to France and Spain. On the return flight to the States from Paris his asthma, which had plagued him all his life, flared up.

On landing in New York he went to the medical centre at the airport, had an X-ray and was given clearance to fly on to San Francisco. In Alan Barley's biography, Brother Martin Ash of Saint Mary's describes what followed: 'About twenty minutes out from New York, Pat was having some difficulty, and was using oxygen. I was sitting next to Pat, but moved as directed, so he would be able to stretch out more and rest. Within two minutes a player told me Pat was having difficulty, and as I stood up to move back I saw Pat stand up, have a sudden spasm and collapse. It took about an hour before the plane landed, and when they took him off the plane I realised there was little hope. Pat passed away at the hospital that Sunday night, April 10.'

The affection felt for Pat Vincent was reflected not only at his funeral at Saint Mary's, attended by hundreds of present and past students, but in a way he would have loved. After six years of fundraising the Patrick Vincent Memorial Field was opened at Saint Mary's in 1989. To this day all the college's home games are played there.

Christchurch Boys' High School teacher Tony Steel has just been selected for the 1966 All Blacks and is hoisted aloft by fellow CBHS masters, both former All Black captains, Pat Vincent (left) and John Graham.

Fergie McCormick, who always believed that backing off from the big men was a mistake, demonstrates his intensity on Otago All Black forward, Gary Seear.

CHAPTER FIVE

FERGIE

Fergie McCormick was once asked how he would have dealt with tackling Jonah Lomu, who had just galvanised the 1995 World Cup in South Africa by running over English fullback, Mike Catt.

Several other former All Blacks, when asked the same question, had joked about the prospect. Get a gun, trip him, look for a big net were all on the agenda. Another, more seriously, suggested trying to get Jonah to go back in field so a covering forward could get him.

Fergie was more blunt: 'Hit him as hard as you can. If someone's coming straight at you, you don't stand still and let him choose which way he'll go. You work him towards the touchline, don't give him a chance to cut back in, and then smack into him just under the ribs. It's no use backing off big guys, you've got to get right into them.'

If you'd never seen McCormick play, you might have thought he was an old warrior dreaming about something he could never have accomplished. But if you saw him during the eighteen seasons he played for Canterbury at fullback, you wouldn't have questioned his methods for a moment. This was a man so hard-edged on the field that his torso was basically a concrete block inside a footy jersey. This was a man so muscular that a French doctor in Biarritz on the 1967 All Black tour, when McCormick was suffering from a throat infection, was unable to give him an injection in his backside. The needle kept bouncing back.

He was the son of a 1925 All Black forward, Archie McCormick, and at least one of his Canterbury team–mates reckoned that Fergie was a forward disguised as a back. McCormick was probably born to play for Canterbury. His mother was a top-level sportsperson too, selected for the 1929 New Zealand hockey team for a tour to South Africa that was eventually cancelled, and a champion sprinter.

Fergie wasn't big when he first played footy. He started in the under-30-kilogram grade as a forward, and had to stand at the front of the lineout because any further back and he couldn't see the ball when it was being thrown in.

He first played for Linwood when he was eight, after his family moved from

Ashburton, where he was born, to a pig farm at Belfast. His father would sit Fergie on the handlebars and pedal him eight kilometres into and back from town.

By 1957 McCormick was an 18-year-old, working as a plasterer and playing his first senior rugby for Linwood, the start of a senior club career that would last for the next nineteen years.

In that year Canterbury showed what a potent team it was. At the end of an unbeaten Australian tour in which they won both tests, the All Blacks played a game at Lancaster Park against Canterbury. The home team was primed for the occasion by stories from Australia that the All Blacks were treating the game as the third test of their tour.

The All Blacks fielded three Canterbury players that day: Tiny Hill, Dennis Young and Wilson Whineray, who had just two seasons with Canterbury, 1956–57, while attending Lincoln College as part of a farm cadetship. As a 23-year-old in 1958 he became All Black captain, a role he would hold until the 1965 series was won against South Africa. Though never a ferocious scrummager, he was a superb footballer, a man ahead of his time with handling and passing skills, and a captain with a remarkable ability to read men and a game.

It was Whineray who gave the game in New Zealand the 'Willie Away' move, which saw a man from the front of the lineout run to take a tap from the back, then set up a ruck in midfield for the second five and fullback to use the wide blind that was created.

Also in the All Blacks was a 20-year-old from a farm outside Te Kuiti, Colin Meads, at that stage, he says himself, 'so shy I wanted to burrow into the wall if anyone I didn't know said "g'day" to me.' He wasn't shy on the paddock though, and while he hadn't settled in as the best lock ever to pull on a black jersey, he was an abrasive No. 8 against Canterbury.

Arrayed against the national team was a crowd of 38,000 people who at times did the unthinkable and booed the All Blacks, and a Canterbury team led by Bob Duff, who had decided after the 1956 Springbok series to end his All Black career and play just one more season for Canterbury.

Duff, for many years an accountant in Lyttelton, was a forward who, in Terry McLean's view, 'while not notably nimble was, as good compensation, strong, intent and dedicated. He mastered the ABC of tight forward play and gave New Zealand outstanding service. He played with determination and integrity.'

The All Blacks may have had Don Clarke, with his ability to kick goals from his own side of the halfway line, but Canterbury could call on Buddy Henderson, the Old Boys second five and centre whose kicking skills were only matched by his try-scoring abilities. His kicking was copybook, as smooth and controlled as a Stephen Fleming off drive. As a runner, he usually carried the ball in both hands, keeping his marker in two minds, and his swerve inside a tackle was devastating. He would score 716 points, including 45 tries, in 91 games for Canterbury.

After John Graham, an inspirational Canterbury and All Black loose forward, retired, he said that, 'the best player, to my mind, who never became an All Black was Buddy Henderson. He was a match-winner.'

Buddy Henderson, playing his 100th game for Canterbury in 1962, leads out the team for a match with New Zealand Universities, led by Richard Hodges. Behind Henderson is Canterbury captain, John Graham, who believed Henderson was "the best player who never became an All Black."

So it proved in 1957. A penalty from near the sideline by Henderson put Canterbury ahead 3–0 at half-time, and after Henderson converted No. 8 Neil Roberts' try and kicked another penalty, Canterbury was able to hold out a late surge by the All Blacks and cling to an 11–9 lead for victory. It was the last time a New Zealand provincial team would beat the All Blacks.

Ironically, Don Clarke had the chance to draw the game, but his attempted conversion of a last-minute Russell Watt try swung to the right of the posts.

In provincial rugby in the 1950s there was still room for top teams like Canterbury to play what are now third-division provinces. So, in 1957, Canterbury's tour of the North Island covered the range of rugby experiences. There was a game at Eden Park with Auckland, lost 16–6, that left Neil Roberts with a dislocated cheekbone, fullback Barry Dineen (in the New Zealand Universities' team that beat the 1956 'Boks) with a dislocated ankle and Tiny Hill in agony with a tooth broken off at the gum.

Two days later Canterbury played East Coast in Ruatoria, scraping home 12–11, despite the home team being cheered on by a spectator on horseback who rode up and down the sideline to follow the play.

Even more distracting to the players in the first contest of 1958, against Buller on

Victoria Square in Westport, was a nearby hotel fire which occurred during the game. Play had hardly begun when a plume of smoke appeared from the town's main street. Flames could soon be clearly seen and before long most of the spectators left the players to their footy. With smoke drifting across the ground and players finding sucking in air an acrid, throat-parching experience, the game lurched to a 6–0 win for Canterbury while the pub burned to the ground.

That was an entertaining day. On the other hand, later in 1958 a game was played that was nominated at the time of the Canterbury Union's centenary in 1979 as the most boring ever played on Lancaster Park.

Taranaki had just beaten Otago and Southland on a South Island tour, and was determined to make it a hat trick. Canterbury was determined not to lose. Both sides decided on a low-risk policy that made full use of the fact that it wasn't until 1969 that there was any penalty for kicking the ball into touch on the full outside your own 25.

A crowd of 16,000 people saw a grand total of 117 lineouts, (on average, one every 41 seconds) as Canterbury struggled to a 9–6 win.

It seems almost proper that Alan Elsom, a player who found humour and a spark in so many things in life, would retire at the end of a season that contained such a dour game. Asked whether he had preferred wing or centre during his career, Elsom, just managing to keep a straight face, said, 'It would have to be centre. I was classed as the best centre in the world, but I was only the second-best wing. Jarden would be just ahead of me there.'

The big target for Canterbury in 1959 was the 25 July game against the touring Lions. It was a chance to demonstrate his abilities that a 20–year–old Fergie McCormick almost missed.

He'd already made an impact in club rugby. In the previous season McCormick found himself at centre marking the much-feared Elsom when Linwood played Albion.

Morrie Dixon ran into Elsom that night, and asked, 'What happened to your face, me old mate? You're a bloody mess.'

Replied Elsom, 'I don't know who the little bastard is, but I'll be finding out.'

Dixon looked up the programme and quoted: 'W. F. McCormick.' 'Never heard of him,' snarled Elsom.

By 1959 McCormick had switched from his usual role in the midfield, or at first five, to fullback, on the advice of a Linwood man, Harry Davis, who back in 1924 was one of the selectors who picked a 19-year-old kid called George Nepia as the only fullback in the Invincibles.

Davis saw a lot of Nepia in the way McCormick played. 'George was a master when confronting opposing forwards with the ball on the ground. He crouched, stepped back and then forward. Attackers were conscious of his movements and inevitably looked up. At that instant George dived at their feet, scooped up the ball and cleared. Fergie was doing this quite naturally. The way he took the ball in a crouch, ready to unwind, was Nepia all over.'

McCormick's first game for Canterbury was against Wellington and he had, as he described it, 'a poor game, where things didn't go right. I was nervous, and half expected to be dropped, but the selectors gave me a lucky break.'

He could thank Pat Vincent, in particular, for his reprieve. Bob Stuart had gone to Wellington and was unimpressed with McCormick's positional play. 'But did he tackle anyone?' asked Vincent. 'He did,' replied Stuart. 'Then as far as I'm concerned he plays against the Lions,' was Vincent's response.

It was the only break McCormick needed. For the next sixteen seasons teams that came to Lancaster Park could expect to find the same ball of angry muscle prowling behind the Canterbury backline, daring an opponent to break through and challenge him one-on-one.

His old mentor, Harry Davis, calmed him down on the morning of the Lions game. 'Do you have butterflies in your guts? Well, don't. It's just a glorified club game. You've got to do the same things. Their wings are sidestepping experts. Watch their hips. If they're going to go one way with their hips, they'll leave you the other way. As soon as their hips move, you move too.'

Olympic sprinter John Young tried twice to sidestep McCormick. Each time he was smashed to the ground. He didn't attempt it a third time.

The 1959 Lions game was notable not only for McCormick's first run in the big league, but for any number of other issues. There was the fact that Canterbury, building on an amazing record against visiting international sides, won 20–14. Also demonstrated was the stupidity of the IRB's rule that didn't allow replacements in such games. For almost all of the second half the Lions played with just 13 men, with flanker George Smith and fullback Ken Scotland both sidelined by injury.

There was the unusual sight, ten minutes before half-time, of referee Colin Robson being told off to a standstill by Canterbury's captain, Tiny Hill. Robson got the full Hill treatment, the baleful stare, the wagging finger and the parade-ground dressing-down. This was all because the Lions forwards were jumping across into the Canterbury lineout. 'If you don't stop them,' said Hill, 'there'll be a bloodbath.' The tourists, it was reported, were furious about Hill's lecture, but the Canterbury captain told the crowd at the after-match function that there had been some problems in the forwards, but 'after I spoke to the ref everything was all right.'

And there was also the slick combination of an outstanding loose-forward trio. The flankers were Kel Tremain (like Wilson Whineray, a farm cadet at Lincoln) and John Graham, a teacher at Boys' High who would captain the All Black in 1964 in a series against Australia, become the headmaster of Auckland Grammar, manage the New Zealand cricket team and be a key figure on panels advising the NZRU on All Black coaches from Wayne Smith to Graham Henry. Less well known, but in 1959 just as effective, was No. 8 Hugh Burry, at the time a general practitioner who was once, it was claimed, called away while playing a club game for New Brighton to deliver a baby.

On the left wing for the Lions was future multi-millionaire, Tony O'Reilly, who was not only the pin-up boy of the tour, with shorter shorts than anyone else on the field and flowing auburn locks, but also an enormously gifted winger, big, fast and elusive.

'O'Reilly beat two Canterbury men by speed and swerve, and was hightailing it for the goal,' wrote Terry McLean in his book on the tour, 'when suddenly he was struck by a Sputnik-type creature which had been orbiting about a yard above the ground for what seemed about half the width of the field. This was Burry, making the tackle of a lifetime.'

In 1981 Burry became the head of the NZRU's medical advisory committee and was a prime mover in successfully slowing the spate of spinal injuries in the game in the early 1990s. His forte as a player, as well as his tackling, was his backing-up, a talent shown by the fact that, despite a groin injury restricting him to only eleven games on the 1960 All Black tour of South Africa, he still scored eight tries.

It was a game on the return from that tour in 1960 that provided one of the most dramatic finishes rugby can offer.

Canterbury had a Ranfurly Shield challenge against Auckland, in a Wednesday game, 27 September. The interest in the game was huge, with the home team's trip from its hotel to Eden Park so snarled up by traffic that the bus arrived half an hour late. There was no time for coach Fred Allen's team talk, and the game started fifteen minutes after the advertised kick off.

Kel Tremain, the year before a hero for Canterbury against the Lions, was actually brought up in Auckland and, because he had been back staying with his family in Auckland for a few weeks after the tour to South Africa, was ruled eligible to play for that province. A man whose rugby talent was matched by his good humour, Tremain would later tell the story of how, quite early in the game, he tried to obstruct Canterbury's captain, Tiny Hill, in a lineout.

'Don't do that,' said Hill.

Tremain, feeling pretty confident after establishing himself as a first-choice test flanker in South Africa, replied, 'What'll you do about it, Granddad?' His next conscious memory was waking up in the Auckland changing shed with a sore head. 'I looked at the mirror, and my black eyes were so swollen, I thought I was looking at a Chinaman.'

The game itself was close throughout, but in the closing minutes, thanks to a try and five penalty goals by Buddy Henderson, Canterbury led by 18–14.

A scrum was awarded to Canterbury just outside its 25 and, with Dennis Young hooking, the game seemed about to be settled. Astonishingly, Auckland hooker Colin Currie won a tighthead. Auckland's halfback, the former Wallaby Des Connor, whipped the ball to Mac Herewini, a mercurial first five who was so highly strung he had been known to burst into tears in the shed before a game.

On this occasion, he coolly lofted the ball into a vacant space just outside the Canterbury line. The ball, *The Press* sadly reported, 'jumped around like a Mexican jumping bean,' away from the clasping hands of Hugh Burry and into the hands of a young Waka Nathan, soon to be famous around the rugby world as the 'Black Panther.'

Close behind Nathan was Wilson Whineray. While Nathan was intent upon simply crossing the tryline, Whineray remembered the scoreboard. 'Behind the posts,' he screamed. Nathan veered in-field and flopped on the ground close to the goalposts. Auckland fullback, Mike Cormack, had no problems with the conversion and the Canterbury challenge fell short by just one point, 19–18.

This was the last game for a man who had first played for Canterbury in 1948, Ashburton-born Ross Smith, a left wing who scored 102 tries (94 for Canterbury) in 152 first-class games. He had one test for the All Blacks, in 1955 against Australia, wasn't sensationally fast, but he was fearless, with a range of ways to beat his marker, and a shrewd worker of angles and timing. In the 1950s shield era, he was a key man in setting up good ball for the team in midfield, running into the backline from the blind, and rarely failing to set up a quick ruck for Pat Vincent and the other backs to feed off.

Vincent, now Canterbury's back coach, provided his usual pithy summation at the end of the 1960 shield challenge: 'It's been a good season for Canterbury. It would have been a great season if the game at Eden Park had finished two minutes earlier.'

However, with Pat Rhind looking after the forwards, and Vincent looking after the backs, Canterbury was to enjoy one of its best-ever years, going unbeaten in 1961 through thirteen games.

There was a victory over Southland, 9–6, the first time Canterbury had beaten the home team there since 1926. Neutral referees then could only be a figment of a losing team's imagination, and in the 1961 game Canterbury players probably felt they were lucky to be awarded seven penalties by the local ref, while he was giving Southland a mere nineteen.

For the survivors of the 1960 challenge against Auckland, the absolute highlight of the following year was the visit to Lancaster Park by Auckland, and the 19–6 drubbing the red and blacks handed out.

McCormick was now well settled as Canterbury's fullback, and he was joined in 1961 by another ferocious tackler, Derek 'Bluey' Arnold, in the midfield. Arnold was smaller than the halfbacks when he toured Britain with the All Blacks in 1963–64, but he played rugby with the fearlessness of a giant prop. So quick that he raced for 30 metres past a succession of potential tacklers in the final trial of 1963 to secure a place in the All Blacks, he was as daring on the paddock as his blazing red hair suggested.

If 1962 wasn't quite the brilliant season 1961 had been, it did include a 5–3 victory over Australia. Canterbury's try was set up by McCormick, thundering up on the blind side, bashing out of tackles and passing to his winger, future All Black Bill Birtwistle. That tied the game up, 3–3, with McCormick's conversion winning it for Canterbury.

John Graham, a flanker or No. 8 of exceptional vision and intelligence, was the Canterbury captain from 1961. Graham was born in Taranaki, gained an honours degree in history in Auckland and then came to Christchurch to teach at Boys' High in 1958.

He had started as a first five for the New Plymouth Boys' High School 1st XV but switched to the forwards, prompted by his school coach, J. J. Stewart, who would later coach the All Blacks. Stewart wrote a letter to Graham saying, 'You are bloody slow as a back, but you'll be very fast as a forward.' In his very first test, against Australia in 1958, Graham showed the skills of a back when he broke from a lineout near the Wallabies 25, kicked over the head of their fullback, Terry Curley, then ran round him, caught the ball on the full on his fingertips and dived over for a try.

Leadership ran in the Graham family. John's eldest brother, Jim, was a prop for Waikato against the 1956 Springboks, and is now Sir James, knighted for services to the dairy industry. A younger Graham brother, Bob, captained the Auckland shield team, despite the presence of Wilson Whineray, from 1960 until after the Log was lost. Whineray was happy to take a break from leadership and Bob Graham was an outstanding captain.

When Canterbury went to Auckland for its 1962 challenge, a still-unique situation saw the holder and the challenger led by brothers. This was Bob's day, with Canterbury turned back, 15–6.

Although Auckland's Ranfurly Shield tenure had been the dominating feature of provincial rugby in the early 1960s, Canterbury's performances rated just as highly when the selection of the 1963–64 All Blacks for Britain was made, with six men named from Canterbury, the leading representation of any province.

Dennis Young was away on his last tour and, at age 33, was still the leading hooker, playing all five tests. John Graham was a test regular, as was Bluey Arnold.

Bruce Watt was a cool, collected first five, whom backs loved playing with because of his simple but deeply effective policy of never passing to someone in a worse position than himself.

Allan Stewart, a 22-year-old lock, had a career that started with blazing promise in Britain but would be over by the end of the 1964 season, while Jules Le Lievre, a tireless prop from Akaroa, would have been a test player on the British tour if he had not faced the competition of captain Whineray and the massively powerful Ken Gray.

Le Lievre was at the centre of one of the more weird incidents in Canterbury rugby history. A 1960 game against Waikato in Hamilton was played in a quagmire. In the course of an outstanding performance, Le Lievre, celebrating his 27th birthday, was concussed and fell like a stone, face down in the water and mud. He was, reports on the day swore, in real danger of drowning. Luckily, play broke down and he was revived, although that night he had no memory of the game or the incident.

The last game Le Lievre would play for Canterbury was against the 1965 Springboks, when he was one of a dozen players in the red and black who had, or would, represent New Zealand.

Playing his first game against an international team that July afternoon was a 20-year-old red-headed flanker from the Glenmark club, Alex Wyllie, who had still to be dubbed 'Grizz'. Wyllie was already a fierce competitor, with a unyielding nature that was extraordinary. When Alex returned from boarding school at St Andrew's College, his father, Joe, remembered an incident that summed up the teenage Wyllie:

'We had an 18-month-old shorthorn heifer. I said to Alex that if we could handle her, she might do well at the Amberley show. She wasn't a dirty beast, she was quite good-tempered, but she was determined to have her own way, and she had a bit of size too. Alex took her out in the paddock and wrestled her to the ground, then he held her there. There were two determined personalities in that paddock, but from then on he was the boss. We took her to the show as a two-year-old and she won supreme champion.'

Wyllie's attitude had impressed Fergie McCormick in his very first game for Canterbury, a 1964 clash with Auckland at Eden Park. The then 19-year-old was marking Lew Fell. A gritty, fierce No. 8, Fell made a blindside run, and was crash-tackled by Wyllie. Fell objected and started firing punches. Wyllie, a schoolboy boxing champion, knocked him to the ground.

At this stage McCormick – he swears with only the most peaceful intentions – came flying in from fullback. 'I thought, "Christ, we can't have the young fella sent off so soon." But the referee, John Pring, just told Alex to go back into position, and he told Fell that if he couldn't take it to go and have a shower.'

John Graham, the captain of the Canterbury team against South Africa, was very familiar with Wyllie. He had been coaching a Boys' High 2nd XV that had played a St Andrew's team with Wyllie in it. 'In those days Alex was really the terror of secondary school rugby. He dominated the game and a lot of the kids genuinely feared him.

'When he began playing for Canterbury he was largely untutored in the finer points of the game, but he had all the skills needed to be a top loose forward. He was quick and strong, with extremely good hands and the natural sense of how play would develop that lifts naturals like Michael Jones and Graham Mourie from being good players to being outstanding.'

The 1965 'Bok game had two extraordinary moments. The first was all delight for Canterbury. Five minutes before half-time the South African flyhalf, Jannie Barnard, broke towards the Canterbury line with four men outside him and just three Canterbury defenders to beat.

He tried to eliminate one of these, Wayne Cottrell, with a looping pass to fullback Lionel Wilson, but ghosting in from the wing was Bill Birtwistle, a former schoolboy sprint champion, so lean he looked gaunt on the field.

Birtwistle was about to wear the All Black jersey and, as he grabbed down Barnard's pass, he showed why he deserved to. Wilson was almost in his path, but Birtwistle stayed cool enough to step to his left, and now there was 90 metres of open space ahead of him. He stayed focused and kept form as he glided to a spot between the posts on the 'Boks' line, with their fastest man, Gert Brynard, chasing every step of the way. McCormick converted and Canterbury was ahead, 5–3. However, the massive lock Tiny Naude kicked a penalty just on half-time, so the teams went into the second half with South Africa holding a one-point lead.

With just minutes to go came the other heart-stopping moment. Captain Graham has centre-kicked for Canterbury, and Wilson and winger Jannie Englebrecht ran, eyes glued on the ball, to make the catch. Before the football landed they smacked into each other with such sickening force that both were knocked cold.

Now there were four Canterbury players – Wyllie, first five Bruce Watt, wing Tony Steel and loose forward Neil Cornelius – and just one South African – centre John Gainsford – near the ball. With 38,000 people screaming their support, Wyllie flicked the ball with his foot towards Steel, a national sprint champion. The Canterbury flier tried to secure possession, but the ball bounced off a knee, spun away and the chance was lost. The 'Boks won, 6–5.

At the time this was rated as one of the best matches of the 1965 tour, but the game with the Lions in the following season made headlines of an entirely different kind.

The match wasn't flash as a spectacle. In fact, it was a shocker. If a footy game was a colour, this one would be grey. There were 113 lineouts, 25 scrums and, when the ball wasn't being thrown in or put into a scrum, one of the 30 penalties awarded by the Otago referee, C. J.McAuley, was being taken. For the record, the Lions won 8–6 on a perfect midwinter's day in front of a 43,500-strong crowd.

It was what happened at the after-match function that stirred most emotions. The Lions manager, Desmond O'Brien, an Irishman based in London, didn't murmur the usual platitudes when it was his time to speak: 'Rugby is a game we love, and a game we enjoy playing,' he started, 'but we are heartily sick of the obstruction, short-armed tackling and other illegal tactics employed by the teams we have met in New Zealand.

'We went out today to counter those tactics, and that is the spirit we intend to preserve in the remaining games. We have had enough. The tour has been enjoyable, apart from the 90 minutes of each game, 80 minutes for playing and ten minutes for the inevitable injuries.'

It was suggested that as he went past his captain of the day, Jim Telfer, O'Brien had said, 'I'm going to say a piece about this, Jimmy. You be kind to them.' Telfer, though, a dour, teetotaller schoolteacher from the Borders district in Scotland, drove the message home harder:

'I don't apologise for the way we played today. It takes two teams to play open rugby. I play match-winning rugby the only way I know. I am not going to say today's game was dirty, because every game we have played on this tour of New Zealand has been dirty.

'When the All Blacks toured Britain [in 1963–64] they were often twenty points up and yet kept the game tight with their stereotyped rugby. So thank you for the way you booed [Lions kicker] Stewart Wilson when he took that vital conversion today.

'I have to propose the toast to the referee, and I might say that it is the manner in which New Zealand referees allow play to run that starts the fighting. I can only wish the referee a safe journey home.'

The response was swift. NZRU president, Harry Blazey, a former referee considered even more cautious in his public statements than his chairman brother, Ces, said that O'Brien's speech was nothing less than a peevish and ill-mannered attack on the referee and refereeing in New Zealand.

'Mr O'Brien's remarks are quite unjustified,' said Harry Blazey, 'and it seems to me that before accusing other teams of illegalities he should look at some of the illegalities the Lions are practising.'

Such as? 'Coming into the rucks on the wrong side, failing to roll clear of the ball and obstructing in the forwards.'

In the following week's *Christchurch Star-Sports*, for which he wrote a column, captain John Graham narrowed the complaints down even more. He accused Howard Norris, described by Terry McLean as the 'not so young Welsh prop with the slipped stomach,' of causing the trouble that began in the front row, and spread through the forward packs. Norris, wrote Graham, 'continually packed in on an angle on the loose head, and he attempted to pull his opposing prop down to the ground by grabbing the front of his jersey.'

Fergie McCormick reckons that Norris was 'a very ordinary rugby player, but an extraordinary bloody nuisance. Most props who have played international rugby know there's only one place for a guy to put his head. It's something props just don't fight about. But Norris pulled this stupid stunt and openly boasted about it. He tried it in the first scrum of the game, and Alister Hopkinson wasn't prepared to let it go beyond that point. He let Norris have one. Who wouldn't?'

Hopkinson was the wrong prop to play silly games with. You won't hear a bad word about 'Hoppy' from anyone who played with him, was coached by him or merely met the man. It was said that thanks to his work as a stock agent there wasn't a person in North Canterbury he didn't know, and not one who didn't like him. A smile or a laugh was never far away with Hopkinson, even in the darker moments.

In 1967, after Colin Meads had been ordered off in the test with Scotland, the All Blacks' bus was a chamber of misery and silence. As Meads got on the bus, the players muttered condolences. Except for Hopkinson: 'Of all the dumb, stupid, useless idiots I've met.'

Meads stopped and the others held their breath. 'What?' Hopkinson was undaunted: 'All you had to do was limp off, you bugger, and the crowd would have clapped you.' Even Meads, in the depths of his misery, had to smile.

If Meads had wanted more advice, Hopkinson might have also recalled Canterbury's game with Buller in Westport at the end of the 1966 season. Hopkinson and the Buller prop, Joe Syron, who had represented New Zealand as a boxer, had been sparring all afternoon. At a lineout, referee Frank Hawes saw Hopkinson throw a punch.

There was no hesitation. Hopkinson was off. He walked a couple of paces, then reconsidered. 'You can't do this,' he told the astonished ref.

Buller's captain, Trevor Craddock, joined in the discussion. Let him stay, he pleaded with the ref. 'You see,' Hopkinson kindly pointed out, 'he wants me to stay too.' With the promise of no more biff, Hopkinson's ordering-off became one of the shortest on record.

Nevertheless, Hoppy's good humour didn't run to being imposed on in a scrum. It was so in 1966 and, as we shall see, very much the case in 1971, when the Lions game with Canterbury would see the home team's play described by a British critic as 'only fit for a psychiatric ward.'

However, that was far in the future as changes to the men running the show were made in 1967. Professor James Stewart, principal of Lincoln University (in 1983 he would become Sir James), was ' Prof' to the Canterbury teams he would select and coach from seven years.

Originally from Wanganui, Jim Stewart came to Canterbury to study agriculture and economics in the late 1940s, and never left. His academic career bloomed, and so did his rugby. Because he wasn't as big as most of the front-rowers he faced, his propping technique had to be impeccable, and he was good enough to tour Australia in 1951 with a New Zealand Universities' team and play 26 games for Canterbury from 1949 to 1956.

Stewart was in the 1953–56 Ranfurly Shield squad, and Dennis Young takes some pleasure in pointing out that two of the forwards, Stewart and Wilson Whineray, would be knighted, and 'not one back.'

As a coach, Stewart was a great mixture of the academic and the practical, a bridge between the hard-bitten farmers of the Wyllie ilk and the more cerebral city boys. Future All Black captain, Ian Kirkpatrick, says that Stewart 'was a truly great coach. He knew so much about forward techniques and their application. He had a good way with the players too.'

It was case of the Prof and the Publican, because the back coach was Morrie Dixon, the livewire wing from the 1950s who retained his energy levels as a coach, as well as his competitive nature.

Captaining the team was Ian Penrose, a born-and-bred New Brighton man who, when he went to Wellington for business for two years in the early 1960s, played as a centre and fullback for Petone.

Ian Penrose bullets a left foot kick, a skill his time at fullback sharpened.

When he returned to the Brighton Club in 1962, he moved to the side of the scrum. Under the coaching of Hugh Burry, Penrose moved to No. 8, where he became a master of cover defence. He had another skill not given to all forwards: a bulleting left-foot kick that could easily tear off 50 metres when his team was on defence.

The Ranfurly Shield was lodged in Hawke's Bay by 1967 and, under the system then operating, there was no challenge for Canterbury in that season or the next, despite the red and blacks being among the guns of provincial rugby.

The best Canterbury could do to prove a point was to provide five players for the 1967 tour of Britain. One was Tony Steel, the New Zealand 100 yards champion in 1965 and 1966, with a best time of 9.6 seconds, which makes him the fastest All Black sprinter of all time. He was powerful too and, after a shaky start to the British tour when his fascination with history led coach Fred Allen to suggest he was 'bloody ancient-monument-happy', his form improved

Tony Steel (left), warming up before a 1964 track meet at Lancaster Park with American Tom Farrell, was a New Zealand champion sprinter, the fastest to ever play for the All Blacks.

so much that the legendary Welshman, Cliff Morgan, described him on the BBC as the 'danger man' of the All Blacks.

The newcomers were loose forward Ian Kirkpatrick, second five Wayne Cottrell and Alister Hopkinson.

Kirkpatrick, with King's College mate, Hamish Macdonald, had driven to Canterbury in a 1958 Holden from his native Poverty Bay to get a taste of South Island farming. It was basically the sort of adventure young blokes look for when they're just out of school, but it would be the football-making of both.

At the Rangiora Club they soon showed their worth and Kirkpatrick, a true athlete with a resting heart rate of 48 (the same as John Walker's when he was the Olympic 1500-metre champion), was just 21 when he toured Britain with the All Blacks. By tour's end Kel Tremain would say, 'I may have been pretty good. I may still be pretty good. But when this kid develops, he'll leave me for dead.'

Cottrell, a baker who played for the Suburbs Club, had such balance, and handled and passed so well that, by the end of the tour, he was seriously challenging vice-captain Ian MacRae for a test spot.

Fergie McCormick was the only fullback chosen in a squad of 30 players. At that point he was 28 years old and had played just one match for the All Blacks, the last test against the 1965 Springboks at Eden Park.

McCormick swears that he replaced Mick Williment in that game on form, although the Wellington man had left the field concussed in the Universities' game with the 'Boks just ten days before the Eden Park test.

Whatever the truth of that issue, Williment had been the first choice of the All Black selectors against the 1966 Lions for all four tests and in the 1967 Jubilee test against Australia, which meant McCormick, in the final trial in Wellington, seemed to be playing, at best, for the deputy role on the British tour.

Not that he saw it that way. After a sleepless night, chatting with room-mate Ian Kirkpatrick, McCormick, after what had become his traditional dry retch just before the game, generally edged Williment in the trial. 'I kept telling myself. "Keep your nose in front. Take your chances."'

When the All Blacks selectors ran through their team in private with the NZRU council before the side was publicly announced, they discovered they'd named 31 players. One was scratched off the list. A decade later, coach Fred Allen would confirm to McCormick's biographer, Alex Veysey, that it was Williment. So when NZRU chairman, Tom Morrison, went through to announce the team in the cavernous function room under the Athletic Park stand, McCormick was in and Williment was out.

To say it was a contentious selection, especially in Wellington, is like saying it gets a bit cold at the South Pole. Even the usually deeply cautious *Rugby Almanack* authors, Arthur Swan and Arthur Carman, were so incensed that they actually wrote of Williment's groin injury, 'his favouring of the injured member became most apparent at a time when it was to his disadvantage.'

Brian O'Brien, the editor of *Sports Digest*, called the choice of McCormick a 'suicidally irresponsible decision . . . one of the most inexplicable . . . in the entire history of rugby selections.'

But Fred Allen's faith in McCormick was rewarded with one golden performance after another in Britain. Two efforts on defence in the final game against the Barbarians, an 11–6 win that sealed an unbeaten tour, bordered on the supernatural.

The Barbarians had two Welsh wingers: Keri Jones, who had run for Wales at the 1966 Commonwealth Games in Jamaica, and Gerald Davies, who the Welsh believed was even faster on a footy field than Jones.

Jones, Fred Allen would record in his book *On Rugby*, was passed the ball two or three metres in-field from the touchline and three or four metres wide of McCormick. 'It was the perfect situation for a sprinter to run round a fullback. Yet McCormick nailed him.'

How did he do it? Allen noted that the 1967 All Blacks had drilled so hard at fitness training that they had all picked up an extra yard of pace, and, just as tellingly, that 'Fergie is a man of character, who believed no one was going to beat him while he was in an All Black uniform.'

Later in the game Davies got the ball several metres to the flank of McCormick. Again the winger was dealt with, throwing a weak pass in-field that was snapped up by supporting All Blacks. This time McCormick used his reputation rather than his body. Colin Meads says that as McCormick, by now famous in the British Isles for his body-shaking tackles, shepherded Davies to the touchline, he was swearing at him, cursing him and telling him what he would do when he got his hands on him. Eventually Davies threw a pass to no–one.

Allen's faith continued to be royally rewarded by McCormick, who kicked 110 points on the 1968 Australian tour by the All Blacks, 28 points in three tests in New Zealand against France, and set a world record with 24 points against the Welsh at Eden Park early in the 1969 season.

Canterbury had a dream finish to the 1960s, although it was hard to predict that during much of the final season of that decade. The team's form had been erratic and, in the lead-up game to a Ranfurly Shield challenge against Hawke's Bay in Napier on 27 September, there was a 20–17 loss to Otago at Lancaster Park. If the TAB had taken bets on rugby in 1969, the odds on Canterbury winning the shield would have doubled overnight.

But coaches Stewart and Morrie Dixon knew that the Otago game was almost a pointer to how Canterbury could deal to a great Bay team, led by Kel Tremain. Tremain was now firmly ensconced as not only the Bay's rugby captain but one of the most successful businessmen in Napier, with a travel agency and a real estate firm.

Bad weather forced the Canterbury team to fly to Palmerston North, not Napier, then chug through a three-hour bus trip and arrive for a brief run in Napier in persistent rain.

But the day of the game was clear and bright, and from the first whistle it was obvious this was Canterbury's day. Driving southern forward play put Hawke's Bay on the back foot from the start, with Hamish Macdonald and Jake Burns, a hard-toiling Marist lock, a steel core in the scrum, and Hopkinson mastering the front of the lineout.

At the back McCormick was in absolutely commanding form, relishing the chances to counterattack given when the Bay, short of options in most areas, decided to get first five Blair Furlong to pepper Canterbury with up-and-unders.

There was even a chance for Bluey Arnold to pull off a superb bit of cheek on his old All Black team-mate, Ian MacRae, the Bay's second five and vice-captain. Chasing a high Canterbury kick, Arnold ran in behind MacRae, and as the ball came down, yelled, 'Mine!' McRae, as a good team man should, stepped aside and let the ball drop to the ground.

Despite a late rally by Hawke's Bay, after being down 18–5 with ten minutes to go, Canterbury was never going to be pegged back and the Log was won, 18–11.

The following morning, at the team's hotel, Arnold found some bottles of sparkling wine. They were soon gone and the party moved on to Kel Tremain's home, where the Bay players had gathered for an end-of-season party.

Somehow the Cantabrians caught the plane for the first leg of their trip home, to Wellington. Faced with a delay of about an hour before the flight to Christchurch, a group including Wyllie, Hopkinson, Burns, Hamish Macdonald, Kerry Tanner and Kirkpatrick decided there was time to go to the Grand Hotel in the city for a few more drinks. 'We got back to the airport,' says Wyllie, 'just in time to say "hooray" to the plane taking off, but we were able to get on the next plane.'

About 10,000 people welcomed the first group home to Harewood Airport, but by the time Wyllie, Hopkinson and company arrived there were just, as Wyllie recalls, a few family members and 'two men and a dog.'

In 1970, when the All Blacks were off on a long tour of South Africa, the Canterbury team that had won the Log was seriously depleted. Bluey Arnold retired and Ian Kirkpatrick had moved back home to Poverty Bay, from where he joined Wyllie, McCormick, Hopkinson, Cottrell and Burns in Africa.

The African tour might have been a triumph for the All Blacks. But Fred Allen, an undefeated New Zealand coach since 1966, heard that he would be dropped before the tour regardless. Outspoken, sometimes brusque, he had stepped on the wrong toes at the NZRU and, to avoid what he absolutely believed would be a humiliating sacking, he stepped down.

Astonishingly, the NZRU appointed a council member, Ivan Vodanovich, who had never been the head coach of a provincial team, to the job. His training runs, so lengthy and tedious that prop Jazz Muller reckoned he needed more games to be able to stand up to them, drained the vitality of the team.

McCormick's tour was even tougher. Not only was the team losing the test series, but he was reviled after an incident in the second test that left South Africa winger, Sid Nomis, spitting his front teeth onto the Newlands turf.

The ball had been kicked through and Nomis and McCormick gave chase. McCormick sensed, but did not see, Nomis behind him. 'I thought I'd make it as hard as possible for him,' said McCormick later. 'There was never any intention to stiff-arm him. I just wanted to slow him down. But as I threw my arm out the elbow caught him right in the face and down he went.'

Nomis went off, McCormick stayed on, and now the crowd was venting all its considerable spleen on the Canterbury man. He was already guaranteed of being the least popular All Black with South African crowds for the rest of the tour when, in the dying minutes of the game, he kicked the penalty that won the test 9–8 and evened the series one all.

It got worse. McCormick was publicly condemned by the team manager, Auckland brewery executive, Ron Burk, who told a press conference that he 'could not have complained if McCormick had been sent off the field. Why on earth did he use a stiff-arm tackle?'

It got worse still. During the week, McCormick told biographer Alex Veysey, Burk came to him and 'stunned me by saying that if he'd been the referee he'd have ordered me off. I asked why and he said, "For the stiff–arm tackle." I said, 'Well, you're just like the other 40,000 who didn't even see what happened.'"

Back in Cape Town, McCormick was approached by a South African journalist, Gerhard Burger, who had stills from a film that showed the Nomis incident from start to finish.

'They showed clearly that I had my back to Nomis the whole time. That at no time did I swing and hit him, that he had actually run full belt into my outstretched arm.

'I took them to Ron Burk in the breakfast room and said, "Ron, these prove I didn't hit Nomis." Ron said, "I saw you hit him." I said, "You didn't, and you owe me an apology for what you said to me in front of the other players. What are you going to do about it?" Ron looked at me and said, "For you, nothing."'

If that hurt emotionally, then in the third test McCormick's pain was very physical. The Springbok forwards, under the benign eye of a South African referee, worked the All Black fullback over on the bottom of a ruck to the point where he needed five stitches in an ear and had two black eyes and what was initially thought to be a hairline fracture of the spine.

He was dropped for the fourth and last test, replaced by Wellington utility, Gerald Kember. The game was lost, 20–17, and with it the series, three to one.

In a very odd twist, there was still a game in 1970 in which McCormick, sneeringly derided as a 'shuffling ruin of an aggressive, teak-tough All Black' by one South African critic at the end of the African tour, could show his home fans that the fires still burned.

The Wellington Ranfurly Shield game on 30 September saw the red-hot challenger, coming to Lancaster Park with a record of just one loss in its last thirteen games, score a try through winger Robert Gray after eight minutes and cling to that 3–0 lead until three minutes from time. With Canterbury awarded a scrum just a few metres from the Wellington line, it was obvious that a dropped goal was the most logical way to draw the match and retain the Log.

What followed was one of the longest scrums that then-new hooker, Tane Norton can ever remember. 'I'd hooked the ball back okay, but it was being held at the back while most of the backs declined to take the kick. The scrum was steadily disintegrating, and I was flat on my back when it was all over.'

Halfback Lyn Davis first called 'Dougie Split.' The ball would go to new first five Doug Bruce, but he didn't want the responsibility. So Davis called 'Baker Split,' a signal that Wayne Cottrell would drop for goal. Cottrell wasn't keen either. In grumped McCormick. 'For Christ's

Tane Norton never gave up on a dream, even if it involved a nine hour trip for training.

sake throw the bloody thing back here, and I'll have a go.'

With both Wellington flankers sprinting at him, McCormick calmly took Davis's pass, sighted, then booted the ball between the uprights for the saving draw. 'I could have cried in sheer frustration,' said Wellington's captain, Graham Williams.

'That was "Fungus" at his greatest,' Canterbury back coach Dixon told author Lindsay Knight. 'He'd taken all the abuse in the world with the business over Nomis, yet he still had to the guts to take that pot. You can imagine the fuss if he'd missed it, yet he never gave it a thought.'

It had been a huge effort by the Canterbury squad to keep the Log through five challenges without the province's touring All Blacks. Coach Stewart came to the end of the season joking that he 'must be getting old. I'm becoming a nervous wreck with all this excitement.'

There had been a brutally unsuccessful northern tour ('Did you win the shield in a raffle?' called one spectator in Palmerston North) before the bulk of the challenges. Illness even forced Canterbury into playing No. 8 and captain Penrose at fullback for an Eden Park game against Auckland that was lost.

It wasn't simple to bring the All Blacks back into the team, either. 'I didn't put Alex and Hoppy into the first challenge (against Southland) after they came back from South Africa,' says Stewart. 'They weren't in great condition. That night Alex was up against a bar, going on about how "bloody Stewart" had dropped him. My wife is a very quiet, Christian lady whom I had never heard swear before. She wheeled around on Alex and said, "Just shut your bloody mouth!" Alex was lost for words.'

Stewart was lavish in his praise for the young players who had dug in while the team was without its All Blacks. 'We asked for a lot. And we got it.'

It was a season that gave two players in particular the chance to show why they should be given a shot at an All Black jersey.

One was Doug Bruce, a laconic first five who grew up in Ashburton and played against Canterbury for Mid-Canterbury from 1967 before moving to Christchurch in 1970.

The other was Tane Norton, and his story is an amazing example of never giving up on a dream. At the age of 12 he was told by his club coach that he was 'just a hooker. Without the other seven forwards you're useless.'

Norton's first provincial game came in 1961 for Mid-Canterbury, when he was an 18-year-old bank clerk in Oamaru. At the time he was training with the local athletic club in Oamaru, then travelling 200 kilometres to Methven every weekend to play with his mates.

When the 1961 Mid-Canterbury coaches had disagreements with both hookers in their squad, Norton suddenly found himself in the front row, including a memorable game with Canterbury marking All Black hooker, Dennis Young. 'I was going to give him the hiding of his life,' recalls Norton. 'Then at one scrum our hooker was about to put the ball in and Dennis asked Canterbury halfback Frank Whitta, "Do you want this one?" "Sure," he replied. So Dennis got it.'

Working for the Bank of New Zealand, Norton moved to Kaikoura in 1962 and made the Canterbury B squad, leaving home by bus at 3p.m. for the training runs and getting back at midnight.

But when he moved to Temuka with the bank, he'd spend three seasons not getting near the South Canterbury squad, and even when he moved to Christchurch, joining Linwood, he'd have three more years as a club player.

Finally, in 1969, eight years since he'd first played provincial rugby, Norton was in the Canterbury squad, a reserve to Gary Bacon, a rising star who, to Norton's delight, moved from Christchurch to Whangarei at the end of the season.

With Norton the player, some things remained constant as his career suddenly bloomed and prospered. He was a superb striker for the ball and his support play was unrelenting. As a person, something else remained the same: a genuine, easy manner that involved true modesty. Years after he was All Black captain in 1977, Norton would say , 'I still can't really believe I became an All Black. It always seemed like something that would happen to someone else, not me.'

In 1971 Canterbury would be a name in bold type in every London paper, but the circumstances were the last the province might have wanted. This was the game in which *The Times* of London claimed the Lions had been 'severely bludgeoned by punching and kicking. The match atmosphere became unspeakable when the open terrace spectators, who numbered most of the 53,000 present, howled for the blood of the Poms.'

The *Daily Telegraph*'s John Reason wrote: 'I'm not surprised Canterbury holds the Ranfurly Shield. The only thing that surprises me is that anyone wants to play them for it. The sight of prop Sandy Carmichael lying collapsed on the masseur's table with his bloodied, broken face packed with ice said all that needed to be said about this shameful brawl.'

Lions No. 8 Mervyn Davies called the match the most 'vicious and ugly . . . I have ever seen,' and flyhalf Barry John accused the Canterbury players of being thugs.

It is true that Carmichael was invalided home after the Canterbury game. It's also true that Canterbury's coach Stewart has always maintained that it was absolute nonsense to suggest Canterbury went out to maim and injure.

Alister Hopkinson swore that the problems started, much as they had in 1966, with the Lions trying to bore in on the Canterbury hooker. Hopkinson had asked coach Stewart what he should do about what he considered illegal tactics by the Lions' props in earlier tour games. Stewart said, 'It's in your hands, but I'm not going to have the whole game ruined by the front row.'

Punches were soon being exchanged, and that's the operative word, 'exchanged.' John Reason claimed that 'it is considered a psychological defect in New Zealand that Carmichael did not hit back. So the other Canterbury forwards jeered at him and the other Lions for being "soft Pommie bastards."'

There was little mention of the other Lions prop, Ray McLoughlin, who was sent home with a broken thumb. He had thrown a punch at Hopkinson, who ducked out of the way. Wyllie was behind his team-mate and McLoughlin's fist crunched into his head, fracturing the bones in his thumb.

Canterbury's captain Penrose claimed it was 'utterly ridiculous to say that Canterbury went on the field with the intention of fighting. It is equally ridiculous to say the team was coached to do this. There was jersey pulling and other petty things from the Lions which do more to irritate players than straight out aggression. John Reason makes it sound as though no punches were thrown by the Lions, apart from when McLaughlin broke his thumb. That's quite incorrect.'

Reason also claimed that Wellington referee, Humphrey Rainey, had called the two captains, Penrose and Welshman John Dawes, together and announced, 'From now on I'm going to follow the ball. If anything else goes on, it's up to you two to sort it out.' In a 1982 book he wrote himself, Rainey fumed at the suggestion: 'What I did say was a normal enough request when a game needs a greater level of control than a referee alone can give. I asked for the help of the captains in controlling their teams, and said, "It's hard enough trying to follow the ball, and at the same time control the players in the mood they're in."'

Rainey had his own theory about the strife between Hopkinson and Carmichael, which he thought dated back to the 1967 All Blacks test with Scotland when Colin Meads had been ordered off. Just before Meads had kicked at the ball near the Scottish halfback and was sent off, Carmichael had kneed the All Black lock in a ruck. A Scottish official would later say that the only mistake referee Kevin Kelleher made was that Carmichael should have been ordered off too.

'I've often wondered,' wrote Rainey, 'whether the animosity between Hopkinson [who had propped for the All Blacks in the Scottish test] had carried over to Lancaster Park in 1971.'

Whatever the extent or the source of the biffo on the field, the game itself was a disappointment for Canterbury. While the forwards won 65 per cent of the possession, the backs couldn't turn it into points and the Lions won 14–3, scoring two tries while Canterbury's only points came from a McCormick penalty goal.

In the grander scheme of things, Welshman Barry John, the gifted Lions flyhalf, under orders from the brilliantly analytical Lions coach, Carwyn James, sat in the stand watching every move McCormick made. They regarded him as one of the greatest potential dangers to the Lions. 'Study his play,' James told John, 'I don't want to see him after next Saturday.'

Duly picked for the first test in Dunedin, McCormick was taunted by John's punts, which dropped just out of the fullback's reach all afternoon. 'It was as if he was guiding the ball by remote control,' recalled McCormick. Two missed penalties, and an exhausting day in the field, saw All Black coach Vodanovich, on his way to a second lost series, dump McCormick in favour of Otago's Laurie Mains.

Three Canterbury players saw out the rest of the series: Wyllie, by now established as a No. 8; Wayne Cottrell; and the only new All Black from Canterbury, Tane Norton, playing the first four of 27 successive tests for New Zealand. The Lions scrumming, he found, was so powerful that he times he found it hard to lift his foot. There was one moment of humour in the second test, at Lancaster Park. Irish prop, Sean Lynch, was angry after a nose-to-nose with Colin Meads, the All Black captain.

'The Lions put in one of their almighty heaves,' says Norton, 'and had us on the retreat again. "How do you like this for scrummaging?" Lynch shouted at Colin. "Very nice," replied Colin. "But we've just scored a try." Sid Going had scooted away while they had their heads down in the scrum and put Bob Burgess in for a try.'

The season also saw the Log go to Auckland. The superstar of the 1970 All Black tour to South Africa, Bryan Williams, did the damage, but not with scorching runs for tries. Williams was nursing a groin injury, which restricted his running, but his long-distance kicking was lethal, penalties from 46, 40 and 42 metres sealing up the game for Auckland, 20–16.

If 1971 had more disappointments than triumphs for the red and blacks, the next two years would see Canterbury rebound to be universally recognised as the best provincial team in the country.

First would come the winning back of the shield from Auckland. It had bounced up to Northland in 1971, but Auckland won it back late in the following season, so at Eden Park on 5 September the Log was up for grabs.

Captaining Canterbury was Grizz Wyllie. Oddly, he doesn't remember his team's victory with anything like affection. The previous Saturday there had been a test against Australia, and the Canterbury All Blacks flew to Auckland to catch up with the rest of the team for an usual Tuesday challenge. (At the time the schedules had been made Auckland didn't have the shield.)

'It wasn't a big crowd,' says Wyllie, 'and it wasn't really a great game. We were defending desperately at the end, and won 12–6.' Fergie McCormick produced the best moment of the day in the changing shed at the end. Pondering the fact the old foe Auckland had been beaten at Eden Park, he growled, 'It couldn't have happened to a nicer pack of bastards.'

So far, so slightly out of the ordinary. Over the next year the history of the Log, and Canterbury, basically went haywire.

Firstly, there was the only non–profit making defence of the shield in history. West Coast had a challenge on Saturday 16 September, which clashed with the live telecast of the third test for the Wallabies at Eden Park. The CRFU gave away free passes to try to bolster the crowd, but just two thousand people, including only thirteen hundred who actually paid, were at Lancaster Park to see the Coast, now an eternity away from the glory days of the 1930s, thrashed 47–3. When they added up the figures at the end of the day, union officials discovered that they had run the game at a loss of $361, described by one cynic at the time as the bar tab for the Canterbury forwards.

Conversely, common sense ruled when an Otago team that had belted Auckland, Wellington and Hawke's Bay during the season was due to challenge on the following Saturday, when the final All Black trial to choose the team to tour Britain was being played. The game was delayed until the Wednesday, by which time it was known that Canterbury had five players in the touring team – Wyllie, Norton, Hamish Macdonald, winger Duncan Hales and midfielder Ian Hurst – and Otago three – halfback Lin Colling and props Keith Murdoch and Jeff Matheson.

Macdonald had been threatening to break through to national level for several years, and once he got there in 1972 he played, as Terry McLean reported after the tour, with a remarkable maturity and 'if anything ranked next to Wyllie among all the forwards in a capacity for sustained aggression.'

Hurst was the bolter in the side. At the age of 19 he had played for North Otago, then for Canterbury Colts and Canterbury B in 1971. But he was almost unknown to the average rugby fan until halfway through 1972.

A competition run by *Rugby News* magazine, to win a free trip for two to Britain drew 15,000 entries, all trying to pick the 30 touring players. Of the 15,000 entries, Hurst was picked by the grand total of seven people. Yet, as McLean wrote, 'He was solid gold. With each match Hurst's qualities, most of them based upon a maturity remarkable in a man of only 22, steadily improved, and he looked to be a player of exceptional possibilities.'

Absolutely unwanted was fullback McCormick, now 33 years old but still as combative as ever. In the shield challenge with Otago he played what many believe was his greatest game. In the process of Canterbury romping to a 23–9 victory, McCormick showed such class that Otago chairman, Charlie Saxton, said that 'he must still be regarded as the best fullback in New Zealand.' Jim Stewart claimed he had never seen a better game by an individual at any level of rugby. Russ Thomas, a great Canterbury administrator and All Black manager, said, 'I have never seen a man have such an influence on a game through skill and courage. I had tears in my eyes as I watched Fergie McCormick that day.'

What did McCormick do? According to John Brooks in *The Press*: 'He must have looked like Lawrence of Arabia to the Otago players as he burst through the clouds of dust on the rock hard ground at the head of men who, if they did not utter wild cries, at least had a light in their eyes that reflected dedication to a cause. McCormick was the source of their inspiration.

'His booming punts for the line brought gasps of anguish from the toiling Otago forwards; his goal kicking was so accurate that the four points he needed to bring up his 1000 for the province presented no problem. And how he ran! Time and again he thrust through the heart of the Otago defence, with the strength and subtlety of a man ten years his junior.'

Wyllie and Macdonald expressed their feelings in a more direct way. To McCormick's acute embarrassment, they hoisted him onto their shoulders and chaired him off the field. Not a man for wearing his heart on his sleeve, McCormick conceded to a reporter after the game that he 'was pretty touched when the boys picked me up. It got at me a bit.'

If doing the dough on the West Coast game, and players chairing a hero off the field, was unusual, what happened in 1973 was just plain weird.

Jim Stewart says the Canterbury team of that year was the best that he had been associated with as player or coach. Keep in mind that he was a squad member during the great 1950s shield era, and keep even more in mind that the 1973 team couldn't keep the Log beyond the very first Ranfurly Shield challenge of the season.

The Marlborough game is one of those occasions talked about so much that if everyone who claimed to have been there actually had been, the official crowd figure of 15,000 should have been more like 100,000. Not that the fans who stayed away were the only ones who underestimated Marlborough.

There's a simple pattern to making sure you have a successful Ranfurly Shield season, and it includes making the first challenges the sort of games that could be won by your colts team. 'I don't think our officials at the time had looked very closely at our programme,' says Grizz Wyllie. 'If they had, I guess they just thought that if we couldn't beat Marlborough there was something very wrong with us.'

It was true that a couple of the Marlborough players had played footy in Canterbury and hadn't made the grade. First five Tony Goddard had never gone beyond club games for Lincoln College. Winger Brian Ford moved from Kaikoura to Christchurch to play for the Shirley Club and had five games for Canterbury in 1971. But while he was a big, strong, fast man, he had hands like clubs and was soon dropped. Back in Kaikoura he threw a tennis ball against the side of a house for hours to improve his hand-eye co-ordination, and when he came back to Christchurch he was in Marlborough colours and ready to do damage.

So, to be fair, was every other man in the Red Devils. Just a few minutes into the game, Jim Joseph, the burly Maori All Black prop whose son Jamie would become a full All Black, crashed into Wyllie on the charge. Making his way to a lineout, Wyllie muttered to his hooker Norton, 'This is going to be a bloody battle.'

The secret weapon that Canterbury didn't know about at the time was Fred Allen. The recently retired All Black coach had been persuaded to go to Blenheim to talk to the players and had then taped an inspirational pre-match talk that ended: 'I know in my own mind, even in the short time I have had with you blokes, that there is every chance of you bringing the shield home. But there will be no short cuts. Everyone must make up their mind they are going to play rugby for 80 minutes, non–stop. Get right in behind Ray [Sutherland, the captain] and Alan [Sutherland, the All Black No. 8]. I expect you to play the game of your life. Spring the surprise and go out and do it. Go to it.'

They did. With eight minutes to go, Marlborough was leading 9–6. Four minutes later Brian Ford ran into Ranfurly Shield history. He set out 70 metres from the Canterbury line, beat a couple of tacklers and was now faced with McCormick.

Keep in mind this was at a time when many of Fergie's team-mates, including Wyllie, reckoned he was in the best form of his long career. Sure, Ford was strong, a truck driver who loved physical contact on the field. He was quick too and had benefited from the coaching in Marlborough of Ralph Caulton, a sinuous wing for the All Blacks in the late 1950s and early 1960s.

Did strength and size worry McCormick? Hardly. Many swear that his greatest-ever tackle was against the giant Hawke's Bay lock, Rod Abel, in 1964 at Lancaster Park. McCormick was spotting Abel just on 25 kilograms that day, when the Bay man, at full gallop, was met three metres from the Canterbury line by McCormick. The fullback crouched so low that coach Morrie Dixon swore 'his bum touched the ground.' Then he uncoiled, his shoulder was buried in Abel's midriff and suddenly the big man was off his feet, driven backwards and slam-dunked into the turf.

As for speed, we've already heard how McCormick disposed of the Welsh flier, Davies, at Twickenham just by shouting at him.

But it didn't happen this time. Ford slowed, then accelerated, and for once McCormick was left grasping air. Try, game, set and match: 13–6.

All that was left for Marlborough fans to do in Canterbury was to drape ribbons, scarves and rosettes on Wyllie Bridge at Omihi on the way home, tip over

Grizz's letterbox and erect a sign at Kaikoura proclaiming: 'You are now entering Ranfurly Shield Country.'

For Canterbury there was a season to rescue. The loss to Marlborough was actually the team's third loss, the first being to Wellington, 37–10 ('At least challengers who watched the game on TV wouldn't have learnt anything about our tactics,' deadpanned Doug Bruce), and then South Canterbury prevailed 15–11 in Timaru. But after the shield debacle there wasn't another game lost for the next twenty matches, stretching over two seasons.

There was running, attacking rugby to burn: Wellington beaten 32–19 at Lancaster Park, while at Carisbrook Otago fell, 17–11. 'The shield,' coach Stewart would note, 'has a rather severe effect on everyone, a must-win, win-at-all-costs effect. Our rugby suffered from being under the shadow of the shield until Marlborough took it.'

Auckland was thrashed 42–3 at Lancaster Park, a game that, in its way, was almost the death of Grizz Wyllie. The day after the Auckland game, and the celebrations that went with it, Canterbury was off to the West Coast for the annual game. 'We left at about 6.30 in the morning, and by the time we got back to town on the bus it was one o'clock on Monday morning when I started driving home. I dozed off near Leithfield. I was heading for a pond, swung it the other way and it looked as if I was going to go through a gateway, but I hit a pole instead.' Although his car was mangled, Wyllie was unhurt.

The most satisfying win for Canterbury in 1973 came at Lancaster Park against a touring England team that would beat the All Blacks 16–10 in a one-off test.

Before the game there were suggestions that, after the 1971 Lions match, it was unwise for Canterbury to be even given the game. In *Rugby News,* editor Bob Howitt wrote: 'It may have been diplomatic for Canterbury to be omitted from England's tour, to allow troubled waters to smooth still further.'

No need. While the Canterbury rucking was the key to the team's success, there were no fist fights and no talk of thugs, just a closely fought game which Canterbury won 19–12, the game sealed by a 50 metre intercept try by Canterbury's left wing, Bruce McPhail, the son of former coach, Neil McPhail, and not to be confused with the Bruce McPhail who played on the wing for Canterbury and the All Blacks in 1959. The 1973 Bruce McPhail had pace too and, although he was chased all the way to the tryline, he was never going to be caught.

The successes kept on coming, with the captaincy of Grizz Wyllie now firmly embedded. Wyllie loved playing for Canterbury, and coach Stewart says that while 'we did have our moments, we established a productive working relationship. Alex had extraordinary commitment, almost unbelievable. We trained three nights a week and on Sunday morning. I can't remember him being late for training, let alone missing one. I've never seen such commitment in rugby.'

Wyllie wasn't one for warm words of fellowship on the field, especially not to backs. His usual vice-captain, Lyn Davis, recalls that 'we argued on the field a lot about how much ball he let the backs have. Basically he wanted the ball to stop at Doug Bruce because Alex reckoned it was "no use giving it to those dumb pricks out there."'

Jim Stewart's association with the team would end with the 1973 season. His great gift to the team had been the scrum that Canterbury developed. When he stepped down as coach he said that 'when the Lions came here in 1971 I learned that we had not been putting enough emphasis on scrummaging. By putting every emphasis on the virtues of good scrummaging, rucking and driving, we've been able to provide the opportunities for our backs to score tries.'

His lessons weren't lost on Wyllie, who, in addition to Norton in the front row, had two powerful All Black props in Bill Bush and Kerry Tanner.

'Tumbles' Tanner was the master not only of the physical needs in the front row but the sledging that saps the will of opponents. In the middle of a 30–0 demolition in 1974, the Waikato scrum was being marched backwards. Trying to rev up his locks, a Waikato prop yelled, 'Weight, weight, where's the weight?' Tanner patted the man's stomach: 'It's here, mate.'

Bill Bush (or, impressively, William Kingi Te Tepohe Bush) grew up in a small Maori settlement in the ranges between Napier and Taupo. He went to Whangarei looking for work when he was barely 15, and soon found himself propping the City Club's senior rugby scrum.

William Kingi Te Tepohe Bush was, his All Black captain Graham Mourie says, "a mighty guy."

He came to Christchurch in 1969 and, at the suggestion of a friend in Whangarei, the New Zealand Maori player Val Baker, went to the Suburbs Club, where his impact was almost immediate. He would move on to Belfast and, in 1971, into the Canterbury team. Strength, size and grit he had already had. The finer points came quickly, under the expert tuition of Jim Stewart.

Bush's 1978 All Black captain, Graham Mourie, wrote in his autobiography that 'if I had been asked before the tour started who I thought might give me the most trouble, it would have been Billy I would have named. If you asked me at the end of the tour who was the ideal man to tour with, the answer would have been the same.

'Bush was a good footballer, able to perform well in the Irish and Welsh tests. If his football had a fault it was that he was too loyal, too honest. The penalty he gave against Wales was for a bit of well-merited retribution.

'In all other aspects of team life, he was exemplary. He seemed to have in the public mind an image as a tough guy, a strong man of the unsmiling giant variety. I suppose that partly grew because of his mien, although, as he promised, when we beat Scotland for the Grand Slam he shaved off his rather fearsome beard.

'Bush's service to the team was an outward manifestation of his outlook on life, his

Three for the training paddock: Fergie McCormick, Lyn Davis and Doug Bruce, together the basis for a tremendous Canterbury backline.

intelligence, and his general curiosity about life. As Doug Rollerson would say, Bush was a "mighty guy".'

The rugby world's axis shifted for Canterbury in 1975. Metric measurement arriving was one dramatic change: now the 25 was the 22 and the footy field was 100 metres, not 110 yards, long. But that was a very minor tremor compared to the seismic upheaval of Fergie McCormick retiring. Fans who had been at intermediate school when he started playing for Canterbury were now bringing their own primary-school-aged kids along to watch him. A Canterbury team-mate, Terry Mitchell, on the wing in 1975 and already an All Black, had been a nine-year-old at Takaka School when the McCormick career began in red and black.

It would be wonderful to record that Fergie McCormick ended his career in triumph, cheered to the echo, the hero of the embankment. But that wasn't the case, or anything much like it.

The highlight of the Canterbury home season in 1975 was a game with Scotland, and the new Canterbury selectors, Tiny Hill and Derek Arnold, made it clear they wanted McCormick there for the big occasion.

Three weeks before the game, McCormick had missed a fly-kick at the ball in a club game for Linwood against High School Old Boys. An Old Boys' forward, diving for the loose ball, landed with all his weight on McCormick's leg. The muscles above the knee were torn and bruised. The next day McCormick could barely walk. After a week of treatment he found he couldn't kick a football more than four or five metres. He ran in the sea to ease it. The Saturday before the Scotland game Linwood played University, and although McCormick played, he found that 'when I kicked, it seemed like my knee had the speed wobbles. I didn't know which way the knee was going, so I didn't know which way the ball was going.'

Hill and Arnold decided to take the chance. It seemed to be all going wrong when McCormick tried to convert a Doug Bruce try near the posts and the ball skewed away. Some of the Lancaster Park crowd forgot the years of sweat and pain that McCormick had poured into the game. They booed him and yelled abuse, asking if he wanted a wheelchair.

Fergie turned the jeers to cheers with a try that won the game for Canterbury. The home team was down 9–8 with ten minutes to play when the ball popped out of a maul and into the hands of a charging Bill Bush. 'I screamed blue bloody murder for the ball,' McCormick told his biographer, Alex Veysey. 'I was on the burst with the ball in my hands when the referee popped up in front of me. I yelled, "Get out of the bloody way," or something like that, but maybe his position was a godsend. It pushed me back towards the posts. I shifted off one defender, then actually got impetus off another as I skewed off him, and the line was there. I was grabbed and held, but it was too late. I was twisting, wrenching at the line. Then I slammed the ball down just as something was starting to say in my skull, "Get the bloody thing down or you'll stuff it up."'

McCormick wasn't able to take the kick at goal. Wyllie, a surprisingly good kicker (his younger sister, Rose, remembers hours in a paddock on the family farm, fetching the ball while her brother practised goal-kicking, 'and being shouted at if

I wasn't quick enough'), slotted the conversion and Canterbury now held the lead, 14–9. That lead would increase, with a try by Bruce and another Wyllie conversion, to 20–9 at full time.

It wasn't that McCormick's knee had blown out that stopped him kicking. It was just that all the emotion and trauma of the previous three weeks had caught up with one of the hardest men in the game. 'I'd never felt so stuffed,' said McCormick. 'It was as if that try proved everything. It sewed up the game for us.'

Ideally, that might have been the end of an astonishing career. But McCormick loved the game, loved the competition, loved the physical encounters too much to call it quits. 'You don't get knocked round in the stand,' he mused. 'You don't wake up in the morning with bruises. But I'd have preferred bruises to that bloody useless business of watching rugby from a safe seat.'

Looking for that game which would restore the form he, and the Canterbury team, yearned for, McCormick kept playing, increasingly frustrated with his own form.

The nadir was reached with his last game for the province, against Northland. 'It had never been part of my game to kick guys on the ground,' said McCormick, but, mad-headed after seeing team-mates booted, he jumped up from a tackle by Rod Macdonald (younger brother of Hamish, who was now playing for Northland) and 'Yes, I slippered him.'

The crowd went mad, and so did the Northland players. Late in the game McCormick, who wasn't ordered off only because the referee hadn't seen him boot Macdonald, was given the chance to clear to touch. Instead he charged straight into the Northland forwards, and was hurled to the ground where he was trampled by his furious Northland opponents.

Fergie wanted to play his last game, which would have been his 223rd for Canterbury, the following Sunday against Taranaki. Coaches Hill and Arnold thought otherwise. 'He was carrying injuries,' says Hill. 'It wasn't fair to the rest of the team to be covering for him.'

Others felt differently, and when McCormick was named in the Canterbury B sevens team it was, wrote John Brooks in *The Press*, 'like asking Sir Laurence Olivier to kiss goodbye to the West End by playing the gravedigger in *Hamlet*. He deserved to be given the chance to play Taranaki, in the team's last home game.'

What seems more important now is that that during McCormick's career for Canterbury, from 1958 to 1975, he not only scored 1297 points but set a benchmark for courage and commitment. He wasn't being serious, but his remark to a frustrated club referee was right on the mark. McCormick had moved on from telling his Linwood backs what to do, to drilling his forwards and then suggesting how the ref should handle the game. 'You're not even the captain,' said the referee. 'No,' replied Fergie. 'I'm the bloody general.'

Fergie McCormick, not the captain, the general.

Alex Wyllie on the farm at Omihi, where they play their rugby hard.

CHAPTER SIX

GRIZZ

It was halfback Lyn Davis who gave Alex Wyllie his famous nickname. During a Town v. Country game at Lancaster Park, the burly Country No. 8 let everybody know he wasn't happy. As the teams left the paddock, Town halfback Davis, his ears still ringing from the verbal attacks, snapped back: 'God, you've done nothing but grizzle, grizzle, grizzle all game.'

So it was that Alexander John Wyllie became 'Grizz' to his mates in Canterbury and All Black rugby, and to a thousand grateful headline writers all over the world.

Alex (his family pronounce the name to rhyme with relic) Wyllie had his own style of leadership forged by his days with the Glenmark Club in North Canterbury. His father, Joe, had been a coach there, playing himself until he was 41, his career finally stopped by a broken leg, which had barely healed before his other leg was broken by a bull when Joe was on a horse cutting out some cattle.

They played rugby hard in Omihi, and clubmates recall one match against the United Club when, ten minutes from the end of play, Alex Wyllie dislocated a thumb that wouldn't go back into place. 'Go off and get it fixed,' they urged. 'No, I'll tuck it under my hand,' said Wyllie, who went on to finish the game.

As his Canterbury career took hold, he inevitably became the Glenmark coach as well as the team's captain. Dave Morris, who coached archrival Amberley as well as running the local hotel, remembered how Wyllie was an expert at mind games: 'Alex would come down to the pub on the Friday night, the cunning bastard, and by the time he'd finished talking to my guys about what he was going to do to them the next day, I'd have half a team. They were never the same.'

Wyllie became Canterbury's captain in 1972 and remained so until he retired from provincial play at the end of the 1979 season. He would become the Canterbury coach in 1982, a choice that wasn't universally applauded at the time. Russell Thomas, one of the great administrators and diplomats of the game, was chairman of the CRFU when Wyllie was appointed coach and noted that 'some people had great difficulty living with the fact that Alex could be a very aggressive personality. To some he used bullying tactics to get his own way, but I think every good administrator in rugby should be able to understand the strengths and weaknesses of the people he's dealing with. You could say some don't like Alex because of his aggressiveness, but that's the man and his nature. That's what lifted him to the top. You can't have it both ways. A passive person gets passive results.'

On his way to the Canterbury coaching job, and the huge success that came with it, Wyllie got a first-hand look at what worked, and what didn't, in provincial rugby during his 214 games, 108 of them as captain, for Canterbury.

If he had a weakness as captain, it was a trait he would not carry into his coaching role with Canterbury. Even fellow forwards thought he liked the idea of dominating the scrums just a little too much. Tane Norton remembers in particular a game with Bay of Plenty in Rotorua: 'We were playing in ankle-deep mud and had a scrum set almost on the halfway mark. Alex wanted us to go for a pushover try! There was no way we were going to be able to do it. We just told him to get stuffed.'

During his last years in the Canterbury team Wyllie led a side coached by Tiny Hill and Derek Arnold in the mid-1970s, then by Hill and Gerald Wilson, who had coached the crack Christchurch Club team earlier in the 1970s.

The best of those years was 1977, when the Canterbury team won the first division of the NPC, a competition that had only started the previous year.

Canterbury had a terrific forward pack that year, with two players at the heart of the tight five who would soon be All Blacks: lock Graeme Higginson and prop John Ashworth.

Higginson, a Rangiora boy, was a grim-faced, taciturn man, and that was just when he was being interviewed. On the field he was even more unforgiving, and on the 1980 All Black tour of Wales he was at the centre of a weird incident that led to an outbreak of referee jokes in Britain.

In the game against Llanelli, touch judge Ian Inglis signalled to Scottish referee Alan Hosie that there had been foul play in a ruck and pointed out Higginson. Hosie spoke sternly to Higginson and pointed to the grandstand. Welsh flyhalf Phil Bennett wasn't the captain of Llanelli, but he was so horrified that Higginson was being sent off that he raced in and joined in a lengthy shouting match with the referee, asking that Higginson be allowed to stay on.

And so he was, but after the game Hosie swore black and blue that the words All Black captain Graham Mourie had heard – 'You're off' – were actually preceded by the warning, 'Once more and . . .'

So why was the discussion so long? It was noisy, said Hosie. Everyone was talking at once, and the noise from the crowd added to the confusion. The pointing arm? The best theory Welsh fans had was that Hosie was saying, 'That's my brother up there in the stand and he needs a ticket for the test.'

Hosie claimed, in what now feels like a sensationally Monty Python moment, that he was just illustrating to Higginson how he would signal the sending-off if Higginson offended again.

When he wasn't bemusing referees, winning lineout ball or doing the hard yards at the centre of rucks and mauls, Higginson was a top-flight polo player, good enough to win a scholarship to Harvard University in the United States to play the game.

John Ashworth, tough-looking, unyielding in the front row, would joke later that he had to leave his original choice of work to match his image on the rugby field. A gifted artist, he was one of just 80 people from the whole of New Zealand accepted for a graphic arts course in Wellington, and when he came back home to Christchurch his skills were used at the *The Press* as a commercial artist. Looking to 'harden up my hands,' he then worked as a truck driver and did seasonal labour at the Kaiapoi freezing works, stacking carcases.

He supplemented his physical work with a big running regime, regularly knocking out eighteen kilometres at a time on the roads of North Canterbury after moving to live at Saltwater Creek, north of Kaiapoi.

The best of the Canterbury forwards for most of those years, however, was Wyllie. He was a devastating runner off the back of the scrum, so well balanced that halfback Davis says Wyllie was 'able to stay on his feet with the ball in his hand, and keep making progress. He had a very hard upper body. He was a bruising bugger.'

Norton, who would captain the All Blacks in all four tests against the Lions in 1977, the year Wyllie led Canterbury to its first NPC title, says that Wyllie 'never wasted words, but what he said had the stamp of authority. He led by example.'

He was ruthless too. While Canterbury was beating Wellington 17–0 at Lancaster Park in 1977, loose forward Mark Stevens slumped to the ground, clutching his face. Wellington halfback Dave Henderson was outraged. 'What dirty bastard did this?' Wyllie stepped forward and announced, 'I did.' Henderson, brave but not suicidal, gulped and said, 'Nice punch, Grizz.'

In 1980, with Wyllie gone, coach Tiny Hill retired and, sticking with a two-man system that had served Canterbury for 40 years, the CRFU appointed Neil Cornelius to coach the team in 1981 with Gerald Wilson.

Cornelius had captained Canterbury in all sixteen games in 1966, as a flanker from the Amberley Club. As a player he was skilled and gutsy. As a captain he was popular but may have lacked the streak of ruthlessness needed for a truly great leader.

Kevin McMenamin, the head rugby writer for *The Press* in the 1980s, would suggest in his book *Shield Fever* that Hill, with his tough parade-ground manner, and Wilson, a quietly spoken, even-natured man, made a great combination as the hard guy and the good guy.

With Cornelius and Wilson, though, there was no bad cop, just two good cops. The stage was reached by the end of the 1981 season where John Ashworth was refusing to drive into town for some training runs because he reckoned nothing worthwhile was coming out of them. The players had lost interest, the coaches couldn't scare any back into them, and the attitude was reflected in three lost games to end the season at Lancaster Park, the last a humiliating 31–6 hiding from Wellington.

It was a grim winter in many ways. During the Springbok tour the grandstand at Rugby Park burnt down less than 12 hours after the All Blacks had trained there, and just three days before the 28 August test at Lancaster Park.

The start of the test was briefly delayed while broken glass, tacks and fish hooks dropped by 40 demonstrators were removed by volunteers (among them Grizz Wyllie.) The tourists had slept the night before on mattresses on the floor of the

Linwood squash courts, and had to arrive at the ground at 9 a.m. to avoid a huge demonstration outside the ground.

Attacked from outside the sport, and with things going dog inside the rep team, the Canterbury Union was ready for a dramatic change.

In 1981 Wyllie was still playing for Glenmark and not only captaining but also coaching the Canterbury Country team. Late in the year the Union decided it would go with a head coach, and Wyllie, prodded in particular by Mike Weir of the Apple and Pear Marketing Board, then Canterbury rugby's major sponsor, finally agreed to put his name forward.

He actually filed his application half an hour later than the 5p.m. deadline, and while the CRFU meeting was going on in Christchurch, Wyllie was unaware that three ballots were being held to narrow it down before he was declared coach for 1982. He was at a Lions Club meeting in the Gretta Valley Tavern when he got the phone call to say he had the job.

In *The Press* the change from Wilson to Wyllie was summed up very simply: 'From a velvet glove to a mailed fist.'

It certainly felt like that to lock Kerry Mitchell early in the Wyllie reign in '82. 'Alex made us train for hours at Rugby Park,' he says. 'I was completely stuffed. My wife had cooked a nice meal at home, and she was really unimpressed when I got home. She thought I'd got boozed after training. I couldn't even explain. I was gone.'

Wyllie had suggested on the night he was appointed coach that 'a bit of discipline wouldn't do any harm' for Canterbury. When the players in his first squad gathered at Amberley, the coach quickly established what that meant. Talk to six players and you'll get six versions of the precise wording of his edict that night about being late for training. One says Wyllie reckoned the only excuses were death or docking; another that it was death or crutching. Wyllie himself can't remember, but the important point, he says, was that there 'were no bloody excuses at all really.'

Wyllie quickly found that he was actually fitter than some of the players in the team, so he began with some long, hard fitness sessions before he moved into any exotic moves or tactics.

'Early in '82 he thrashed the hell out of us at training,' John Ashworth told author Lindsay Knight. 'We spent so much time training I thought about taking my sleeping bag with me. I used to come home so exhausted that all I could eat for tea was a plate of ice-cream.'

Two men would become key off-the-field mentors. One was Doug Bruce, who Ashworth says was 'a great blend with Grizz. Dougie was almost the exact opposite, so quiet and so reassuring.'

Bruce had finally got his due as the top first five with the All Blacks in the late 1970s, one of the *Rugby Annual*'s five players of the year for 1977, when Bob Howitt wrote: 'Mr Cool emerged as a commanding figure in 1977, possessing flawless hands and the most telling boot in the country.'

Bruce's All Black captain, Graham Mourie, says that without him 'the 1978 Grand Slam tour would have faltered after we lost to Munster [in the fifth game of the tour]. He had an educated left and well-mannered right boot plus an outstanding tactical sense.'

Cynics reckoned one reason Wyllie wanted Bruce was that he had always been a heavy smoker, as was Grizz, so Wyllie knew he would never be short of a cigarette. A more honest answer would have been that they thought as one about rugby, without ever having to spell it out. In 1982 they ran trials for the Canterbury team, and the day after the final trial, without prior consultation, Wyllie rang Bruce and asked him if he'd worked out his top fifteen players. Bruce had. Read them out, asked Wyllie. Every time a name matched one on Wyllie's list a tick went on the paper. By the time Bruce had finished there were fifteen ticks beside the fifteen names Wyllie had decided on.

Bruce has always downplayed his role with the team. When I was working on Wyllie's biography in 1991, Bruce claimed that his main job was 'protecting the backs from Alex.' Pressed for more detail, he said that 'when the backs were working on their moves, their patterns, most of the time I was with them. If they'd stuffed up something during a game, Alex would come over and tell the backs about it. I could see what they'd done wrong as well, but it suited me to have him give them the edge of his tongue.'

The other key man off the paddock was more unexpected. About the only thing Jim Blair had in common with Wyllie and Bruce was that he was a heavy smoker.

Blair was a former professional soccer player from Scotland, now based in Auckland as a physical education lecturer at the North Shore Teachers' Training College. Wyllie heard him speak at a national promising players' camp at Lincoln and liked the sound of the specialised fitness techniques Blair was outlining.

Worried that other provincial coaches at the camp might have the same idea, Wyllie waited until Blair headed to the urinals, then made him an offer to work with Canterbury while Blair, who would later confess he was scared he'd offended Wyllie in some way, stood nervously facing the porcelain.

'I told the Canterbury Union I wanted this joker down to do some tests, and that's how it started,' says Wyllie.

Blair introduced, and Canterbury became the first provincial team in New Zealand to use, the grid exercises that are now an accepted part of rugby in New Zealand, from the All Blacks down. It was something Wyllie knew would bemuse some: 'I think some people, even today, see the grids and say that it's kids' stuff. They don't realise how competitive it can be among the team, and how you can improve your skills handling and passing the ball.'

Nobody was more surprised than Blair that Wyllie accepted what was then a revolutionary way of preparing a rugby team: 'If you think about it, for somebody like Alex, who seemed to epitomise everything that was traditional and uncompromising and hard about New Zealand rugby, to pick up what is supposed to be a radical approach from a guy who has never played a game of rugby in his life, worse still, a soccer player, from the poofs' game, is quite remarkable. Really, he was taking a hell of a chance.'

If Blair was surprised, so were some of the players when Wyllie didn't insist on a dour, tight style of play.

Wayne Smith, later an All Black coach, had been a skinny, unknown 21-year-old from Putaruru when he chugged into Christchurch in a battered old Valiant to start

Wayne Smith chugged into Christchurch in an old Valiant, and stayed to carve up opposing backlines.

a course at teachers' college. He was dismayed to find 90 players at a trial for the Christchurch Club, but was told that at Belfast there was a good forward pack, led by Billy Bush, but hardly any backs. 'I said, "This'll do me."' By the end of the season he'd made a meteoric rise to the Canterbury team, and was put on stand-by for the All Blacks tour to Britain.

Smith found quickly that Wyllie the captain wasn't to be trifled with. He once called a blindside move from a scrum, but, with the skipper's head in the scrum, the left wing over-ruled the call and Smith kicked the ball into touch.

An angry Wyllie asked what had happened. Smith said the wing had over-ruled the call because it was early in the game on a cold wet day, and the wing wasn't ready. 'Is that so,' said Wyllie. He marched to the winger. 'I wasn't ready,' said the wing. 'In that case,' growled Wyllie, 'you can **** off!' To the astonishment of all concerned, given that tactical substitutions were not then allowed by the rules, Wyllie signalled, and got, a replacement from the stands.

It was totally Wyllie's show, Smith says, but while that might have been a problem, it wasn't because Wyllie had 'amazing vision and understood the game totally.'

What Wyllie wanted when he became coach was very straightforward. 'If you've got the ball your opponent hasn't, so the first thing is to win the ball. Then, after that, if you can keep hold of it, you shouldn't lose. It's easier to say than to do, but that's the guts of it.'

Given that in his last years as captain Wyllie played the game close to the forwards, to the point where Lyn Davis thinks he slowed games down to suit his own pace, it was perhaps little wonder that backs like Wayne Smith didn't immediately realise that Wyllie the coach wanted them to attack more.

In his first game with Wyllie coaching, says Smith, 'He'd said to me, "Only run twice in the game." After five minutes I'd had my two runs and I was buggered for the rest of the game. We won handily and there was a do at the Hornby Lodge. Alex got me in a corner, poked the finger at me and told me he was relying on me as a decision-maker. I grew up a bit that day I suppose. He put a lot of responsibility on me.

'The next game was against Queensland at Lancaster Park, and it was a great game, probably one of the best of that era with Alex. They came here with all the guns, and we took them apart, 23–4. That day the waiting list for the Supporters' Club jumped up to 150 people. Suddenly people realised there was something special going on.'

Wyllie had several aces up his sleeve with the team. One was a former Christ's College cricket star called Robbie Deans, a boarder from Cheviot, who as a batsman was good enough to make the 1977 New Zealand Secondary Schools' team. At Christ's College he was usually a five-eighths, and only an occasional goal kicker. He became a regular kicker not by choice but under orders from his Canterbury Colts coach, Fergie McCormick.

'Fergie helped me a lot initially,' says Deans. 'His philosophy on kicking is in his book, and it's simply that the more you practise, the more luck you have. You work until you reduce the range of error, to the point where you hit the post and it goes in, rather than hitting the post and going out. He helped me in my attitude.

'For the rest, you largely have to work it out for yourself. You can feel it when you hit the ball, you know when it feels right. If you copy somebody else all the time, you'll never arrive.'

They would write a song about the prolific Robbie Deans, 'Give it a Boot, Robbie', before the shield era was over, and even his brother-in-law, Canterbury and All Black flanker, Jock Hobbs, gave him some grief about goal kickers getting all the glory. Mind you, when a penalty was needed to draw one game and save the Log, Hobbs would tell Deans, 'Have all the glory you want, just kick the bloody thing.'

Another ace in Wyllie's hand was his captain, flanker Don Hayes. A West Melton farmer who once denied the reason he was the slowest tractor driver on the Canterbury Plains was because he was so cautious ('It's just that I seem to fall asleep on the tractor, particularly after lunch'), Hayes, in Wyllie's view, 'did the grafting stuff, not the sort of fancy stuff that shines for a lot of people. He was always right in the thick of it, setting up the ball for other people to work with.'

At the end of the 1981 season Hayes, who had taken over the captaincy when Wyllie retired in 1979, was sick of the job: 'When we were losing I felt responsible, and it was hard to take the criticism.' Wyllie knew that Hayes was actually thinking about quitting top-level rugby altogether.

Hayes himself had a great line in self-depreciation. 'I like to make up my mind before I make a decision, and that doesn't always please Alex.' So why was he considered such a good captain? he was asked in 1985. 'That's a hard question and I can't answer the hard questions. It's probably the pressure from Alex Wyllie. I can still feel him out there on the paddock. He and Dougie Bruce are the inspiration behind the team, not me.'

Wyllie, on the other hand, thought that Hayes was good enough to be an All Black, and was certainly good enough to be the Canterbury captain. 'You wouldn't ever get a more respected captain,' said Wyllie. 'He led by example.'

In the midfield Wyllie had Smith, by now an All Black after the 1980 tour of Australia, and Warwick Taylor, a Matamata schoolboy star who came to Christchurch via Otago University, where he trained as a physical education teacher. His older brother Murray, also a five-eighths, had made the All Blacks from the Waikato, and it was soon obvious that Warwick had the right stuff too.

What struck Wyllie immediately was Taylor's dedication: 'He put challenges on himself, and lifted his game that way. To develop his kicking he used to work by himself with an old ball filled with wet hay. That's the sort of effort he made.'

Wyllie had never seen Craig Green play on the wing when he put him there. Green had been a midfielder, usually a second five, from his days at Shirley Boys' High School. But Wyllie had Taylor as his second five and thought that Green would make

Warwick Taylor, fending off Auckland's Kurt Sherlock, worked on his kicking with a football stuffed with wet hay.

a good winger because he was such a strong runner who was extremely difficult to knock off his feet.

As a wing he became a try-scoring machine. John Kirwan, who played on the other wing to Green in the 1987 World Cup-winning All Blacks, says that 'the secret of his success is the way he uses his angles on attack, which makes him so difficult to mark. Greeno runs to the inside or the outside of you before he actually takes the pass. He's a master at it, which is why so many wings suddenly find themselves out of position for the tackle when they're up against him.'

Every memorable team has a larger-than-life figure on the field. Often he's a player who polarises fans, thrilling with his courage one moment and outraging them with his wild-headed ways the next. In the case of the Canterbury team of the 1980s, that man was Victor Simpson. However, near the end of the 1982 season Simpson, a University centre with the sort of let-it-rip attitude that made McCormick a hero of the 1970s, was almost kicked out of the Canterbury team before the real success had arrived.

Wyllie wanted him to play on the wing. Simpson wanted to play at centre. In Whangarei he played on the wing against Northland. When Wyllie said that was where he would be for the rest of the season, Simpson was enraged by the suggestion. Later in the evening John Ashworth helpfully upended a bucket of ice on his head to help him cool off. Simpson demanded an air ticket back to Christchurch. He didn't get it and the following day, at Auckland airport, Wyllie told Simpson that Green would play on the wing and 'he'll be in the All Blacks before you will.'

Nevertheless, despite the acrimony at the time, Simpson stayed at centre in the Canterbury team and, with success and maturity, he would become not only friends with Wyllie ('If he said die, I would die,' Simpson swore in 1984), but, at the end of 1985, an All Black.

Although Canterbury made obvious improvements in 1982, with wins over Waikato (27–16), Otago (25–18) and Auckland (19–15), not everyone rated the side's chances for the 8 September Ranfurly Shield challenge against Wellington.

One doubter was Wellington's fullback, Allan Hewson. Hewson was a man with a keen sense of humour, so he may have been kidding when he was interviewed by Christchurch radio commentator, Ken Anderson, in the week before the challenge. Asked what he thought the best plan for Canterbury in the game would be, Hewson replied, 'Jump on the ferry and go home.'

On the Thursday before the challengers left Christchurch, Wyllie had Alistair Hopkinson and Professor Jim Stewart talk with the players. Hopkinson warned the players how quickly time would pass and how important it was not to miss any scoring chances.

Stewart riveted the side. 'Most great sportspeople,' he told them, 'get a chance at greatness, and this is your chance. If you miss it, you may never get another one. For the rest of your lives you may wonder if there was anything more you could have done.' There was a steely silence when Stewart had finished. Nothing more could be done in Christchurch.

But there was one more tweak in Wellington. 'On the day of the game,' says Victor Simpson, 'Grizz played us the tape Ken Anderson had made with Allan Hewson.

You should have seen it. The boys went from 70 per cent to 110 by the time they left that room. The timing was perfect.'

Hayes and Wyllie discussed what they would do if Canterbury had a choice of the stiff breeze. 'Grizz's inclination was to take the wind,' says Hayes, 'but he said the final decision was mine. I decided to play into it in the first half. I had a feeling we were the fitter side, and it's so much harder playing into the wind when you're tired.'

Early in the match Hewson was tackled hard by Ashworth and left the field with concussion. One Canterbury player couldn't resist asking, 'Off to catch the ferry, Hewie?'

Wellington at the time had an outstanding backline, but Taylor, efficient and tireless, and Simpson, volatile and ferocious, covered them, as Robbie Deans recalls, 'like a glove. They had such a good understanding, and they did the damage, knocking the Wellington guys down.'

At half-time the challenger was down 9–4, but soon after the break Deans kicked two penalty goals to put Canterbury ahead, 10–9.

At this point Hayes left the field. 'My ribs were injured and I was useless in scrums, and all I could do on defence was run into people. John Ashworth persuaded me to stay on until we were ahead, and then I went. It was painful to go off, but it was no time for passengers.' Huddled miserably in the dank concrete changing room under the Athletic Park stand, Hayes heard the Wellington crowd roar as a penalty by Hewson's replacement, Brian Cederwall, put Wellington back into the lead, 12–10.

Robbie Deans, who followed Fergie McCormick's advice that the more you practise kicking the more luck you get.

With eight minutes to go, Wayne Smith was feeling terrible: 'I'd just lost a try for Craig Green. I passed too late, and the chance was gone. I kept thinking to myself that my mistake had cost us the shield.'

Then Canterbury won a lineout on Wellington's 22 and Smith started to run to his left. In the memory of TVNZ commentator, Keith Quinn, who was calling the game: 'He ran an unusual angle, and just kept going and going and going. As I recall he wasn't dummying, but the Wellington guys were hanging off because Craig Green and a whole bunch of other talented guys were outside him. It just opened up and away he went.' Smith says, 'You don't always get a second chance in a game, but that afternoon I did.'

The wide-angled conversion was one of Robbie Deans' most satisfying kicks of the whole shield era. 'Kicking the conversion meant that Wellington had to score a try to save the shield, as opposed to kicking a penalty goal. They had a kickable penalty awarded, but had to tap it and attempt the try.'

All John Ashworth can recall of the last frantic minutes is Jock Hobbs screaming, 'Tackle, tackle, tackle!' At last referee Colin Gregan blew for full time with Canterbury ahead by 16–12, and the Log was on its way to Christchurch.

Spookily enough, Wyllie had agreed to a Fresh-Up commercial being filmed in the changing room immediately after the game. Years later he still finds his own actions slightly strange: 'You usually hate that sort of thing, but I just had a feeling everything would go all right.' A delighted sponsor gets a commercial that includes the Ranfurly Shield. Jock Hobbs had the last word: 'I think I'm juice logged.'

When the players arrived back to Christchurch airport that night they got a hint of what they had unleashed. Thousands of fans were there to greet them, and Wayne Smith could only get his car away from the throng by driving over a flowerbed.

The first defence of the shield was against Counties, and the Canterbury team, at this time used to playing in front of crowds of about five thousand people, was told to assemble at Lancaster Park by 2p.m. At about 1:45 a panicky Wayne Smith found himself driving round the streets outside the park, looking for a space. There were 37,000 people jammed into the ground and the players didn't have car passes. 'I had to race down the street with people slapping me on the back and wishing me well,' recalls Smith. 'It was getting later and later. This was the most important game of our lives, and almost all of us were running late.'

The night before the game Wyllie bumped into the referee, Southland's Kerry Henderson, together with Canterbury referee Tom Doocey, who introduced the pair. 'Keep an eye on those bloody Counties backs tomorrow,' Wyllie suggested. 'They stand offside a lot.'

Counties, a team that included future All Black captain, Andy Dalton, plus the only man George Nepia claimed was in the class of Bert Cooke, Bruce Robertson, ripped into Canterbury and with two minutes to go the men from Pukekohe led 15–12. It looked like Marlborough all over again when All Black winger, Robert Kururangi, swooped in for an intercept and set off on a 60-metre dash for a certain try.

Back on the 10 metre mark stood referee Henderson, his arm raised for a penalty to Canterbury. The offence? The Counties backs standing offside. Seven days after his vital conversion in Wellington, Deans stepped up for another heart-stopping kick.

'Your routine is vital if you're a kicker,' says Deans. 'When you're kicking well, it just starts to happen. You shouldn't try to isolate the elements. It takes away your fears. You can say, "Just do what you've always done, and you know you'll get the results."'

The kick flew between the posts and the shield was saved. Wyllie's Canterbury squad will never assemble at the ground again. In future the players would book into a hotel (initially the Shirley Lodge, and then at the New Caledonian) on the Friday night and travel by bus to the ground.

Wairarapa-Bush were despatched 51–6, and then there was a summer for Wyllie and his men to really get used to the idea that they were the holders of the Ranfurly Shield.

The 1983 season would prove to be the highpoint of the Wyllie era. Every game was won, the shield retained and the Lions were beaten.

In the process, Wyllie's selecting and coaching skills were be demonstrated in several ways. He had fitness expert, Jim Blair, coming to Christchurch on most weekends, running fitness tests on the players and setting up special individual programmes. 'I know now that we've had the chance to talk over the years,' says Blair, 'that even as a young man Alex was intuitively doing the training that was right for him. I think what stuck in his mind was that rugby training runs are for everyone, and some of the training wasn't suited to him. His body knew what was right for him. Once you get to know him you realise that Alex's a much maligned man as far as his intelligence goes. He has a very conceptual approach to rugby, and you can't have that unless you're a deep thinker.'

As for selection, let's take just one example: a 28-year-old winger from the Marist club, Gary Hooper, who had played nine years of senior footy without ever progressing beyond the Canterbury B team. Wyllie wanted speed on the wings, and that was something that Hooper certainly had. Given a shot at the big time when Victor Simpson pulled out of a trial at Denton Park in 1982, Hooper managed three tries and would play 27 games for Canterbury over the next two years, scoring a total of twenty tries.

In the book *The Geriatrics*, by Lindsay Knight, John Ashworth tells one of the great Wyllie stories, with Hooper the other central figure:

'He was a good player, Hoops, but he'd taken a while to get into the Canterbury A team, and it was Grizz who finally gave him his chance. Hoops had some problems in his first couple of games. He wore contact lenses and these hadn't been working properly for some reason and during a game he'd dropped the ball a couple of times with the line open. After the match, Grizz and Hoops happened to visit the toilet at the same time, and found themselves standing side by side. Embarrassed by his mistakes, Hoops told Grizz he was sorry for dropping the ball but he was having trouble with his sight, although he was sure it was fixed and would be right now. 'Grizz said, "Well, I hope you get your eyes fixed sooner or later, because right now you're pissing down my trouser leg."'

There was also an X–factor with Wyllie the coach, that flash of inspiration that turns out to be a key element in a special victory.

Such a moment came in the 1983 challenge from Auckland. There was a routine that the Canterbury team had slotted into with shield games. It was never broken.

Rugby players are creatures of habit, so on the Saturday morning the players' cars would be driven to the ground and parked. Back at the hotel at lunchtime, getting ready for a 3p.m. kick off, there would be a team meeting. Some players would get a roasting, and some actually wanted it. 'For some reason,' Hayes would muse, 'I react better if I'm being told off than when I'm being praised. If I'm complimented I tend to nod off.'

Warwick Taylor, usually found, he says, hiding in the background at the meeting, notes that 'Alex knew which guys he could rev shit out of, and which ones to leave alone. He never put down the guys who would have frozen.'

On the bus the same route was always followed. 'It felt good,' says Wayne Smith. 'It was like going to the office every day. The same stop signs. The same little old lady working in her garden.'

Gear bags would be dropped in the changing shed and then the players would get together again, the shield on a chair at the front of the meeting room above the stand, while Wyllie and Bruce had another say.

Then it was back to the shed and another set of rituals. At some point Victor Simpson, storming around the room in just a pair of shorts, would pick up one of the management group, Les McFadden, and quickly do ten squats with McFadden across his shoulders. Meanwhile, Wyllie would be circling through the room, stopping for a word here, a cuff on the shoulder there.

Just before the 1983 game with Auckland, a side unbeaten to that point in the season, Wyllie decided upon a dramatic, and extraordinarily late, change to the Canterbury game plan. Says Smith, 'We were in the tunnel, waiting to go on the field. Alex suddenly grabbed my jersey and said, "Run it from everywhere." He just had a feeling and at the last second decided it was on to run it all day.'

And that's exactly what Canterbury did. Auckland coach, John Hart, had Buck Shelford playing on the blind side that season, not at No. 8. Shelford's courage, strength and determination made him a great No. 8, but he wasn't quite nimble enough on the side of the scrum to stop Canterbury halfback Bruce Deans, Robbie's gifted younger brother, from making a string of searing blindside breaks. By the time the game was over, Canterbury had scored five tries, Auckland none, and the result was a remarkable 31–9.

There were some unusual aspects to the game against the 1983 Lions. For a start, the match was played on a Tuesday, with the third test against the All Blacks the following Saturday. And it was a pleasant change that in the lead-up to the game it was the visiting players who were defending themselves against allegations of foul play.

In the 21–12 win over North Auckland three days before they played Canterbury, Lions lock, Steve Bainbridge, was caught on video head-butting Northland's Alistair Robinson.

The Lions' manager was Willie John McBride, who had locked the scrum in both the 1966 and the 1971 Lions games with Canterbury. In 1983, with the charge of dirty play levelled at one of his men, McBride went ballistic. 'I have not seen the [Bainbridge] incident on video,' he told a press conference when the team arrived in Christchurch, 'and nor do I intend to. I think it's disgusting that we are being made out to be the aggressors by the New Zealand media. Frankly I'm sick of it. The New Zealand media are killing rugby. I have nothing more to say because I've had a gutsful.'

As it happens, the game did involve a weird foul-play touch, when Irish centre David Irwin, outraged at Warwick Taylor jostling Roger Baird as the Scottish winger was running to drop out from the Lions 22, elbow-jolted Taylor so hard he was knocked to the ground. Robbie Deans, who had already scored a try, which he converted, and kicked three penalty goals, kicked another penalty from the Irwin offence to put Canterbury ahead 22–16, with seven minutes to play.

Irwin had the satisfaction of then running in a try that gave Irish fullback, Hugo MacNeill, the chance to draw the game with a last-minute conversion halfway between the posts and the sideline on the right side of the field. MacNeill, 'never one to do things by halves,' as one commentator noted, took the ball four or five metres back from the 22 and belted it with everything he had. A right-foot instep kicker, he sank to his knees when he saw the ball curl from right to left and keep on its path across the face of the goal posts. Canterbury had the game, 22–20.

An outstanding figure for Canterbury in the Lions game, as he was throughout the shield era, was Dale Atkins. Big, burly and a consistent try scorer, he became, in Wyllie's view, up there with Buck Shelford as a No. 8 capable of driving off the back of a scrum near the line.

Auckland All Black, A. J. Whetton, would single out Atkins in a select list of his most difficult opponents: 'Dale was always difficult to mark because of his size. He wasn't a tall man, but he was very powerful and he could jump in the lineout and run with the ball. When he left the back of a scrum with the ball he was an awesome character. I always had my hands full when I played against him.'

What Canterbury and Wyllie also showed during the 1982 and 1983 seasons was that anyone who had the idea their style would be limited to forwards grunting the ball up the middle of the field, with the backs there to make tackles and fill up the gaps in the top half of the programme's team list, was very wrong.

A shot that's extremely rare. Usually when Dale Atkins ran from No.8 he was the one knocking someone over.

Wyllie himself says he knew that 'outside Canterbury there were comments when I got the coaching job that Canterbury would go back to playing it tight. That was never the case with us.'

Robbie Deans is blunt about the perceptions: 'If you believed the media you would think Alex was just a rough oaf. His tactical appreciation is often underestimated. He's forever thinking about the game and areas that can be exploited. With Canterbury, he looked at what he had and where he wanted to go. He wanted to play 15-man rugby, and he slotted those players in to fit. In his last days as a player that wasn't how the game was played. It was possibly a reflection of the state of his own body that [as a captain] he didn't look for a lot of running.'

Victor Simpson gets almost as fierce as he was when he was playing: 'We only closed the game down when the opposition team wouldn't play the attacking game. We were more mobile than our opponents, we were fitter and we ran it wider. In 1983 Craig Green scored more tries [sixteen] than any other winger in New Zealand. There were no pushover tries for us!'

If the Counties game was the near-miss of 1982, the game that stretched the fabric in 1983 was the match with Wellington. This was the chance for Wellington to not only win the Log but to gain revenge for losing it the previous year. The shield rumour mill in Canterbury ran wild. At the heart of the gossip was the suggestion that the arrogant Wellington Union regarded the victory as a done deal.

The new Michael Fowler Centre in Wellington was being officially opened on the night of the game, and probably the wildest rumour in Canterbury had Wellington officials planning for the Log to arrive at the Centre on a pre-booked helicopter to kick-start the celebrations. If that story had even a grain of truth, it wasn't to be.

There was talent all through the Wellington side, from Allan Hewson at fullback, to Bernie Fraser and Stu Wilson on the wings, to Murray Mexted at No. 8, and future World Cup-winning lock, Murray Pierce, in the middle of the scrum. But he would be gone twenty minutes from the end, with a broken jaw, after dominating the lineout for the previous hour. At the time, and since, Wellingtonians have believed that he was deliberately bashed out of the game.

The man who threw the punch, prop Murray Davie, swore to Kevin McMenamin that wasn't the case. Davie agreed that he punched Pierce but said it wasn't a specific attack to get Pierce out of the game. 'I was hit from behind, and I simply retaliated in the direction the blow came from. Pierce just happened to be the man on the receiving end.'

What was more damaging to the Wellington cause was a try lost just before half-time when Hewson, a hugely gifted player so skinny that it was once suggested he had to run round in a shower to get wet, speared through a kick for Fraser to run on to. The Wellington fullback was leaping in the air in celebration when, to his absolute horror, he saw Fraser snatch at the ball and knock it on.

At half-time, says Victor Simpson, he was tightening his sprigs and 'as Alex was going off he said, "We've got these pricks. Get into them." I thought to myself, "You've got me." I admired our forwards. You could bend them for 60 minutes of a game, but then they'd get up and bend the other side.'

Late in the game, with his team still ahead 16–13, Wellington captain, Paul Quinn, urged his forwards on with the words, 'Nothing silly now. We've got this game won.' Hayes, with a sense of humour drier than a West Melton hay paddock in late January, mused later whether Wellington giving away a penalty just outside its half, duly kicked by Deans to tie the game up 16–16, was something 'silly' or not.

Eight minutes from the end, Hayes sealed the game with a try near the corner. Wyllie's reaction? 'He wanted to know why I didn't score under the posts.'

It was the last of just two amazing years for Gary Hooper, the man who proved that there's always hope of bigger things as long as you're playing. While Hooper turned to his other major love, cricket, Robbie Deans toured Britain with the All Blacks, along with Craig Green, Warwick Taylor, Wayne Smith, Jock Hobbs, Albert Anderson and Murray Davie.

Deans stayed on in Europe to play a season with the Grenoble Club in France, which provided him with one of the classic rugby stories: 'It was my first game, and in the shed the coach was going hell for leather and I couldn't understand a word he was saying. I could see from the response of the rest of the team that it was pretty emotional stuff. Then I went and relieved myself in what I found, from the gestures of the officials, was the wrong place. Those French toilets are very complex.

'When I got back to the team they were all sitting on the floor, doing a rowing exercise in pairs. I had to row with a front-row prop who was built like Alex Wyllie. He was really wound up, and basically bounced me all around the room. Once I'd staggered to my feet and got ready to leave the shed, the masseur came up and kissed me on both cheeks. I was pretty relieved to step onto the field.'

If 1983 was the absolute golden year for the Canterbury side, the following wasn't too shabby either, although there were early signs that it wasn't going to be quite the thriller '83 had been. One ominous sign came at Eden Park, where Auckland, so well whipped the year before, rebounded with a 32–3 thrashing.

There were many theories as to why the turnaround had been so dramatic. One was that Jim Blair was now supplying fitness programmes to Auckland as well as Canterbury. Blair himself believes that Wyllie's love of a training run may have had something to do with it: 'I'm very much against players training on the day before a game. When Alex came to Auckland in '84 he rang me and said they were going to have a training run on the Friday. I said, "Alex, you know how I feel about that." He said, "It'll only be light. Come and have a look for yourself."

'Well, he totally redefined the word "light". They'd trained on a fairly heavy ground, and I believe the match with Auckland was lost on the Friday. I feel they lacked in sharpness on Saturday, they appeared dead in the legs and the game was lost.'

Oddly enough, the loss, which broke a 29-game winning sequence, wasn't a source of huge remorse for the Canterbury team. In a brutally honest comment in 1984, Don Hayes noted, 'When you're winning, even the idiots want to be your mates.'

The pressure that builds on players in Canterbury rugby is possibly greater than in any other province. A community feeling that embraces the team can be stifling as well as supportive. The centre of a lot of that attention in the 1980s was Robbie Deans, and he sums it up as well as anyone: 'The Ranfurly Shield transformed everything. Goal-kicking tends to focus attention on a player and, as the Canterbury goal-kicker, that gradually happened to me. Living on the farm, I was in the fortunate position of being able to get out of town and away from all the attention. At times life must have been hell for those jokers in Christchurch. I knew how much attention the shield was getting from going in for the games, but I didn't have it rammed down my throat. At 3ZB they did a marvellous job for the game, but the pressure was relentless.'

With one monkey – the record streak of victories – off their back, the red and blacks had to regroup with the selection of seven Cantabrians in the All Blacks to tour Australia: Deans, Green, Taylor, Smith, Hobbs, Anderson and Ashworth.

Jock Hobbs was another key player in the shield reign, an openside flanker and another former Christ's College cricket star, like Robbie and Bruce Deans, who would eventually make his national mark at rugby.

Speed and fearlessness were two marks of Hobbs' play and, although that fearlessness would later lead to concussions that robbed him of a possible captain's role at the 1987 World Cup, his talents made him an All Black in all four tests against the 1983 Lions.

He had vivid memories of his first test, played at Lancaster Park, of seeing his parents from the bus window as they walked to the ground, and then playing a test on the side of a potent All Black scrum, a feeling he described as 'like sitting in the front row of a Rolls-Royce.'

Hobbs would go on to play a major role in the signing of wavering All Blacks to the NZRU in 1995, trying to make sure they wouldn't be swept away by the privately owned World Rugby Corporation. His reward for weeks of sleepless nights, frantic travelling and nerve-racking negotiations was to be voted off the NZRU council after just eight months in the job. His remarkable rehabilitation to the boardroom would come seven years later when, in the wake of the World Cup-hosting debacle and the damning Eichelbaum Report, he was swept back into power as chairman of an all-new NZRU board.

New to the Canterbury team in 1984 was a man whose style was a world away from the urbane lawyer, Hobbs. Andy Earl, who grew up in the Hawarden area, went north as a 17-year-old to work on farms in the Wairarapa. When he returned to Canterbury, to run a Rotherham dairy farm and play for the Glenmark club, he was still only 21. But he was already so sinewy and strong that he was quickly welcomed into the Canterbury pack. 'A lot of us were pretty raw talent, keen as hell,' says Earl. 'We were lucky that we had a few older guys like Donny [Hayes] and Wishy [Ashworth] that we had a lot of respect for. But nobody was treated, or acted, as being better than anyone else.'

Jock Hobbs, fast, fearless, and denied by injury the chance to captain the All Blacks at the first World Cup.

Also making a claim for another member of a famous family to be in the All Blacks was halfback Bruce Deans, the younger brother of fullback Robbie. 'Diesel' Deans, like Earl, stayed working as a farmer throughout the Wyllie era, and his selection ahead of Steve Scott, a 1980 All Black from the Shirley Club, was a major talking point when the new coach took over.

Wyllie had still been playing for Glenmark when the teenage Bruce Deans first played halfback at the club, and he had no doubts over Deans' qualities: 'I knew Bruce's game pretty well, and he had the variations for what we wanted to do on the field. He was strong, he could run, he could kick over the top and he had a pass that was a lot quicker than people initially gave him credit for. He wasn't just a halfback for the forwards.'

For the first two challenges of 1984 there was a radically different look about the Canterbury team. Rod Latham, better known as a determined all-rounder in the New Zealand one-day cricket team, was at fullback against Nelson Bays (won 34–10) and Buller (57–13), along with men who would remain top-flight club players, such as University prop Phil Robson, Old Boys midfielder James Leggat, Suburbs flanker Barry White and Shirley hooker Barry Dixon.

When the All Blacks returned from Australia, a softer side of Wyllie emerged. The coach found it so hard to tell the players he had used for Canterbury while the All Blacks were away that they were no longer needed. There was hardly room on the training field for the extended squad. Eventually the job of breaking the news to the players who weren't wanted was assigned to Doug Bruce.

With all the All Blacks back in the fold, West Coast (68–3) and Wairarapa–Bush (24–6) were dealt with, and the season highlight came with a 44–3 whipping of Otago.

This was the chance for Canterbury to show that skilled back play and elaborate moves were part of the armoury.

A try by Andrew McMaster, an air force man who Wyllie reckoned would have been a leading contender for the 1985 tour of South Africa if he had not left for Britain for a training course with the RAF, drove the 35,000 fans into a frenzy. Smith, Taylor and Simpson worked a double scissors move that culminated with Robbie Deans hitting a Simpson pass at full speed and making the final pass to McMaster.

All five tries that day were scored by backs, but the forwards had dominated too, winning ten of the eleven lineouts in the second half and providing such quick ruck ball to Bruce Deans that the play was described by one critic as 'rugby in excelsus.'

Waikato, unheralded before the game, got close at 16–10, and it took seven penalty goals from Robbie Deans to turn away Counties, who scored three tries to Canterbury's one, going down 27–19.

The closest shave came in the last challenge of the year, against Bay of Plenty. The Bay arrived with little fanfare, having just been spanked 65–9 by Auckland, the seventh loss in their nine first-division games in 1984. The day before the game they took a leisurely bus trip to Akaroa, prompting the *Christchurch Star* to ask whether the visitors were in town for a shield game or as a tourist party.

What Bay of Plenty did have was a rugged forward pack, with an All Black, Frank Shelford (a cousin of Buck's), on the flank, an All Black lock, Gary Braid, and one of the most publicised forwards of the time, Hika Reid, or Hika the Happy Hooker from Ngongotaha, as he was branded on a brilliant debut tour with the All Blacks in 1980. Adding to the mix as a prop was a 23-year-old part-time pub bouncer from Rotorua, a New Zealand judo champion called Steve McDowell.

The Bay forwards played in a frenzy for all of the game, winning a tighthead in the fourth minute to set up a try for winger John Hanley, and then storming the Canterbury line again and again in the closing minutes, down 18–13 and needing a converted try for the win and the shield.

With time showing on the clock, the Bay tapped eight metres out and Peter Kennedy, a barrel-chested 107 kilogram prop, flung himself at the line. Behind him captain Hayes thought, 'What a bugger, losing it in the last minute of the last game of the season.' But two Canterbury players, Wayne Smith and Andy Earl, were doing everything they could to stop Kennedy.

Smith told Kevin McManemin that all he was trying to do was pull the ball clear. 'Considering the differences in our sizes there was no way I could have held him up.' Earl had different plans. With his bare left arm wrapped around Kennedy's chest, he somehow pushed the Bay man off his dive. Kennedy was adamant that he had scored. Smith was equally convinced he was inches short.

With video replays and television match officials still more than a decade away, Smith says that 'My biggest fear was that the referee [Hawke's Bay's Geoff Smith] would not be in a position to see the gap. But then I saw his feet close by and I knew we would be okay. He was perfectly positioned to see what happened, and we very lucky that he was.'

Not so fortunate was Robbie Deans, who in this game tore an anterior cruciate ligament, the medial ligament and the cartilage in his right knee. It would be the last day of July the following year before he would be able to return to the Canterbury team. The distance he could goal kick had been reduced by about ten metres. 'When you kick with an

Andy Earl, raw, sinewy and "keen as hell."

uninjured leg, the leg actually hyperextends to a few degrees beyond 180. After the operation you should really keep the leg a few degrees below 180. So there's a natural loss of power.'

Nevertheless, the fans wanted Deans back in the Canterbury colours much sooner than Wyllie did, and the fullback was turning out for Glenmark as early as 15 June. Wyllie was unmoved. Deans wasn't, he believed, fully fit after his knee rehabilitation, so first utility Keiran Keane and then Rod Latham, who had already told Wyllie he wanted to only play club football to concentrate on his cricket, was at fullback when challengers King Country (33–0), Taranaki (27–3) and Southland (53–0) were all rebuffed.

Deans returned for a 42–4 win over Marlborough, with Craig Green scoring five tries, a mediocre 17–7 win over Mid-Canterbury and the despatch of North Auckland, 29–3.

That game equalled the record of 25 shield defences set by the Fred Allen-coached Auckland team of the 1960s, and set things up perfectly for the challenge from Auckland on 14 September, which had already been billed the previous year as the game of the century.

It was a brave and generous gesture by the Canterbury Union. The Union could easily have slipped in a midweek game against a third-division union and picked up the record. Instead, just as Auckland in 1963 had given Hawke's Bay, who in the 1920s had set a record of 24 defences, the chance to defend its own record, Canterbury chose to do the same with Auckland.

There was controversy before the sold-out game, which drew 52,000 spectators, when the NZRU decided against allowing a live telecast. Wyllie was happy for the game to be shown live, even suggesting a switch to a Sunday challenge, so it wouldn't clash with live rugby elsewhere in the country.

While the Canterbury players could only try to avoid the hype, Auckland actually did. Their squad had a low-key meeting with players from the 1963 team at Eden Park, then slipped away to Christchurch that Friday afternoon. A media ban was enforced, most notably on Auckland captain Andy Haden, who before the 1983 challenge had rarely been off the phone satisfying interview requests.

On the other hand, the Canterbury players, as Wyllie remembers, 'were like me, we didn't seem to have a minute to spare.' Captain Hayes recalls, 'The days you play very well everyone has thought about the game, and everything seems to go right all down the line. We just had a lot of little things that didn't click before the Auckland game.'

Hayes won the toss and, just as he had back in 1982 when Canterbury had won the Log from Wellington, decided to play into the wind.

The first half was a nightmare for Canterbury. Robbie Deans, usually as safe as a bank, fumbled a high kick, and Auckland's centre Joe Stanley pointed with his free hand at a gap that opened, then ran into it for a try. Winger Terry Wright chased his own kick for another. Victor Simpson tried to run out of the Canterbury 22, was caught, the ball was wrestled off him by Steve McDowell (who, largely on the basis of his outstanding game the previous year in the Bay of Plenty shield challenge, had been wooed to Auckland), and quickly passed to John Kirwan for a try. Just before half-time Kirwan made another break and prop John Drake was on hand for

Auckland's fourth try. The dead-eye Grant Fox had added two penalty goals and a conversion, and the half-time score was Auckland 24, Canterbury 0. The match of the century looked like developing into the farce of the century.

It was a time for a cool Canterbury head, and, to the surprise of some, it was Wyllie who provided it.

He did so under unique pressure. In the stand during that hectic first half, a group of gang members, one of whom thirteen days later murdered a complete stranger with a shotgun at the Woolston Tavern, blocked Wyllie's view of the game. Asked to move, one of them wrapped a chain around his hand and urged Wyllie to come down and fight. Police moved the group, but not out of the ground.

As Wyllie and Bruce made their way to the middle of the park at half-time, Wyllie was punched in the side of his back. 'People in front us had parted to let Doug and myself through. When I was hit I half turned and brushed the joker who had hit me out of the way.' That backhand was caught on television and led to stories that Wyllie had been so angry he'd backhanded an innocent spectator. In fact it was one of the gang.

Wyllie says he was disappointed for his team, not in any way angry. 'They were letting themselves down after doing so much for the game in Canterbury. After proving themselves and getting as far as they did, it was looking as if they might lose by 40 points. It was just a matter of me saying, "Auckland has scored 24 points, there's no reason why you can't. The ball's there, just get the bloody thing and start scoring points!"'

Skipper Hayes started the comeback. Six minutes into the half he flung himself at a Fox clearing kick and charged it down. The ball bounced wildly and was grabbed by Bruce Deans, who dived the Auckland line.

Four minutes later, Auckland won a lineout on Canterbury's 22. Openside flanker Mark Brooke-Cowden surged ahead and set up a ruck. Drake flicked the ball between his legs to McDowell and he plunged over for the try. The score was now 28–4. In the stand Wyllie thought, 'Hell, the half-time talk hasn't worked at all.'

But on fifteen minutes Robbie Deans darted on the blind and kicked the ball ahead for Green to gather and score near the corner flag. Deans kicked a magnificent conversion. Seven minutes later, the Canterbury fullback kicked a penalty: 28–13.

With just five minutes to go it was obvious that the steam was starting to run out of the Auckland team, and the Canterbury players were rampant. Smith worked miracles at first five, running to the blind, setting up a ruck, then getting back to set up a maul on the open side. He wrenched himself free, took the pass from halfback Deans, kicked to the right wing and backed up Hobbs, who scrambled the ball to Smith for a try: 28–17.

The Aucklanders were stunned. Joe Stanley said later, 'I just couldn't believe it was possible when Wayne Smith got the try and it was down to eleven points. They must have been stuffed, but they kept on coming.'

Three minutes to go and Robbie Deans hoisted an up-and-under from a penalty. Green beat Auckland hands to the ball and fed prop Chris Earl, who bashed up-field before passing to lock Albert Anderson.

Anderson was a huge man but extremely fit. Wayne Smith remembers blessing

Coach Alex Wyllie knew the range of qualities that Bruce Deans brought to the halfback position.

him and fellow lock Kerry Mitchell early in the shield era. 'Sometimes I think if it hadn't been for them we'd have all been dead. They were the biggest and they were often last in the sprints, so Alex would say, "Anderson, I told you not to be last, and here you are at the back. Do it again." We'd have a bit of a break. Time and again I'd look at Victor and say, "Thank goodness for Bert and Mitch."'

All that work paid off when Anderson saw only Grant Fox between him and the line. Fox was brave and went low, but there was a 35 kilogram weight difference between the two and Anderson had enough energy left to fling himself into the air at the line. Fox had no chance, the try was scored and Deans converted: 28–23.

Now there was dread in the Auckland squad. Joe Stanley recalls thinking, 'We could lose this. Twenty minutes before we'd been up by nearly twenty points, and now all they needed was a converted try to win.'

When Canterbury won a lineout 30 metres from the Auckland line, Smith kicked high. The ball bounced in front of the Auckland posts and gently looped over the line. Canterbury's Green and Auckland's Kirwan and Fox all grasped for the ball, but Kirwan got his fingertips to it, slapped it over the deadball line and referee Bob Francis blew full time.

Later, there was a brief flurry of controversy over whether there should have been a couple of minutes left to play because a digital timer on the delayed television coverage showed a full three minutes remaining.

If there had been a five-metre scrum, Auckland's All Black flanker, A. J. Whetton, confessed straight after the game, he wouldn't have had the strength left to lift up his arms for a tackle if Bruce Deans had run on his side of the scrum.

But there will never be any whining from the Canterbury squad. Reflecting on the game, Warwick Taylor says that 'if we'd lost it playing badly we would have all felt bitter about it. As it was, it hurt, but we didn't feel let down. Alex had always said he didn't mind if we lost it, as long as we played well. And we did play well.'

In the course of holding the shield from 1982 to 1985, Canterbury scored 938 points, with 214 scored against them, clocking up 140 tries while conceding just nineteen, five of them to Auckland in the final defence. Robbie Deans scored 332 points in his 22 games, while Craig Green played 24 games and scored 24 tries. The 26 games at Lancaster Park drew a total of 490,000 people.

But it wasn't the statistics that players like Victor Simpson will remember: 'The biggest thing was the friendships. We're all still mates. We've gone our ways, but when we get together we're like a band of brothers.'

John Ashworth thinks the era meant more to Canterbury than just the rugby: 'A lot of people, especially in the rural sector, were hurting at the time. When the shield came along it was something that everybody could grasp a part of and share in the pleasure. People could take their minds off the daily struggle and identify with a physical thing, where everyone could express themselves during that 80 minutes.'

The best off-field story must remain, as it probably should, with self-effacing captain, Don Hayes. There was a tradition of Sunday drinks at Lancaster Park, during which practical jokes were the rule of the day. Hayes and his wife Jenny went to their car one Sunday to find the front seats covered to window level with rubbish from a skip at the park. Hayes cleared just enough space to get into the car, turned to his wife and said, 'Gee, Jenny, the car's untidy.'

Canterbury's great captain Don Hayes (right) was always ready to tidy up, whether, as in this case, a pass from Jock Hobbs, or the front seat of his car.

Andrew Mehrtens, a player with Canterbury bloodlines over three generations.

CHAPTER SEVEN

BATTLELINES

The kid was likely to drive you mad. The second his father was home from teaching at Woodend School, Andrew Mehrtens was at him to come outside and kick the brown plastic ball his son had got when he was two.

Terry Mehrtens, who had played for the Junior All Blacks at first five, usually obliged. And young Andrew wasn't bad either. Before he started school he was booting the ball over the fence at the back of the schoolhouse. It didn't take long for the passion for kicking to assert itself. 'Right through, in all my teams, I've always made it known I wanted to be the kicker, even before they'd asked for volunteers,' says Mehrtens.

At Christchurch Boys' High he was a very good tennis player but rugby was always going to be the calling. When your grandfather, George, was an All Black fullback, your father was playing for Natal against the All Blacks while he and your mother, Sandra, were on a working holiday in South Africa, and you were born in Durban, there's not much chance rugby won't be in the blood.

Add into the mix his hero worship of a 1980s playing icon, Robbie Deans, and a nearly fanatical support of the Canterbury team in general. A full-page poster of Deans from the *Christchurch Star* took pride of place on young Andrew's wall. In the middle of the television coverage of the amazing 1985 game with Auckland at Lancaster Park, in the wake of the Craig Green try that sparked Canterbury's second-half comeback, the screen is suddenly filled with a 12–year–old Andrew Mehrtens flinging himself out of the sideline crowd to express his ecstasy.

At high school, Mehrtens was good enough to make an impression at First XV level, and played well enough for Canterbury at an under-18 tournament in 1991, but he didn't make it to national schools' level.

So in 1992, when he went to Wellington to trials for the New Zealand under-19 team, it felt like all the other trial players knew each other from the schools' teams. 'Somehow I made the New Zealand team,' says Mehrtens, 'which I'm sure was as big a surprise to all the other trialists as it was to me.'

The coach of the team was Vance Stewart, and here's where the story gets really interesting. Vance Stewart wasn't your normal rugby coach.

It was Stewart who introduced Mark Mayerhofler to Canterbury from North Harbour, going to the trouble of organising cross-credits for training college to make sure Mayerhofler didn't suffer academically when he shifted. Stewart encouraged Justin Marshall to rehabilitate a niggling groin injury in Canterbury, rather than in his native Southland. Stewart elevated Mehrtens, Tabai Matson, Daryl Gibson and Angus Gardiner from local club competitions.

Mark Mayerhofler, so quiet off the field, but on the paddock Bubs was a rock in Canterbury's midfield.

If you'd never met Stewart, it would be easy to form a mental image of a man who locked the scrum 80 times in the 1970s for Canterbury, twelve times for the All Blacks and ran a business trading in metals. What would you think? A hairy-fisted, bull-necked, ruffian?

Nothing could be further from the truth. Softly spoken, well read and an immaculate dresser, Stewart arrives as Canterbury coach in 1993 after a long period where getting it right on the field is proving as hard to grab as quicksilver.

Since 1986 there has been almost a revolving-door policy with coaches until Stewart is appointed. Grizz Wyllie stays on for one more season after the shield has gone in 1985 before he becomes, in 1987, an All Black selector at the first World Cup and then the All Black coach.

In that last Wyllie season, 1986, Canterbury beat a touring Wallabies team 30–10 and have a shot at the Ranfurly Shield in a fierce game at Eden Park, won 28–15 by Auckland.

Wyllie draws on 35 players during the year, exactly the same number he had needed for all 27 games during the shield era. One reason for casting the net so wide is that eight Canterbury players are in South Africa during April and May with a team called the Cavaliers, organised in the wake of an All Black tour in 1985 being cancelled by a court injunction brought by anti-apartheid activists.

One of the Cavaliers is Robbie Deans. The trip to South Africa, largely organised in secret by Andy Dalton and Andy Haden, comes like a bolt from the blue to Deans. Deans is playing cricket at Scargill one day when he sees Jock Hobbs drive up. A South African tour is the last thing on Deans' mind.

Deans thinks, 'What the hell's going on?' Jock Hobbs walks over and says, 'I've come up to ruin your summer. It's on again.' Until the day the Cavaliers leave, Deans never really believes it will happen.

What Deans does know is that he would never go on an unofficial tour again. 'We tried to create the atmosphere of playing for your country, but not having that silver fern on really does make a difference. You can't replace the feeling of representing your own country.'

The upside to the Cavaliers tour for New Zealand rugby in 1986 is the play of the team that became the Baby Blacks and includes ten new test players, (the Cavaliers are all banned for two tests by the NZRU), coached by Brian Lochore and captained by David Kirk. Against almost all expectations, the All Blacks score a famous victory over the French at Lancaster Park on 28 June, winning 18–9.

It isn't so exciting for Canterbury. Doug Bruce's two years as head coach in the wake of Wyllie start well in 1987, with victory in the South Pacific championship, an early-season tournament that involves Auckland, Wellington, Canterbury, Queensland, New South Wales and the Fijian national team.

But even that victory has a strange tinge to it. The final game, against Auckland, is won 21–16, but Auckland's fourteen and Canterbury's five World Cup All Blacks are all in camp and unavailable.

The rest of the season is unremarkable, Canterbury sliding to fifth in the NPC, and at one stage there are even fears of relegation. Don Hayes has retired, Jock Hobbs moves to Wellington before concussion problems force him from the game, and Craig Green plays six games and then goes to Italy. With rugby still in a quasi-amateur era, Green is basically forced out of the sport. 'I was working as a contract roofer in 1987, which meant that if you're not there to do the work, you don't get paid. I used to work flat out during the summer just to be able to live and play rugby in the winter. There was one year when I only made $6000.'

If 1987 isn't flash, 1988 is to be even worse. The team slips back to fourth in the South Pacific championship, and late in the season drops to sixth in the NPC, with the worst loss a 31–10 flogging by Auckland in a Ranfurly Shield challenge.

Change is on the way and the Union turns to Frank Jack, a man whose work in the prison service doesn't curtail a keen, deadpan sense of humour.

There is a graphic example of it after a sweaty pre–season game in Brisbane. Todd Blackadder is playing openside flanker and the temperature is about 38 degrees. There's no air-conditioning in the changing room and the players feel they're just about dying.

Frank Jack comes up to Blackadder and says, 'Do you love the heat, Toddy?' That becomes their joke. Blackadder responds, 'Yeah, yeah, I love the heat.'

Later, Queensland play Canterbury at Lancaster Park and the weather is so cold several of the visitors are treated for hypothermia.

Jack comes up to Blackadder that day too. 'Do you love the cold, Toddy?' he asks. When Blackadder replies, 'Yeah, I love the cold,' Jack says, 'What? Do you love the hot *and* the cold?' Jack keeps a deeply serious look on his face while Hamish Murray and Blackadder, sitting next to each other, fall about with laughter.

Jack's brother-in-law, Alister Hopkinson, is co-opted as Jack's assistant and, after a disastrous South Pacific championship with every single game lost, there is a dramatic improvement in the NPC, Canterbury finishing second to Auckland.

A master-stroke is getting Robbie Deans back into the squad. Having to work harder at training since his major knee injury in 1984, Deans has lost interest in the grind of travel and training, and in 1988 opts to play just for Glenmark.

He has the same plans for the following year until he turns out for an invitation side against Canterbury in a pre-season game at Loburn. He is standing next to the microphone when the Canterbury squad is named, and he is in it.

'Talk about red in the face!' says Deans. 'If Frank had come up to me quietly and asked me, I probably would have said I wasn't available. But I couldn't very well turn him down in front of a hall full of people.'

Deans ends the season with 279 points for Canterbury, his highest-ever tally, but pinpoints wing Paula Bale, Marist's flying Fijian, as the matchwinner in the side. 'He scored 24 tries and could turn a game with one bit of brilliance.'

The start of the 1990s sees Jack and Hopkinson in charge again, Canterbury score just one win in the South Pacific championship, slip from second to fourth place in the NPC, and become the target of the worst sledging the team has ever struck in the wake of a bizarre 'no scrums' Ranfurly Shield challenge at Eden Park.

It was true that Lions teams had bagged Canterbury for rough play and that the neutrality of Canterbury referees had been questioned, but nobody had ever suggested that a team in red and black was less than manly until 6 October 1990.

In the fourth minute of the shield challenge against Auckland, hooker John Buchan is ordered off by referee Keith Lawrence for kicking Gary Whetton in a ruck. That in itself is controversial. Whetton had just been penalised for stomping a Canterbury player, lock Ian Fleming, when he is knocked over and kicked in the shoulder by Buchan.

As he leaves the field Buchan passes his replacement, Phil Cropper, who will later become headline news in Australia when he is named as one of the men who is alleged to have tried to blackmail film star Russell Crowe over video footage of a nightclub brawl. He has played twelve times already for Canterbury in 1990, all of them as a flanker, but coach Jack considers him as Canterbury's reserve hooker too.

The New Zealand Union has instituted a rule, for the safety of players, that if a front-rower is ordered off he has to be substituted by another front-rower.

An Auckland official will later claim that, as the two Cantabrians pass in the tunnel, Buchan said to Cropper, 'Don't play any scrums.'

On the field Cropper tells pack leader Rob Penney and captain Robbie Deans that 'Frank [Jack] says I don't have to hook.' The coach, sitting in the No. 1 Stand high above the ground with no communication with the reserves bench, is as surprised as anyone else with what follows.

When the first scrum is called with Cropper on the field, nine minutes into the game, Penney tells referee Lawrence that Cropper isn't a specialist hooker. Cropper is asked, and confirms that he isn't a hooker. This is news to Auckland's hooker, Sean Fitzpatrick, who had captained a New Zealand Colts team in 1984 that had included Cropper as his back-up hooker.

There are no more scrums. When one is called for, Lawrence orders a tap-kick. The result is a strange hybrid of touch football, league and rugby.

Auckland is ahead 15–0 at half-time, and wins 33–18. Fans boo and jeer, and many leave well before the end. Straight after the game Auckland's captain, Gary Whetton, is scathing. 'They wouldn't scrum. They had a spare prop in the stand, but they wouldn't scrum. This was Canterbury, for God's sake, where men are supposed to be men.'

The atmosphere is still white-hot at the after-match function, where Jack mutters to one of his players, 'Watch your back here, this could blow up.'

It's the last game of the season for Jack, and also the end of what has been a promising coaching career, which has seen him assist with coaching All Black trial teams.

That all comes to a juddering halt after the no-scrums game. Jack is told by a Canterbury official that 'someone has to take the blame, and you're the fall guy.' He is not asked to explain at any point what happened at Eden Park but is sacked and replaced by John Phillips, an appointment that itself will also end in tears.

Phillips, a tough, fearless flanker had played 99 games for Canterbury when he was dropped on the verge of his 100th game by selector Gerald Wilson.

When he discovers that Wilson will be his manager with the Canterbury team, Phillips is told by his wife that he should decline the coaching position. Not wanting to 'upset the apple cart,' he goes ahead anyway.

Andy Earl is one who thinks that Phillips should not have been sacked: 'We had the basis of a pretty good young team. We finished fourth in the NPC, had a good tour away in the North Island. Then the management had a bit of wayward thinking.

'To me, John was even better than Alex Wyllie. I've been coached by B. J. Lochore, and he was a good man because he could relate on any level. Alex could only relate on the level of "do it or else". Some could handle it, but some couldn't. John had a similar attitude to Lohore. He'd always put the players first, which I think is bloody important. If he'd been given another year, who knows? Things were just starting to roll.'

Phillips is a man who has no time for glamour boys. 'At the end of the day,' he says on his appointment, 'you can have the fabulously skilled players who just won't take the crunch. When it comes to the real crunch tackle they're too worried about their pretty little faces. You must have some hard nuts, who don't mind jumping off that big fence and dying for the team.'

The Bay of Plenty game, which Canterbury lose 28–13, is the last of the season, and it will prove to be Phillips's last game as Canterbury coach. Despite mediocre games at the tail-end of the NPC, Canterbury actually finish fourth in the competition.

What sinks Phillips are suggestions of untoward behaviour off the field. He will later deny rumours of damage to hotels and motels while the team is on the road, and says he was never confronted with any suggestions of personal misconduct. 'I wouldn't have minded if I'd got a phone call saying, "Look, these claims have been made against you." Then I'd have had a chance to reply. I am bitter about what happened. I was in England and rang from a public phone box near Heathrow to find out what had happened about the coaching.'

A young Todd Blackadder, at this stage a No.8, shows some of the pace that saw him play sevens rugby for New Zealand.

What Phillips discovers is that he's been replaced by former All Black prop, Alistair Hopkinson.

In a twist not without its own ironies, Hopkinson then brings in Frank Jack, sacked to make way for Phillips, as his assistant. Hopkinson is a coach players want to play for, but the results, as Canterbury try to rebuild, are mediocre.

There is a decency and spark about 'Hoppy' that is impossible to resist. His humour is typified by the suggestion, possibly true, that as coach he kept track of possible candidates for Canterbury by writing their names on the wall of his woolshed.

It will prove to be a brutal season for Canterbury in 1992 but somehow Hopkinson keeps his famous good nature intact. 'You sort of got the feeling that no matter what the results were, he loved you anyway,' says Todd Blackadder. 'You had undying respect for him. When you look back on it, 1992 was the year Canterbury was nearly relegated. We were staring down the barrel of second division.'

If there is a bright spot, it's a 38–13 whipping of Ireland, which saw Canterbury ahead 30–7 at half-time and complete humiliation for the visiting team on the cards.

But even that victory is soured to a degree when Andy Earl is cited, then suspended for two weeks by the Canterbury Union, for clearing Irishman Richard Wallace out of a ruck with a swinging arm. The big problem is that Wallace has suffered a hairline fracture of the jaw in the process, although, as loyal as ever, coach Hopkinson says he suspected the facture had come in an earlier attempted tackle on Canterbury fullback Andrew McCormick, Fergie's gifted son.

The year marks one of the few times when Canterbury fans, usually so fanatical in their support, virtually turn their back on the team. Even the lure of free drink and food at after-match functions isn't enough to fill the Lancaster Park social room, where old players and officials actually hiss 'gutless' at the current team as they shuffle in after yet another loss. It is just as lonely on the park.

In games against Queensland and North Harbour, the ground announcer says that everyone can go into the stand. No more than two thousand people end up huddled up together, trying to keep warm.

'Every single home game,' says Todd Blackadder, then in his first full season for Canterbury, 'the weather was crappy, sleet and rain. People didn't turn up, and we played wet-weather rugby, badly. You could run out there and point out your family. You could see your mum and dad and your brothers.'

The only NPC games Canterbury win are against Hawke's Bay and North Harbour. The game against King Country (lost 24–20) is Andy Earl's last, and losing at Lancaster Park is probably the worst performance of the season.

'There were also a few little divisions inside the team that year,' says Blackadder. 'Some of the side were experienced and had played a lot together, and another group of younger guys had just come in. When things aren't going too well on the field, the shit hits the fan a bit. There weren't major things. Groups who sometimes did their own thing, which wasn't conducive to team work.'

It is the year of the big snow in 1992 in Canterbury, which leads to one of the great Andy Earl stories. Earl's rough-and-ready appearance belies the man's intelligence but does give some hint of how much courage and commitment he brings to the table.

During that winter, the All Blacks are touring Australia and new coach Laurie Mains finds himself with an injury crisis in the loose forwards with the second test in Brisbane about to be played.

He rings Earl at his Rotheram farm. We want you to come to Brisbane to play in the test, says Mains, then you can get back home. 'It's your call,' responds Earl. 'But if I don't go on to South Africa I won't come to Brisbane. You have to decide whether you want me or not.'

Mains, not a man used to being questioned over his decisions, asks how fit Earl is. Has he been playing? Yes, Earl replies, he has. Unspoken was that, well, he *would* have been playing, except for the snow, during which he has worked for weeks with others in the area to help save stock. But he had been playing before that. So his answer isn't exactly untrue.

Earl flies to Brisbane and, on a steamy, sweaty Sunday, by sheer force of will, is one of the better All Black players, making a covering tackle late in the game to save a try. How tired is he at the end? 'My backside was hanging round my ankles by the time I came off. Perhaps I shouldn't have played it, but there were test matches I thought I should have played that I didn't, so to me I was just getting one back.'

Graeme Bachop and his brother, Stephen, began breaking things playing in their Lyttelton house as kids. Graeme came through the road tunnel as a teenager and became a great Canterbury and All Black halfback.

Hopkinson is voted out after 1992, the third Canterbury coach to lose his job in three seasons. He reacts without bitterness: 'I'll be at Lancaster Park watching as usual, but instead of sitting in the No. 3 Stand, I'll be on the bank.'

If Hoppy is sanguine about being dropped, there is little dancing in the streets of Christchurch with the appointment of Vance Stewart and his assistant coach, Aussie McLean, for the 1993 season. 'At least we'll have the best-dressed NPC coach in New Zealand,' is the bitter reaction of one club coach. It isn't that Stewart is actively disliked, just that he seems very low-key compared to the personality of a Wyllie or a Hopkinson.

As well as Stewart, Mike Brewer will be a powerful figure during what will prove to be his brief spell in Christchurch. The captain of Otago for seven years from the time he was twenty, Brewer would have been Laurie Mains' All Black captain from 1992 except for his appalling luck with injuries, which had already kept him out of the 1987 and 1991 World Cups.

Work for the Canterbury International Clothing Company brings him to Christchurch in 1993, and his All Black mate, halfback Graeme Bachop, is able to talk Brewer into stopping a six-days-a-week work regime to play the last three games of the season when regular flanker, Greg Smith, leaves to play in Japan.

Brewer's first impressions aren't good: 'The whole environment, it seemed to me, was ripe for a team to fail. Ill discipline was rife. Midweek training was always due to start at 6p.m. I was having to leave work a lot earlier than usual to make the start time, but then we all had to wait while some guys rolled in at ten past 6, even quarter-past.

'That lack of commitment to the team at training carried through onto the field. Guys gave away penalties when they didn't have to, they got offside, they dropped passes, they missed tackles. There seemed to be no rules and no disciplines to meet.'

For the 1994 season, coach Stewart has decided that Brewer is going to be his captain, replacing Rob Penney: 'Some people saw it as an outsider becoming captain in a limited time, but there was never a question over whether Mike should be captain. There was never a question raised by the players over whether he was acceptable. He was the obvious choice and the team would have followed him off a cliff.'

Stewart and Brewer even go to the lengths of having a signed covenant for the team. 'The covenant was something of a flow-through from the previous years when things hadn't been going well,' says Stewart. 'I wouldn't say there was dissent within the team, but within the Canterbury rugby community there was a lot of comment about who was being selected and who wasn't.

'Some of the reserves were going to their club representatives about the Union and having a go there. Things were being slipped to the media that should have been kept in house. So, to a degree, we were beating ourselves to death.

'We sat down and talked about something that I think Benjamin Franklin said when signing the American Declaration of Independence: "We shall all hang together, lest we all hang separately."

'We looked at the whole season, set our goals and decided what we needed to put in place. Then we declared that we'd be loyal to each other. No matter what happened we wouldn't go sniping at each other through the media. That formed the basis of our covenant.

'We had a meeting of the senior players, who all had their ideas. Then we put it all in writing, Mike read it and agreed with what was in it. Then we all signed it. It was a secret document. Even some of the officials of the Union haven't read it. If people didn't want to sign, they weren't in the team.'

For Todd Blackadder, Brewer, a hard taskmaster with a personal taste for hard training that even Laurie Mains would say 'bordered on the masochistic,' was 'absolutely outstanding. He was the first guy that gave us real direction. He brought intelligence into the side and we started to do things for a reason.

'He also started pointing the finger at guys and putting pressure on them to perform for the team. Until then there was too much of an attitude that it was good enough just to be in the side.

'I learnt more from Mike than I had at any other time. He did back then what we do now with players – make them feel welcome and give them as much help as you can to make them part of the environment. To treat them as you would want to be treated yourself. Mike was a lot like that.

'In previous years I'd felt a bit like an outsider. Perhaps you only notice those things if you're sensitive to them. But with Mike I certainly enjoyed it, playing with an experienced All Black, with a guy who was so forthcoming and who took the time for me. He was really an inspiration for me.'

In 1994 the Canterbury squad has a powerful core of key players, some of them introduced, some of them home-grown, but all about to flourish in the new regime.

At the front there is prop Richard Loe, back where he grew up after years in the Waikato and the All Blacks. He returns to the Canterbury fold after being banned for six months for eye-gouging while playing for Waikato in the 1993 NPC final.

During the ban, journalist Trevor McKewen writes a story in Australian *Penthouse* magazine in which Aussie prop, Tony Daly, suggests that, as his career went on, Loe had turned from a 'tough customer into a dirtier and slimier player.'

At the time Loe was 33, and Daly no doubt thought he would stay in retirement. To his horror Daly finds himself packing down for New South Wales against Loe in a pre-season game in Christchurch. Other Canterbury players recall how Loe greets Daly with the words, 'Hello, Fatty, I read what you said about me in the magazine.' The best Daly can manage is a squeaked, 'I was misquoted!'

It would have surprised many that one man who swears by Richard Loe is Jonah Lomu. Asked after the 1995 World Cup if there were any players who went out of their way to share their experience with the then very inexperienced wing, Lomu doesn't hesitate. 'A lot of credit has got to go to Loey. Everybody keeps on talking about him, and rough play and things like that. But deep down he's a great guy. When I had the last sprints to do at the training camps, Loey was always there with me, even when he'd finished his. He'd turn around and help whoever was last. It didn't matter who it was. I would say I know him pretty well, having been on tour with him for seven weeks, and he's a superb guy.'

On his return to Canterbury, Loe makes it clear he isn't going to end up in judicial trouble again. 'I have to realise,' he says, 'that there are some people out there with bent imaginations who think they can provoke Richard Loe, and maybe get him in the crap again. I'm not going to have any part of that.' He doesn't.

At No. 8 is Todd Blackadder, whose career had caught fire while working on a dairy farm in Collingwood, where he played for Nelson-Bays. On his return home to Rangiora he soon found himself in the Canterbury B side, and then, for one game against Bay of Plenty, John Phillips's A side in 1991.

Wayne Smith is the B team coach in 1991, and at one stage is talking to his assistant coach, John Mills, about some concerns he has at openside. Mills points to blindside flanker Blackadder and says, 'Look at him, mate, we don't need an openside, he does both jobs.'

It takes little time for Blackadder, with his distinctive loping run, fierce tackling and ceaseless pursuit of the ball, to become a special favourite of Canterbury crowds, a status that will soon grow to huge proportions.

'Some of the younger players in the team were pretty constricted at that stage,' says Vance Stewart. 'But Toddy wasn't. He was a blood-and-guts man. It was a case of "Give me the ball and I'll smash it up the field." He was aggressive around the rucks and mauls, as you'd expect a country forward to be.'

Halfback Graeme Bachop has been an All Black since 1988, and fought back into the side in 1993 after new coach Laurie Mains had concerns over how quickly he cleared the ball.

Quiet and reserved with outsiders, Bachop develops into a confident playmaker, with not only great speed but strength way beyond his size. In one All Black exercise of the 1990s, which involved two players putting both their hands on the ball, then trying to wrestle it away, the only man in the whole squad to get the better of Bachop was Zinzan Brooke.

He sharpened up his skills as a child in Lyttleton, ('Always breaking things in the house,' says Graeme), playing football with his older brother, Stephen, who would become an All Black in 1992 out of Otago after playing for Manu Samoa at the 1991 World Cup.

As a high school pupil, Graeme goes through the tunnel to play with Linwood, where he has the good fortune to be coached by 1967 Junior All Black halfback, Brent Elder, who 'soon fixed the fact I couldn't pass both ways'. It is Elder who gives him the nickname 'Grim' for the serious look Bachop often wears.

By contrast, outside Grim is a perky No. 10 from Old Boys, Andrew Mehrtens, whom Stewart has started in three games at first five and three games at fullback in 1993. In one of the better rugby quotes, Stewart reckoned that Mehrtens is 'so intelligent that he likes to present challenges for himself. If there's an easy way and a difficult way to do something, Mehrts will chose the hard way.'

If Stewart has any doubts about whether Mehrtens has a unique approach to football, they will be dispelled when, while studying a video of a game at Lancaster Park, he spots the first five, on the field during a stoppage in play, joining the crowd in a Mexican wave.

Tabai Matson, so strong at centre just one tackler won't bring him down.

Mehrtens' combination with Bachop starts at Old Boys, when the halfback moves from his Linwood Club, and is important, says Mehrtens, in the development of his career. 'Bach is the sort of player that takes a lot of pressure off a first five because he can run, he can kick and he takes good options. It was helpful just to see when he did things.'

Stiffening up the midfield is a man who coach Stewart had in his New Zealand under-19 team in 1991, Mark 'Bubs' Mayerhofler. A product of Henderson High School, Michael Jones's old school, Mayerhofler grew up in west Auckland, then played rugby in North Harbour, where his way is blocked by All Blacks Walter Little and Frank Bunce.

Still only 21 in 1994, he agonised for most of the summer of 1993–94 before making the move, and it was quickly clear why Stewart wanted him. Todd Blackadder remembers an occasion when 'Bubs saved a certain try by catching a player, turning him on his back, and dragging him with one hand back from the line. I never saw anyone more committed than him. When he played it was almost like having another loose forward who was out in the backline.'

Outside Mayerhofler at centre is a big, former Christ's College winger with the wonderful name of John Tabaiwalu Fakavale Matson, or 'Tabs' for short. Matson is a school hurdles champion with a stride so raking and easy that he is constantly being accused of not giving it 100 per cent when he plays. The fact he can still run away from opponents is often forgotten.

As to his strength, that is extraordinary. One of the most amazing moments in New Zealand rugby in the 1990s comes during the Canterbury v. North Harbour game at the Onewa Domain in 1994. Matson makes a clean break by fending off Frank Bunce. The All Black centre, never bested in a physical contest during a great career, grits his teeth and comes roaring back at Matson, only to be smacked by another fend that this time sits him on his back.

Todd Blackadder later notes that Matson 'had a great ability in that he was strong enough to stay on his feet, he was balanced and he was extremely skilful. He created space for his wingers. What more could you want out of a world-class centre?'

Captain Brewer says the 1994 season will be divided into three mini-seasons, starting with the warm-up games, followed by the game with South Africa, and then the NPC, including a Ranfurly Shield challenge with Waikato, which has finally prised the Log out of Auckland's hands in 1993 after a record 61 defences.

The week before Canterbury play the 'Boks, Otago has beaten them. It was claimed that Otago coach, Gordon Hunter, walked into the changing shed before the game, hammered a nail in the wall at the height you'd mount a trophy Springbok head, and walked out again.

There is nothing so dramatic from Stewart with Canterbury, but he does give his midfielders, the Three Ms as they are known to the team, a free hand to play the game as they chose to.

It's a decision endorsed by his captain, Brewer. 'They went out on a pretty wet and muddy Lancaster Park and tried all their moves. When they didn't work, nobody got frustrated. If you hammer young guys for mistakes when they're trying a move, you stamp the flair out of them.

'Our forwards learnt a good lesson from the game. They didn't attack the 'Boks at the start the way they would have taken on a first-division side. As the game went on they realised that if you play against a decent team and let them play the way they want to, they're difficult to contain. So we were a bit tentative at the start and, by the time we got a roll on it was too late.'

South Africa win 20–10, but the real target for the season is waiting in Hamilton.

'A bit of steel was coming into our team,' says Brewer. 'It began with Richard Loe in the front row. In the middle of your tight five he's like a big steel girder. Having him packing down against his old forward pack was a huge psychological boost for us.'

In the week before Canterbury goes to Hamilton they have one of the 1980s heroes, captain Don Hayes, in to talk about the game.

Hayes comes in on the Thursday night. He begins by saying that he isn't very good at delivering a talk, then pulls out a few notes on a bit of paper.

When he speaks he doesn't mince any words, and the players realise that he's reliving what it had been like for him. Brewer finds the hair on the back of his neck starting to stand.

Hayes talks about the build-up, winning the shield and defending it. Brewer knows that he and Stewart could have gone on for hours about some of the points

Hayes makes, but the sincerity of the man, and hearing it from someone who has done it, is a real boost for the team.

At Hamilton's Rugby Park the day before the game, Brewer observes how the different players tune in. Mark Hammett and some of the younger players kick a hackey sack around. Mehrtens has a few kicks, then jokes with Matson. The most obviously churned up is Paula Bale, who walks away by himself.

Brewer wakes on the Saturday, 3 September, feeling very confident and receives a fax in his room from Grizz Wyllie, then coaching in South Africa. In bold capital letters Wyllie finishes by writing: 'ATTACK, ATTACK, ATTACK!'

The weather is perfect in Hamilton, and so is the occasion for Canterbury. After 30 minutes the score is 22–8 and the cowbells are largely silent. Waikato score first, but then there's a penalty try, awarded when Mehrtens, with a clear overlap ahead, is tackled by an offside player. A 50 metre break by fullback Simon Forrest puts Paula Bale in, and possibly the most exciting try of the day is run in by Brewer after Mayhofler first slices through the Waikato midfield inside the Canterbury half, then wrong-foots Waikato fullback, Todd Miller, and feeds his captain, who is untouched over the last 25 metres to the line.

Waikato creeps back into the game, but never threatens to win. At full time Canterbury has the game, 29–26, and Waikato captain, John Mitchell, hands over the Log to Brewer. Mehrtens tells an interviewer, 'It's good you're talking to me now while I'm still sober,' and in the early hours of the morning one of the shyest men in the team, Mayerhofler, is standing on a bar counter in a Hamilton pub singing karaoke to a packed room.

On the Sunday morning the Boeing 737 flight lands in Christchurch to be greeted by a crowd of at least four thousand people. One of the survivors from the plague year of 1992 mutters, 'Hell, there are more people here than used to come to the park to see us play.'

Brewer says, 'I think the confidence that had been building inside the team was now being reflected by the public. The players seen as the stars – the Blackadders, the Matsons, the Mehrtens – were the ones who performed in Hamilton.'

On the Sunday morning after the shield is won, the players, their families, partners and some friends gather at the Russley Hotel for a quiet celebration. To everyone's surprise the shield itself, on close inspection, proves to be badly dented and has a crack that threatens to snap it in two.

'Scotty England, who's a woodturner, did a lot for the shield and New Zealand rugby in restoring the Log,' says Todd Blackadder. 'We didn't only win it, but reconditioned it as well!'

There are 30,000 spectators on hand for the first challenge, from Counties, and for Brewer there is confirmation that the young Canterbury players are quickly learning how to cope with a test-match-like atmosphere.

'Canterbury would get the ball early on and attack one area of the opposition, whether it was a high kick into the box, a wipers or an attack in the midfield. They'd attack one area, and whoof, everyone would be there, going for the jugular.'

That's exactly how it goes against Counties. Pressure is quickly followed by points, and by the end of the game Counties have been demolished 42–16, Mehrtens has equalled his boyhood hero Robbie Deans's Canterbury shield record of 32 points in a game, and Counties coach, Ross Cooper, says, 'Today we saw the emergence of a star of New Zealand rugby in Andrew Mehrtens. He's outstandingly talented.'

Ahead lies the Otago challenge. 'It became the one game that the whole season relied on,' says Brewer. 'Our aim in '94 was to be in the semifinal of the NPC, to win and hold the shield, and to be unbeaten at home. If we'd lost to Otago, all those things would have gone.

'We had a long training run on the Tuesday, which was a little bit flat, and we still weren't pinging on the Thursday the way we had been before the Waikato challenge. But I was still reasonably happy. The pressure was probably more on Otago than on us. Most people expected them to win.'

Otago prop Nick Moore agrees: 'The public felt we could win. They probably got that impression through the media. In the team we were confident, but I don't think we were as confident as everybody else. There was a lot of hype before the game, and quite a few of the boys had family come from all over the country.'

Gordon Hunter says that Otago's lead-up was mismanaged: 'There were articles written by people who were probably well-meaning, taking an interest in the side having an historic win. It probably went over the top.

'I can recall one interview where I was completely misquoted. It was a major error by me, not knowing the person I was speaking to. Bruiser [Brewer] would have just needed to take the paper into his team room and thrown it down. That's all he would have needed for a team talk.

'There were articles in the *Otago Daily Times* about ticker-tape parades being planned. The media could have been handled far more constructively. You learn, I suppose, and in hindsight I would have taken a far stronger hand and eliminated the outside influences.'

The hype becomes so intense that, after a Christchurch radio station produces a song with nonsensical lyrics teasing the Otago players, 'Goldie' Wilson appears on television with the incredible caption on screen: 'Jeff Wilson – accused of having a small ding-a-ling.' Wilson snarls that words wouldn't hurt him.

Russell Vine, running the Lancaster Park Sports Museum, finds that on the Friday before the game and on the Saturday itself he is selling 800 Canterbury jerseys. By comparison, in the first year of Super 12 and throughout the NPC, he sells just a single jersey. Vine's counterpart in Dunedin sends up boxes of Otago stuff, and he sells all that out too. With the help of the city council, Vine sells two thousand rosettes. People get dressed up and wear their provincial colours with pride.

Mike Brewer says, 'We were ready physically. It was just a matter of getting ready mentally. On the Friday night at the captain's meeting I got five senior players to speak. For the first time there was some electricity in the air.

'Then, on Saturday morning in his team talk, Vance topped it off with his pre-match speech. He talked about his father, and when we left the room I wasn't the only one choking back a tear. After that we were rock solid.'

Blackadder recalls that Stewart 'delivered one of his all-time best speeches. It was absolutely inspiring, about how there are times in your life when you've got to make a stand.'

Despite the emotion, it is Otago who score first. 'The talk had been about how the game would be a case of what they were going to do us and, sure enough, they scored a try in the first couple of minutes,' says Blackadder.

Otago's Jamie Joseph dives over right between the sticks. Standing behind the posts, Blackadder thinks, 'Shit!' He has a tingling feeling that someone is walking over his grave, in front of a full house.

Five years later he watches a video of the game and is amazed at how young the team was, a bunch of kids. They got through, he realises, on sheer emotion and enthusiasm, and, buoyed on by the crowd, produced a remarkable performance.

Brewer knows Canterbury can beat Otago if the players can keep their discipline and concentrate on their defensive screens. The Otago players, he knows, are never afraid to move the ball back before they move it up. When they move the ball away from one side, Canterbury keep pushing up, and when the ball swings back Canterbury are ready to knock Otago over.

The only time Brewer thinks Canterbury might lose the game is when Stu Forster scores five minutes after half-time. At 20–10 Canterbury will be rocky if Otago scores again, and they break up the left touch almost immediately. But Canterbury regroups, bang the ball down the Otago end, and the challenger's chance is gone.

Nick Moore felt certain that Otago was in control right up to the last couple of minutes, and Canterbury hooker Matt Sexton agrees: 'We were just hanging on for dear life in that first half. They were all over us. We were reasonably composed but were hanging on by our fingernails.'

Brewer recalls that 'before the game it'd been said that Andrew Mehrtens was the key to Otago winning the shield. He wasn't an All Black then, just a promising newcomer. The theory was that he wouldn't have another good game with the pressure that Otago was going to put on him. Well, the game was as close to a test match as you would ever get, and he did have another good game.'

With ten minutes to go Canterbury is a point down. It sounds hard to believe, but Brewer isn't stressed. He's been in similar positions before, and with just three points needed to keep the shield, at the back of his mind is something Canterbury has tried out at training.

He knows they've worked at taking a penalty near halfway, kicking the ball to touch for their throw-in, winning the lineout and then setting up a ruck in the midfield for Mehrtens to drop a goal.

'Referees are not inclined to give penalties at such a late stage in the game,' says Brewer. 'With Mehrts, you can usually guarantee that four out of five dropped-goal attempts will succeed. We ran exactly that pattern five minutes from the end, but this was a one in five for Mehrts. He missed the dropped goal.'

Sexton remembers how, when Canterbury got the penalty, Brewer called all the team in, and he was staggered at how cool a head his captain maintained under pressure.

Brewer says, 'Right, this is the plan. Mehrts is going to kick to the right-hand corner. We'll throw back lob on Scotty England, then set up a midfield ruck and keep at them until they make a mistake or we score.'

In the last couple of minutes Canterbury has a lineout throw just metres from the Otago line. Brewer knows that Mehrtens is 'a very intelligent guy.' They don't have to speak because Mehrtens knows exactly what Brewer's thinking.

Referee Colin Hawke looks at his watch with about eight minutes to go and thinks, 'Let's not have a 50-50 penalty that can have a major influence on the match.' He wants to let the players decide the outcome.

Then a ruck develops and Hawke realises it's on for a Mehrtens dropped goal. He can't believe it when Otago captain, David Latta, dives through the ruck offside almost at the ref's feet. Nobody in the Otago team says anything when Hawke blows for the penalty. There isn't any point in playing an advantage, Hawke knows, because the ball has been killed.

Nick Moore says that 'when the penalty was given we knew that was it. "Crazy" Latta gives so much to a game and was so well liked in the team. It was sad more than anything.'

Hunter reckons that 'going into that room after the game was like being with people whose dads had all died at the same time. I'd never had an experience like it before. It was a hell of a day.'

Latta, almost the blueprint for a real southern man, agrees: 'It was like a bereavement in the family in the shed after the game. I thought the ball was out of the ruck so I chanced my arm. I was the offender and I'm disappointed with that. But we were forced into a lot of errors in the game, and that was just one of them.'

For Brewer there are mixed feelings: 'I knew how much football meant to the Otago team, how much they committed themselves and how hard they trained. While I was sorry for them, I was really happy it was my team who won.'

Todd Blackadder will recall that holding the shield 'was an amazing effort when you look back on it. Those games go so quickly. You're absolutely crapping yourself. You've got all the nerves and expectations, and you're playing against what is probably a better side. The game itself was just ferocious. Absolutely ferocious. It went so hell for leather it was a fleeting memory.'

Sexton remembers not just the game but how the night ends. The team goes out on the town after the game, sharing the moment with everyone, rather than just keeping it to themselves. Sexton's wife, Kate, is from Otago, and they have a lot of blue and gold supporters staying with them. Sexton gets home at about four in the morning, switches on all the lights and shouts, 'We won, we won!' He has to fling his arms up to ward off a shower of Speight's cans.

The winning of the shield will be a vindication of everything Vance Stewart has done in his first two years as coach.

Blackadder believes that Stewart 'introduced a lot of things that have since happened in professional rugby. He set goals, which we'd never done before. If someone had asked what a goal was, we would have said it was something you kicked between the posts.

'He brought a lot of intellect into our side. We had been pretty much just blood and guts, and we played more just on emotions. I think I played the first few years on pure emotion. We didn't really devise game plans.

'I can remember his team talks before the games distinctly. He'd recite, for example, something out of Charles Upham's book. He'd obviously done a lot of reading, and there were things he picked up on. I found his talks inspirational.'

Canterbury has a chance to be in the NPC final, travelling to Takapuna to play North Harbour in a semifinal.

There are moments to remember from the game for Canterbury, but only moments, as they lose 59–27. 'We were never in the same ballpark,' says Blackadder. 'Our season had ended after that Otago shield game. We'd put all our emotions, all our energies into that game. We were a young side, we'd given it our all, and there was nothing left.'

For Canterbury the 1995 season begins with Super 10. Any confusion with the professional approach to Super 12 as we know it now should be discounted immediately. 'We had one training run the week before we played Queensland in Brisbane,' says Todd Blackadder. 'That was our whole pre-session campaign.'

The Crusaders lose 24–6 to Queensland and, when a front-rower is binned, experience for the first time having to send another player off to bring on a front-rower for the sake of safety. All the players mill around as Mike Brewer tries to decide who to send off. Nobody wants to catch his eye and then lock Scott England says, 'Oh, bloody hell, I s'pose it's bloody me,' and storms off the field.

The next day a trip to the Gold Coast is planned, and most of the team expect a pleasant day at the beach, but Brewer is a very grumpy man after the loss, and makes the bus driver stop at a little public park on the side of the road. The players find themselves doing down-and-ups, sprints, the whole brutal, sweaty repertoire of a man who has learnt his techniques at the feet of Laurie Mains.

Canterbury will end up with just one win, against Tonga, in Super 10, which included South African teams, so it was the NPC and defending the Ranfurly Shield that would make or break the season.

With the Log, there is a defence on the road in Ashburton against Mid-Canterbury, won 64–19, and at home against Nelson-Bays (43–17), Marlborough (79–0) and South Canterbury (72–27).

A new boy in the ranks in 1995 is a tough, feisty halfback from Southland, Justin Marshall, who takes little time to make an impression.

When Marshall arrives from Southland, he takes some stick for what the team calls his mudflap, long hair at the back that covers a lot of his neck. He doesn't let any of it suppress his natural confidence. Canterbury is training at Rugby Park and Richard Loe is telling Marshall how to put the ball in. Marshall snaps back, 'Just shut up and push. I'll put the bloody ball in.' Loe, as startled as anyone, zips it.

Marshall is in Christchurch largely because Stewart knows his worth from the same 1992 New Zealand Colts team that included Andrew Mehrtens.

Marshall had a junior career that almost stalled at the Southland stage. Called into the provincial training squad for an under-18 tournament, Justin and two Mataura mates arrived an hour late for a training session at Drummond. The coach of the team is former All Black, Leicester Rutledge, who says they justified being late because they'd got lost trying to find the ground.

'I told them to get changed, and we'd do some scrum practice,' Rutledge told author Bob Howitt. 'As the first scrum went to go down I was overwhelmed by beer fumes. I asked the Mataura guys what the hell they'd been up to. "We had to stop at a pub to ask directions," said Justin. I gave them a decent strum up.'

A young Richard Loe shows the strength that makes him the wrong man to tip a beer over.

Marshall always has a keen sense of humour. In an early player profile he is asked to name his favourite restaurant, and says, 'The Gore pie cart. You're always satisfied.' His personal goals are to try to establish himself as an All Black halfback, and to keep his legs browner than Andrew Mehrtens, who strikes back by claiming the worst thing in rugby is 'Justin Marshall's swede breath.'

An early threat to Marshall's career comes with an injury at the end of the 1994 season. By now the first-choice halfback for Southland, he is given little help when chronic groin muscle injuries make it impossible for him to walk properly, much less play footy.

At the instigation of Stewart, the Canterbury Union brings Marshall to Christchurch, flies Sydney surgeon, Neil Halpin, across the Tasman to examine him, and then sends Marshall to Sydney for an operation that will prove a complete success.

Ironically, Marshall's first game in the NPC for Canterbury will be against Southland, won 27–22, at Lancaster Park.

A 58–30 hiding for Waikato in a Lancaster Park shield challenge is followed by a loss to Counties, 41–39, with a new rugby legend, World Cup star Jonah Lomu, scoring one try for Counties and future All Black, Joeli Vidiri, scoring another on the opposite wing, and then an abysmal 48–28 defeat at the hands of King Country in Te Kuiti. It is one of just two wins in the NPC for King Country, the other being a one-point victory with a last-second penalty against Southland.

Todd Blackadder is rested for the King Country game and watches from the stand in dismay. 'We thought we were a better side than that, but we got cleaned out. We were still going through that potential tag where "potentially" we were a good side. I don't like that word "potential" because it means you haven't actually done the job. We were one of those teams that would win the tough games, then lose the games we shouldn't lose.

'I remember reading that Grant Fox said good teams win the games they should win. You lift yourself for the big ones, no matter who you are, but you must win the games you should win.'

The night of the King Country disappointment there's a massive court session in the team's hotel, during which Andrew Mehrtens' career is nearly snuffed out by Richard Loe after he suddenly tips a full glass of beer over the big prop's head.

As Justin Marshall recalls it, 'Loey jumped up roaring and grabbed Mehrts by the throat. All of a sudden Mehrts just slumped, out to it. Mehrts had thought it was so amusing tipping his beer over Loey's head, and he got the sleeper hold put on him. Eventually he came round and he certainly never tipped beer on Loey again.'

The Wellington Ranfurly Shield challenge the following week will again prove that Loe isn't a man to trifle with.

Wellington has a massive Fijian prop, Bill Cavubati, who is never far from the headlines, whether it's trying to drop some of the 135 kilograms he is reputed to weigh, or darting away for a futile attempt to rebuild his career in Sydney when he feels he is unappreciated in Wellington.

Before the challenge at Lancaster Park, Cavubati is seen on television and on newspaper front pages grilling Canterbury lamb, which he suggests is what he'll do to the red and black front row.

Wellington is whipped, 66–17, and Loe brings Cavubati to his knees in the scrums. Mike Brewer will say after the game that when Cavubati met Loe, 'we saw the difference between an international prop and a provincial prop.'

The last game of the season is on 23 September against the old foe, Auckland, and it isn't pretty. The challengers are coached by Graham Henry, a shrewd reader of the game, and an extremely pragmatic one too. Auckland might have a firecracker first five in Carlos Spencer, but on this afternoon there isn't going to be any fancy stuff.

Under the rules of 1995, it is possible to kick the ball over the opposition's deadball line, and, as long as it isn't on the full, play restarts with a drop-out.

The Auckland pack is composed, to a man, of All Blacks: from Zinzan Brooke at No. 8, Michael Jones and Dylan Mika on the flanks, Robin Brooke and Richard Fromont locking, and Olo Brown, Sean Fitzpatrick and Craig Dowd in the front row.

All afternoon Spencer kicks the ball dead. All afternoon Auckland retrieves the ball from the drop-out and either scores, wins a penalty or kicks it dead to start the cycle over again. To add to the misery, Mehrtens is late charged by Robin Brooke. On the sideline, commenting for local television channel CTV, the man whose place Mehrtens had taken in the Canterbury team, Greg Coffey, blanches as tape is wrapped around Mehrtens' ribs. 'My God, this is not a good look,' he mutters.

So it proves. Mehrtens is gone and so is the game, 35–0, and the shield.

'Basically Auckland taught us one hell of a lesson,' says Todd Blackadder. 'That game highlighted where we were and where they were. We were basically playing on guts and pride, we hadn't fully worked out our tactics yet. We wanted to play an expansive game, but when they shut us down we ran out of plans. We didn't have a Plan B.'

Canterbury finishes fifth in the NPC. Ahead lies professionalism and some more bitter lessons.

It's 1994 and Mike Brewer experiences the joy that bringing the Ranfurly Shield back from Hamilton can bring.

CHAPTER EIGHT

MONEY

Mike Brewer has enormous command over the Canterbury rugby team in 1995, so when he asks players to defy the New Zealand Rugby Union, not one player breaks ranks.

Money talks louder in rugby in 1995 than it has for a century. In 1893, a dispute between the English Rugby Union and twenty clubs in Yorkshire and Lancashire arose over a request for players in the north, where rugby was the sport of working men, to be paid for time off work to play on a Saturday.

In the south, where the game was the sport of the moneyed classes, the request was turned down by a vote of 282 to 136. Up north, the clubs didn't waste time fruitlessly arguing with the toffs in London. Instead, the Yorkshire and Lancashire clubs broke away to form the Northern Union in 1895. Eleven years later, to mark the difference between its teams and rugby union teams, the number of players per team was reduced to thirteen and rugby league, as we know it, was born.

In 1995, it is the southern hemisphere unions of South Africa, Australia and New Zealand who stun the rugby world by announcing, just the day before the World Cup final at Ellis Park, that the sport in their countries is going fully professional.

The president of the South African Rugby Union, Louis Luyt, leads the charge at the IRB. 'I started with England,' he tells TVNZ's Keith Quinn in 1999, 'and asked if they'd paid their players. They said they hadn't, but they gave money to trust funds, which they admitted went to the players. It went round the table. It turned out that only Argentina didn't pay a cent. They were the only ones. So I asked who we were fooling. It turned out we were all paying under the table anyhow.'

A deal is struck with Rupert Murdoch's News Corp and, on that fateful Friday afternoon in Johannesburg, it is announced that, for a total price of $US550 million, television rights to all domestic games in Australia, New Zealand and South Africa for the ten years starting in 1996 are being sold to Murdoch.

In itself that seems staggering enough. The money boggles the mind. What is almost as astonishing is that a rival organisation, the World Rugby Corporation, linked to another Aussie media giant, Kerry Packer, has been working behind the scenes to snatch away the very players who Murdoch's outfit thinks they have bought the unchallenged rights to.

The WRC is the brainchild of a quiet South African-born Sydney lawyer, Geoff Levy, in association with former Wallaby prop, Ross 'Mad Dog' Turnbull. They swoop in and sign up players all over the rugby world, and in New Zealand some of the most enthusiastic proponents of switching allegiance to the WRC are senior All Blacks.

In Canterbury the point man for WRC is Brewer, whose contract is to be $US1 million a year for three years, and at a training run he hands out contracts to a group of nine or ten players. There are a lot of dropped lips because some of the squad don't get contracts. Not everybody is downhearted, however. Todd Blackadder, meeting the family bills by frantically running a courier van with his wife, finds himself with a $US100,000 a year contract, in his words, 'a hell of a lot of money.'

The contracts eventually become a bit of a joke inside the squad, but what it finally boils down to is that basically the whole team is offered a WRC contract as a Canterbury team. Brewer convinces the players that, if the pay-for-play concept is going to work, they should all stick together as a team. They have three or four meetings and agree to hold out. In hindsight it's obvious that the WRC has gone to the top players, like Brewer and Sean Fitzpatrick, sorted them out with very good contracts, and then looked for the rest of the players to follow.

The day after the World Cup final, key players in the All Blacks are approached by Levy, and then the bargaining gets fierce.

Richie Guy, the chairman of the NZRU in 1995, is surprised by the reaction of the All Blacks when he tells them in Johannesburg that the Union will be able to offer contracts for $150,000 a year.

Nobody says anything about another business in the market, but Guy, who expects a rush of players saying, 'We'll sign now,' gets instead a cool reception and knows that something very significant is secretly going on.

The battle, in fact, is just beginning, and will thrash on for weeks until, it appears, a deal is struck between Rupert Murdoch and Kerry Packer for the latter to drop out of the rugby money war. Geoff Levy, for one, appears to believe that such a deal was struck, but notes that 'it's only hearsay for me to state what happened in a hotel room in London.'

What is absolute fact is that the Canterbury players stay staunch to the bitter end. Jock Hobbs, a former Canterbury and All Black captain, comes to Christchurch as part of his exhausting travels round New Zealand to sign up players for the NZRU, but he's wasting his time. 'We held out,' says Blackadder. 'We went through thick and thin together, and not one guy went the NZRU way. That was one of the biggest mistakes we ever made.'

In Canterbury the story is all over *The Press* about how leading players like Otago All Blacks, Josh Kronfeld and Jeff Wilson, and Counties captain, Errol Brain, have signed with the NZRU.

'Obviously the guys who signed then were on very good contracts,' says Todd Blackadder. 'We were probably the last team to hold out. By then it was all over and when all our boys signed up I think every one of us signed up on the basic $65,000 contract.

'I know that we were penalised because we hung together as a team to the bitter end. In one way that's commendable, but in another way perhaps we should have had the common sense to know that the world was turning.

'They were three-year contracts too, so for those three years from 1996, the majority of the Canterbury players, with the exception of the All Blacks, were on $65,000.'

When Super 12 begins in New Zealand there is plenty of cynicism, and certainly no guarantee that it will be a success.

Had there been enough lead-up time? Even Peter Thorburn, who is given the title of Super 12 commissioner and told to fix the fine details, confesses not long before kick off that there are elements of the competition that will have to be worked out as they go along.

The Crusaders franchise is set up in Christchurch, involving with Canterbury, the provinces of Marlborough, Nelson-Bays, West Coast, Buller, South Canterbury and Mid-Canterbury.

If anything, the Crusaders operation is the slowest in the country to get rolling. There isn't any lack of interest, just some bemusement about how to go about it.

The first Crusaders coach, Vance Stewart, says, 'We did a lot of fitness work, and I think we were the fittest team in New Zealand in Super 12, but we just didn't have the right balance. We'd just gone into a new era, facing a lot of demands, and as soon as the season started we knew what we were in for.

'We went through 35 players that season, and in many areas we were trying to be professional but missing the mark a bit. You can see how much things have changed since 1996 just by looking at our list of officials. Andrew Mehrtens, who was getting over his knee injury from the previous year's All Black tour, was our media liaison man.'

The first game of the Super 12 for the Crusaders is a Sunday match in Hamilton against the Waikato Chiefs, and the Crusaders soon get a taste of nightmares ahead. They are almost alone in the country in not falling in love with the game's new showpiece.

Into the last minute they're leading 26–24, when a touch judge flags Crusaders wing, Adrian Tukaki, for a late charge on Eric Rush. Ian Foster kicks the penalty, and the Crusaders have lost 27–26.

A new squad trying to find its feet, the Crusaders have a lot of injuries and, as a side, don't really know each other. Certainly there are some unexpected names in the Crusaders of 1996. Only a rugby-quiz fanatic would know that Pita Alatini, Deon Muir, Pat Lam and Danny Love are all Crusaders in this first year.

After the close shave with the Chiefs, the next Super 12 game, in Christchurch, sees the Auckland Blues cleaning out the Crusaders, 49–18. Coach Stewart, asked after the game what positives the Crusaders would take from it, can only manage a sad shake of the head. The relentless pressure continues. The Crusaders fly to Brisbane to play the Queensland Reds in conditions that see the temperature at 35 degrees and the humidity 76 per cent. There are suggestions that the Crusaders have slowed to a walk by the time they reach halfway for the kick off. The Reds whip them 52–16. 'The sweat,' says one Crusader, 'pulsed out of your body in time with your heartbeat.'

Back in Christchurch, brutal realities are about to be faced inside the team, and, to the surprise of the Crusaders, the whole town will soon know about them.

On the Tuesday night after the thrashing in Brisbane, the rugby writer for *The Press*, Bob Schumacher, gets a very unexpected scoop.

It's a miserable sort of night and he finds himself the only reporter at the park, waiting for the Crusaders to emerge from training. 'They didn't come out of the changing room and I was standing there on a lonely vigil that went on for ages.' Then Schumacher starts to hear voices, raised in anger, with accusations and counter accusations flying back and forth. 'I overheard what was being said, and started to take notes. I guess some might say I was eavesdropping, but that wasn't why I was there. It was a case of happening to be in the right place at the right time.'

Eventually the Crusaders manager, Chris Wilson, comes out and tells Scumacher that after a long soul-searching session, with 'full and frank discussions,' it has been decided to delay naming the team until later in the week.

The next morning a story appears in *The Press*, so the verbal confrontations are now public and, while the Crusaders aren't delighted at their publication, not one can say the story isn't accurate.

In 1996 there is little time for video analysis of opposing teams, now a staple of pre-match preparation. The Crusaders battle with getting their own house in order, as changes to their starting line-up are forced on them by a string of injuries, and also dictated by efforts to get a winning combination on the paddock.

In the middle of it all, the Crusaders have to stitch together as a unified group player who come from all over the country, without any lengthy pre-season camp to set standards and establish any sort of group culture.

Playing Western Province at Lancaster Park is a chance for the Crusaders to redeem themselves with the home fans. They're ahead 16–9 until, with just eleven seconds left on the ground clock, the visitors score a converted try to draw the game.

Better times come against New South Wales, a night game won 21–16, which features the return of Tabai Matson from injury, Mark Weedon and Con Barrell from suspension, and Greg Coffey, at age 31, out of first-class football for two years, and only playing club rugby in 1996 to help out Marist.

Matson has a blinder, while Coffey is remarkably composed with his play and goal-kicking, and delighted with a match fee, which he reckons will move house improvements up the family agenda.

But it's back to the pits again the following week against Northern Transvaal. Led by the fierce Springbok flanker Reuben Kruger, they whip the Crusaders, 34–18.

Next up is a clash with the Brumbies, not yet the force they will become in later years, and the Crusaders might have taken the game. Instead they lose 29–7 and captain Richard Loe is sinbinned for hitting an offside Brumbies flanker. The timing is a nightmare. A penalty for the blow over-rules a try the Crusaders are scoring near the posts, so it's basically a ten-point punch.

Loe is stood down from the starting XV, and Blackadder is made captain for the next game, with the Hurricanes in New Plymouth. 'I was pretty nervous,' says Blackadder. 'It was all blood and guts, and Richard Loe took a count in my pre-game speech and said I had a record of 36 f's, so you can imagine what the tone was. Richard would have liked to have played, you always do, but he didn't say anything to me or make me uncomfortable.'

In the middle of the Blackadder oration comes one of the memorable team-talk moments. It involves Con Barrell, an endlessly cheerful prop from Northland who had come to Canterbury in 1995 and made the All Blacks the following year.

Blackadder, wound up to a high pitch, is saying, 'I want you to perform, Con. I want a real gutsy effort. No "beep" taking it easy.'

Barell starts sniffing and his eyes lose contact with Blackadder's. The talk grinds to a halt. 'Mmmmm,' says Barrell, 'I can smell hot dogs.'

Even Blackadder has to laugh. He says to Barrell, 'Mate, if we win today I'll buy you as many hot dogs as you like!'

Bring in the hot-dog stand. Turning the Hurricanes ball over 30 times in general play and winning seven of the Hurricanes throws to lineouts, the Crusaders romp away to a 36–13 victory.

The delight doesn't last long. Transvaal, coached by former Canterbury legend Grizz Wyllie, is always going to be difficult to handle at Ellis Park. But a gastric epidemic inside the squad gives the Crusaders no chance at all.

Emergency medical treatment from the team doctor can only do so much and on the way to the game players are throwing up in the team bus. Stu Loe, on the sideline as a reserve, actually vomits while the game is being played. It's little wonder the Crusaders lose, 55–23.

Natal cleans them up in Durban, 58–26, and back home at Lancaster Park there isn't a shred of luck when what looks to be a last-minute try by Justin Marshall is disallowed and the Highlanders scrape in by 29–27. Super 12 is over for the Crusaders, flat last on the round-robin table, with just two wins and a draw to look back on with any pleasure from eleven games.

Vance Stewart is also coaching the 1996 NPC team, but he has a new assistant, former Canterbury B captain Steve Hansen. In Stewart's mind it's also time for a change of captain.

'We got ravaged in that first year of Super 12. We were understrength and, as hard as we tried, we got to the stage where we were playing international teams and we just didn't have players of that ability.

'In that pressure situation some people react in ways you don't expect them to – their demeanour can deteriorate – but Toddy's strengthened.

'At the end of it he seemed to be thinking, "I can do a better job leading this team. I'm keen to do it." In fact the captaincy side on the field and at training wasn't a really big issue to him. What terrified him more was the role speaking in public and fronting the media. He saw himself as a country boy, with a country background, and this was a thing for townies to do. You had the people around him like Andrew Mehrtens, who are pretty slick speakers, good with off-the-cuff remarks, and Toddy struggled with that. But he was prepared at that stage to say, "I'll do the best I can for the team, and I'll overcome the hurdle of speaking for the sake of the team."

'In the team situation he was top-notch. It was a quiet way that Toddy did it. There wasn't a lot of yelling or screaming or swearing. He was all blood and guts on the field, so he could afford to talk quietly to the players, because they knew the standards he played to.

'He had a very good skill level, which was often hidden because he didn't always show what he could do. It wasn't Todd's way to flick the reverse pass behind his back, or the big overhead pass, or the wide skip pass. A lot of the time he was buried in the middle of the rucks with elbows and knees going.'

Blackadder recalls that after the Super 12 of 1996, he was happy to take on the Canterbury captain's role. 'I felt that after what we'd been through, with no disrespect to anyone else, that I could do a good job. It was just a feeling I had. I know it's a slightly strange thing to say but, although I'd never really captained any other side, I felt I was ready. When Vance asked me, I was as keen as mustard.'

Dave Hewett (left) and Brad Thorn hoist their captain, Todd Blackadder, aloft after his last game for Canterbury, winning the 2001 NPC final.

Another change for Blackadder is in the position he will play. Canterbury suffers a run of injuries in the middle of the scrum, so Blackadder plays the remaining seven games of the NPC locking with Steve Lancaster.

'Todd's best position at the time was certainly No. 6,' says coach Stewart, 'but he was always prepared to help out. I know when we lost the shield to Auckland at the end of 1995 they intimidated us and we crumbled a bit. Our locks then were never really hard men. The likes of Robin Brooke could really get on top of them.

'When it came to the NPC, I wanted somebody who would look across at the likes of Robin Brooke and not be bullied. Todd was the man. He had flint hardness and could dominate opponents the way Colin Meads was able to in his day. He was also a very good lineout jumper. Our tests showed that he had the best elevation of any of our forwards.'

With Blackadder locking, Scott Robertson goes to the blindside, Angus Gardiner is at openside, and a newcomer to Canterbury, Steve Surridge, is at No. 8.

At first glance, Surridge may seem an unlikely person to have ended up a Canterbury stalwart. Born and brought up in Auckland, he was an academic with two degrees, one from Cambridge University. An outstanding sportsman in several fields, Surridge retired from rugby in 1993 to concentrate on rowing. Then he went to

Cambridge University, got back into rugby there and decided he'd like a shot at the new professional game in New Zealand.

Surridge becomes famous in the Canterbury team for treating his body the way a Formula One mechanic would treat a finely-tuned Ferrari. One morning Canterbury trainer Mike Anthony is rung up by Surridge who says his pulse when he'd first woken was a bit high. 'That means you're training too much,' says Anthony, so Surridge goes back to bed and has a sleep.

The most notable Surridge incident involves Crusaders assistant coach Peter Sloane, a former builder. Sloane went round to help him build his kitchen, but then Surridge said he had to have a sleep because his pulse was up a bit. Sloane was left to work in the bathroom on his own.

Scott 'Razor' Robertson was a self-described 'surfer boy' at Mt Maunganui College when his rugby career started in the centres or on the wing. In 1991, Craig Ross, a former New Zealand Colts loose forward, became his First XV coach. He was, says Robertson, exactly the right guy at the right time for him. It was Ross who moved the big, fast kid from the three-quarters to the back of the scrum.

By the time he was twenty, Robertson was attracting a lot of attention as a flanker for Bay of Plenty and he was in the New Zealand Colts team that was unbeaten at the first international under-21 tournament, played in 1995 in Argentina, after spending a summer in Sydney training with the Balmain Tigers league club.

Stewart recruits him for Canterbury, and he fits in from the start. 'You could not help but love him,' says Blackadder. 'His whole enthusiasm, he's just a pumped up sort of guy, always smiling, with a boyish keenness. In the changing room it'll go round and everyone will say their bit. Razor will talk about "keeping things tight, you know what I mean?" He'll thump his chest and say, "Keep it real."'

Family is important to Robertson, and one family connection he's proud of is his late uncle, Greg Davis, who tragically died of a brain tumour in 1979 at the age of 39. Born in Matamata, Davis moved to Australia in his early 20s and captained the Wallabies sixteen times from the side of the scrum.

'He was married to my Mum's sister, Claire. I was aware of him when I was growing up, and when I played in Australia people made the connection. He was obviously a great Australian player, captain of the Wallabies and a World XV.'

That Angus Gardiner is playing at all in 1996 is a tribute to the skill of surgeons, who had to reconstruct a knee shattered in his first club game of 1995, and his own will.

Gardiner was born in England while his parents were working there, and his path to the forwards was shaped by future New Zealand cricket coach, Denis Aberhart, who saw him playing fullback in a primary school trial but chose him as a lock. At Christhurch Boys' High he moved to the flank, which remained his position.

After a slow start by Canterbury in the 1996 NPC, there are signs of a spark in a second-half recovery against Auckland which leads 30–3 at half-time on Eden Park. Instead of a rout, the second half sees the only points, a converted try, scored by Canterbury and Auckland coach, Graham Henry, suggesting that he was glad his team built up such a good lead in the first 40.

In the next NPC game, a thriller at Lancaster Park with Otago beaten 43–22,

Andrew Mehrtens returns to the Canterbury team for the first time since the All Black tour, where he'd badly injured his knee in Italy. He not only kicks eighteen points, but gives the backline a confidence that has been lacking earlier in the competition.

By now Canterbury is heading towards a semifinal spot, and a 38–21 win against Taranaki in New Plymouth, then a powerful victory over North Harbour in Christchurch, 43–20, confirms the team's ability.

Stu Loe and Mark Mayerhofler both enjoy milestones in the Harbour match, Loe playing his 100th game for the province, Mayerhofler his 50th.

Loe, a cousin of Richard Loe, combined his rugby with working on a farm in the Glenmark area, saying once that while he didn't always run to keep his fitness up, he would 'park the truck and walk for an hour' to stay in nick.

Travelling a round trip of 175 kilometres to training sessions didn't concern him, ('There's nothing to watch on TV anyway'), and the combination of his positive attitude and competitive skill on the field made him a special mate of captain Blackadder. 'Stu's a bloody good man, the salt of the earth.'

Bubs Mayerholfer comes to be described, quite fairly, by Justin Marshall as the 'rock of our backline. It's a measure of how much respect he's held in that, whenever he says anything at a team meeting, you can hear a pin drop.'

There is one more round left in the NPC in 1996, and it's a battle against Waikato at Rugby Park in Hamilton, eventually won 29–20. So Canterbury finishes third in the round robin and travels to Pukekohe to play Counties in the semifinal.

'We so much wanted to win for Vance in the semi,' says Blackadder. 'We knew that he was retiring after the season finished. He implemented so much for Canterbury that he doesn't get credit for, and we went through the wringer with him.'

That dream will not be realised. The team has its chances in the semifinal, but Counties have a lethal backline, including future French international, Tony Marsh, at second five, Manu Samoa's blockbusting centre, George Leaupepe, and on the wings All Blacks, Joeli Vidiri and the sensation of the previous year's World Cup, Jonah Lomu. This is Vidiri's day in particular, with his four tries spearheading a 46–33 victory.

For Canterbury and Crusaders players, 1997 will be the year professionalism is grasped. There are changes all round in the coaching staff. At the Crusaders, Wayne Smith, back from a stint coaching in Italy, is joined by a former Northland and All Black hooker, Peter Sloane. The manager of the Crusaders, Robbie Deans, is appointed NPC coach, a job in which he is assisted by Steve Hansen.

As a player Wayne Smith was known for not only his attacking and tactical skills, but also his courage. His Canterbury captain, Don Hayes, says that he was amazed at the way Smith would fling himself at the biggest opponent. 'I'd say you could probably write the number of guys he really bowled on a fly's eyebrow, but he was committed to it and always had a go.'

Smith's partner at the Crusaders in 1997 is a man with an attitude that forwards could relate to, especially when at training Sloane growls at the backs in mock anger, 'Get out of the way, you little lizards, or you'll get crushed.'

Training for the Crusaders starts on 6 January, and the team goes to the people of the catchment area, playing warm-up games in Nelson and Greymouth, and holding

Norm Maxwell began as a "six foot tall, six inches wide" schoolboy, but he became a test lock with pace and grit.

practice sessions in Westport, Blenheim, Ashburton and Timaru.

New stars will emerge during the year. One is Leon MacDonald, whose tackling has been scarily aggressive from the time he was a kid growing up in Blenheim.

Kieran Keane, a former All Black, played with some pretty tough jokers for the Canterbury team in the late 1970s and early '80s but when he saw the teenage MacDonald in Blenheim, even Keane was startled: 'When Leon was only fourteen I put him in the First XV at Marlborough Boys.' Sometimes, to be honest, I used to cringe. He was so fearless. In those days there wasn't a lot of refinement – he was like a rampaging bull.'

Like MacDonald, lock Norm Maxwell is a tackler with no apparent concern for his own safety. Maxwell developed his tackling playing league until he was thirteen for the Otaika Eagles Club. At Whangarei Boys' High he was introduced to rugby by a teacher, Te Wai Piripi: 'Norm's problem was that he was six foot tall, which is exceptional for a 13-year-old but he was about six inches wide. Being so gangly, he was uncomfortable about playing rugby, but I knew very quickly I had a future All Black on my hands. He flew into everything at a million miles an hour.'

In his first year of senior rugby, aged just eighteen, Maxwell was invited to play in a Vikings team as a curtainraiser to the final 1995 World Cup trial. He caused his first stir with Vikings team-mates like Counties captain, Errol Brain, by turning up with his gear in a Pak 'n' Save plastic shopping bag. 'I didn't own a gear bag at the time.' There was a further stir when he dominated the lineouts. Vance Stewart, once again a perceptive talent scout, offered him a role in the Canterbury system.

To Blackadder, appointed captain of the Crusaders for the first time, the arrival of Smith and Sloane 'was so refreshing. I think it was the first time we had really worked on our skills at a different level. Smithy kept reiterating what he wanted from the forwards – vision and good handling. It was the start of a new era.'

If you were up against the bruising, battling Mark Hammet "you'd know you were going to get something you wouldn't want."

The players thrive on the reception they get in smaller centres. 'We fed off going round the regions,' says Blackadder. 'I guess the support they gave us made us feel loved for the first time. It was quite a change from 1996, when nobody really wanted to know us apart from our own families.

'They were even talking about starting up a Hurricanes supporters' club in Nelson, and down at the bottom end of the West Coast, where it gets near to Otago, they were starting to look at linking up with the team next door, the Highlanders.'

The whole preparation was, Blackadder remembers, 'bloody hard work. But there was nothing else for us to do. We'd been at the bottom and the only thing we could do was fight our way up.'

There's a win in the first game, 19–17, against the Hurricanes, but games in Australia are lost to the Waratahs, 25–8, and the Brumbies, 49–29.

The heat of public expectation is certainly on when the Super 12 show moves into Timaru for a night game against the Chiefs played in front of a capacity crowd of eight thousand people.

'Before the game I was sitting on the bench and we were under real pressure,' recalls Blackadder. 'It was a must-win game. Robbie Deans came and sat beside me and put his hand on my shoulder. It was a welcome gesture I remember clearly.'

The Crusaders are down to fourteen men for the last 38 minutes, with hooker Mark Hammett ordered off for an alleged punch that video evidence would later reveal was a slap. There was no suspension. Despite that, the Crusaders hold out for a 24–15 victory.

Although the next game, against the Auckland Blues, is lost 29–28, it is still one of the best performances the Crusaders have displayed so far in Super 12.

The Blues at the time are defending champions and have a team loaded with some of the best players in New Zealand rugby. Their forward pack against the Crusaders contains eight All Blacks, from Zinzan Brooke captaining the team at No. 8 right through to Sean Fitzpatrick at hooker.

How astonishing that the Crusaders would come away feeling unlucky not to win, and to have had, in the view of most critics, the better of the forward battle.

'That was the year when our self-belief started to develop,' says Blackadder. 'We went so close against the Blues, and none played better than our No. 8, Clark McLeod. He was absolutely superb.'

McLeod, previously unknown outside Christchurch, was one of the young players Smith and Hansen had taken away on a development trip to Argentina at the end of 1996. That team, captained by Blackadder, was a mixture of NPC players and Canterbury Colts, and won three out of four games on tour. McLeod's play was so outstanding on tour that he had to be included in the Super 12 squad. 'I was going to have to move back home,' he remarked at the squad announcement, 'but now I guess I can afford a flat.'

A key moment in the Blues game is when Leon MacDonald is taken out ten minutes before half-time with a shoulder charge by Robin Brooke. Down 13–6 at the time, the Blues strike back with two quick tries, the second, while the Crusaders are still trying to get their fullback back on the field, scored by Brooke in the same spot where he had flattened MacDonald. Brooke is suspended for two weeks after the game but is not even binned on the night.

After the excitement of the game with the Blues, the trip to Dunedin to play the Highlanders will end in deep disappointment. Up 17–0 after just eight minutes, the Crusaders let the Highlanders edge back into the match, and eventually lose 37–29.

There are certainly signs of an improving attitude in the next game, in Christchurch against the Sharks, who had been finalists in 1996 and had whipped the Crusaders in Durban that year.

This time the game is drawn, 26–26, and Stu Loe suffers the ignominy of being ordered off just twenty minutes into the game. If the consequences hadn't been so serious, the incident would have been like a surreal comedy. The big Crusaders lock, Mark Weedon, was stepping over a ruck when his boot landed on the back of Sharks captain, Gary Teichman's head. Tiechman wasn't hurt, but in the heat of the moment referee Paddy O'Brien thought the boot that touched his head belonged to Loe, so he called the prop out. It's true that many players feign innocence when a referee is lecturing them, but Loe's stunned look and his anguished 'What have I done?' were for real. Loe went to the sideline not knowing what on earth was going on.

Weedon wrote to the judiciary saying that if anyone was guilty he was, not Loe. Despite that Loe was initially suspended for a week, a ban quickly lifted on appeal.

In filthy weather at Lancaster Park, the Gauteng Lions are beaten 23–0, and there's a close loss, 23–22, to Northern Transvaal, then a 16–11 win over Free State on the road in South Africa.

The game that promises a new dawn is the last of the Super 12 round-robin matches, against the Queensland Reds at Lancaster Park. The visitors are whipped, 48–3, and now, with a sixth-place finish in the round robin, there is a new belief among the Crusaders.

NPC coaches Deans and Hansen decide to run a midwinter three-day camp at Hanmer to build team spirit. The players bike through snow, carry the bikes through freezing streams, stumble into live electric fences and divide into four teams for the stretcher carry. For this little treat, the heaviest man in each team is directed to lie on a sack with two manuka poles threaded through it. The rest of the team has to carry the big man over a four kilometre course. Just to add to the occasion, it's actually a race.

To the astonishment of everyone, not least himself, even Bubs Mayerhofler, the sunniest player in the team, snaps at one point when Hansen goads him to put in more effort once too often and is verbally dispatched with a torrent of abuse.

According to Blackadder, 'The time we spent up there was one of the most beneficial things we've ever done. It taught us to be out of our comfort zone. We had quite hard outdoor activities and also mental activities. The management did all the cooking. There was no TV, and we set up all our season. We were up in the snow and everyone was freezing and hungry, tired and a bit grumpy. At the end it was all summed up in a debrief and put into perspective. We learnt a lot from each other up there.'

There is also a theme that a few years later would be used by an advertising agency to lift the nation's mood. A video shows geese flying in formation, explaining how they take turns to take the brunt of a head wind, how they honk to each other when in trouble and go back to assist a sick or injured comrade.

It is agreed that under times of stress on the field, a player will honk and others will honk back to let him know he isn't alone. The first opposing team to strike a bunch of sweaty rugby players honking must have been rocked back just by the sheer weirdness of it.

Robbie Deans says that when he started coaching in 1997, 'Our key thrust was attitude. There was a belief from the marketers that winning was the key in getting people along to the games, but I felt it was attitude.

'So we tried to identify the ideal attitudes and then, as a team, aspired to live by those attitudes. As a group we really put an emphasis on how we were going to include everyone. Toddy was the archetypal Canterbury man, so he was a superb guy to have leading the show. That whole emphasis brought the best out of him.

'A distinction between the amateur days and the professional era is that, in the past, respect for the jersey and what it meant developed by osmosis. As you came into the team you were educated by various means.' Deans began as a young fullback for Canterbury in 1980, when some of the hard men of the game made damn sure that the new boys toed the team line, which decreed that if you weren't prepared to bleed for the jersey you could bugger off.

Now it's the new age. Says Deans, 'We identified the need to consider, rather than take for granted, that our culture – the one we wanted and needed – would happen.'

Deans has his own carefully formed opinions about the worth of Blackadder as a captain. 'There's an awareness more and more that there are two kinds of

As a coach, Robbie Deans' "key thrust was attitude."

intelligence. There's the traditional IQ and there's the EQ, the emotional quotient. Todd's got that in abundance. In the pragmatism of life, Todd's outstanding. Your academics may have an ability to acquire and then regurgitate a mass of information, but they don't necessarily identify what's important at a particular moment in time.

'His emotional intelligence makes him very perceptive with people, and you have to be as a leader. You have to be able to understand where people are coming from to be able to move them to where you want them to go when you come together as a group.

'One of his great skills as a captain was to be able to observe. He wasn't a guy who was verbose, he was very dry-humoured, witty in his own way. He'd use humour to prompt people into action.

'From a coaching perspective he was a great link because he could relate to us and always had a handle on what we were looking for, so he was a great conduit between us and the players.'

The first game in the NPC sees a dream start, a 73–7 demolition of Wellington. Southland is beaten 42–20 in Invercargill, but then Waikato comes to Lancaster Park and gives the Canterbury side a wake-up-call, a 24–18 defeat.

Two good wins on the road show that the Waikato lessons have been learnt. Counties-Manukau is beaten 30–18 in Pukekohe, and North Harbour 20–3 at Albany.

Now it's time for the biggest test of the season, a clash with Auckland at Lancaster Park. It has always been a big game, but by 1997 Auckland has dominated New Zealand provincial rugby for more than a decade and assumed almost mythical proportions. The Queen City has the dash, the cash and the flash, and for many fans in Canterbury that's not so much a fact of life as a personal insult.

Coach Deans startles Blackadder when he says of the Auckland game, 'This is the easy step. We'll be motivated, we've got a good side, we'll be fired up, and we've got them on our park for 90 minutes. They'll stay out there for ten minutes at half-time. And they'll be ours.'

The game will be the drought-breaker, the first victory over Auckland for Canterbury for fourteen years.

The 20–9 victory is everything the capacity crowd of 32,500 people could have wished for. In the first half the Canterbury scrum, facing an Auckland pack missing only an injured Sean Fitzpatrick, turns the blue and white forwards inside out.

Angus Gardiner is omnipresent, making 24 tackles and being directly responsible for five turnovers. So there is strength, there is passion, and there is class too. Six minutes into the second half Tabai Matson angles into the backline at pace, Mehrtens times his short pass perfectly, and the big centre dots down between the posts.

After the win, coach Deans is as pragmatic as he's ever been. He hastens to the media benches to point out, 'We'll enjoy the moment tonight, but this win will mean nothing if we lose to Auckland in a semifinal, or a final.'

The next game, against Otago, is best summed up by Carisbrook's hero of the night, Brendan 'Chainsaw' Laney, a rollicking, irrepressible utility back who will later play for Scotland. 'Jeez,' he says to a reporter after the match, 'that was bloody amazing, wasn't it?'

Indeed. The Canterbury camp thought Laney, a late replacement for an injured Tony Brown, would be so one-dimensional that he'd be easy to deal with. Having rarely played at first five, all he'd do, they figured, was run. And he does.

The trick is that nobody in red and black can catch him. At half-time it's 19–6 to Otago. In the Canterbury huddle the message is simple: 'We've got to score first.' Less than a minute after the start of the second spell Jeff Wilson crosses in the corner, and Otago goes on to win, 35–13.

Canterbury has to beat Taranaki to get a home semifinal, and does just that, winning 40–21, which sets up rematch with Auckland.

On tour with the All Blacks in previous years, Auckland captain Zinzan Brooke, a compulsive teaser, had reminded Blackadder and Justin Marshall on several occasions that he has never played in an Auckland team that had been beaten by Canterbury, and that as long as he was playing, Canterbury would never win.

The game itself could have defined the word 'passion.' Blackadder compares the atmosphere to a test match and says the intensity was almost brutal.

There's some baggage brought to the game by Brooke, who has announced this will be his last game in New Zealand before he takes up a contract with the Harlequins, and he and referee Paddy O'Brien are quickly at each other's throats. From the referee's microphone you can clearly hear Brooke swearing at O'Brien, at one stage screaming, 'Come on, come on, you're a ****ing joke.' O'Brien yells back, 'We'll see who's right!'

Blackadder says, 'That was the game when Zinzan lost it. I don't think I could get a word in that night, with Zinny and Paddy O'Brien going at it hammer and tongs. They certainly weren't helping each other out.'

One of the more astonishing moments in the game comes when Fitzpatrick, famous as the most expert sledger in New Zealand rugby, is goaded into conceding a penalty to Canterbury by his 25-year-old opponent, Mark Hammett. Eight minutes from the end, with the scores locked at 15–15, Hammett is penalised as Fitzpatrick tries to wrestle the ball away from him after a tackle near the Auckland 22. Words are exchanged and then, after Hammett levers himself up by placing an elbow on Fitzpatrick's chest, Fitzpatrick elbows Hammett, right under the nose of referee

O'Brien. The penalty is reversed and Mehrtens kicks the goal for Canterbury.

What did Hammett say? Blackadder says he thinks 'the two of them were probably exchanging cake recipes.' If that's the case, other Canterbury players reckon Hammett's recipe included ingredients like 'you're too old' and 'past it.'

It was certainly a turning point in the match, says Blackadder, and 'it takes a good man to get the better of Fitzy. Hammer is a balls-out sort of a guy, a gutsy player. He'd be a terrible bugger to play against. You'd know you were going to get something you wouldn't want. I certainly wouldn't like to be marking him.'

One of the more extraordinary examples from rugby of sheer determination working medical wonders comes during the eight days between the semifinal with Auckland and the final against Counties-Manukau.

It involves Kevin Nepia, the 123 kilogram prop who moved to Canterbury from Auckland at the start of 1996, his way in his home town blocked by All Black props, Olo Brown and Craig Dowd.

In the semifinal the medial ligament in his right knee is injured so badly it's just one grade off being snapped and in need of immediate surgery. From the moment he comes off just before half-time all that is on his mind is playing in the final. 'All weekend my wife, Lisa, was icing my knee every three hours, right round the clock, until Monday morning. When we got to the specialist the prognosis was grim. It was a tear and there was no rigidity in the knee at all. There was virtually no tendon holding it on.'

The first specialist says it will be six weeks before Nepia can play again. A second gives the opinion that it will be four weeks before he can even run, much less think about playing rugby.

'On the Monday I could hardly walk. I had my knee in a brace and I was using crutches. On the Tuesday it was painful, but I was able to get on a bike in the gym. On Wednesday I was walking without a brace. At the gym I kept the brace on and was able to use a rebounder.

'All through the week Lisa kept icing the knee and I was taking anti-inflammatories to keep the swelling down. On the Friday I took the brace off and had the knee strapped. That night I got through a team training and they said, "Yep, you can play."'

The mental pressure on the Canterbury players is intense. Blackadder finds himself sweating so much before the game he asks Steve Hansen if he can find another dress shirt to change into. At 2.35p.m. the knock comes on the Canterbury changing-room door and Blackadder leads his men down the chipped grey concrete tunnel onto the park. It's a moment he has always relished.

'There's no better feeling in the world than to lead your Canterbury team out in Christchurch. You've got your butterflies and your nerves, and then you get the ball and you just want to get out onto the ground. There's a "whoosh" of noise when you come out of the tunnel, and the blood pumps through the veins.'

The final is barely under way when Leon MacDonald is faced with George Leaupepe, the brutally strong Counties and Manu Samoa centre, on the rampage. MacDonald, at this stage still not out of his teens, is called Rangi, after the maniacal tackling Maori kid in the *Footrot Flats* cartoon.

They called Leon MacDonald "Rangi" after the maniacal tackling kid in the cartoon strip "Footrot Flats".

Leaupepe has the goal line in his sights when MacDonald hits him at chest height in a tackle so fierce it actually bowls the powerfully built centre off his feet. 'Canterbury are renowned for their defence,' yells Murray Mexted in the television commentary box. 'Have a look at this! What a way to stop your opponent when he has a clear run at the line.'

In the heat of a game, says Blackadder, 'you haven't got a lot of time to reflect on things, but when Leon makes a tackle like that it shows his level of intensity, and it rubs off on everyone. You saw Fats [So'oalo] hanging on to Jonah Lomu, Mehrts tackling Jonah. Any other day they would have been swatted like flies. But because the team was so committed and driven to winning that game they hung on.'

At half-time Canterbury holds a 19–3 lead and coach Robbie Deans is as fired up as any player. He walks into the changing room, and when the players are hushed to listen to what he has to say, sweeps the health drinks off the top of the old fridge in the centre of the room. As the plastic bottles bounce on the floor, he points at the bare top and snarls, 'That bloody trophy belongs here.'

Five minutes after half-time Tony Marsh, the talented Counties second five, slices open the Canterbury backline and, on the 22-metre mark, feeds his flanker, Craig Glendinning. Somehow Angus Gardiner digs out another yard of pace and pulls out a try-saving tackle. He then bounces back up and wins the ball back for Canterbury.

In the stands, coach Deans is delighted with the decisions his captain is making. If Blackadder, quite rightly, sees the Gardiner tackle on Glendinning as a crucial time, Deans believes a call Blackadder makes to tap and run in the 60th minute as another major moment.

At the time Counties have come back to be nine points behind. An easy three points are on offer for Canterbury when Counties players are caught offside right in front of their posts by referee Colin Hawke. 'Most captains would have taken the shot at goal,' says Deans. 'But Toddy recognised that it was time to put the foot on the throat, and that's what the game is all about.

'He started to back himself and his own judgement. If you're hesitant, you're off your game. But if you back yourself and have belief in yourself, then others will see that in you. As you start to get success that belief snowballs.'

Lock Graham Jack, older brother of 2001 All Black Chris, is a special hero to the people in the Canterbury team who know what he's overcome to play the season out to the death. He has been ill with a blood disorder that isn't diagnosed for a long time, but keeps fighting to play, often locking the scrum with a quiet, young guy from the Old Boys club, Reuben Thorne.

As an 18-year-old fresh out of New Plymouth Boys' High School, Thorne had headed south, enrolling at Lincoln University for a resource management course. Most of his New Plymouth mates went to Massey, but he had hankered after a return to Canterbury for some time. 'I was born here and all my family came from here too,' says Thorne. 'My granddad used to be the Woolston butcher. We moved north when I was about four or five with my Dad's work. He worked in Wellington for a while, then branched out into farming and ended up in Taranaki.'

There are men like Jack and Thorne playing their hearts out right through the Canterbury line-up, and one of the more amazing tributes comes when prop Nepia's knee finally gives out fifteen minutes from time. As he is assisted to the sideline by Don Hayes, the 1980s skipper remarks in amazement that Nepia is 'the first bloody Aucklander to ever get a standing ovation at Lancaster Park.'

To Blackadder there are obvious heroes, and some not so obvious. 'We had our world-class players, like Justin and Mehrts; Afato So'oalo that year was a pocket dynamo on the wing; and Angus Gardiner played so well in 1997 that he and Josh Kronfeld were by far the best No. 7s in New Zealand.

'But there were other guys not many people would even have known about. Right through the season, we had five or six guys who were tackling-bag holders, who would do a lot of physical work with us so we weren't smashing ourselves up. They turned out to be a sort of thermometer to see whether we were actually doing the work or not. They knew when we were at our best from how hard the hits were going in. They were club players and guys on the fringe of the team, and were crucial in our NPC win.'

The Canterbury team has made a statement in the NPC. The Crusaders are about to make an even bigger impact.

Caleb Ralph (backed up by Andrew Mehrtens) thrived on the family atmosphere in Canterbury.

CHAPTER NINE

TITLES

A lot of words might spring to mind when you think of Todd Blackadder: brave, hard-working, honest, likeable, decent . . . But mystical? Sure, and Grizz Wyllie's favourite pastime off the field was macramé.

Nevertheless, the man from Rangiora has a dream before the 1998 Super 12 final, one that will be repeated for the 1999 and 2000 finals.

He's not sure himself whether he actually dreams it at night while asleep, or sees it when he's dozing, or just visualises it until it seems real. All he knows is that in his mind's eye, on the Monday or Tuesday before every Super 12 final in which he captains the Crusaders, he can clearly picture himself holding up the trophy at the end of the game.

Only Justin Marshall is ever told about the Blackadder vision, and he probably thinks the captain is joking when he tells Marshall before the 1999 final in Dunedin, 'Don't worry about this one, I've dreamt about it.'

If Blackadder literally has a dream, so, metaphorically, do the people who are running Canterbury rugby. There had been management changes in 1996, with Mike Eagle, a stalwart lock for the Albion Club for years and now a successful electrical contractor, heading a board that decides it is time to embrace the professional era.

Chief executive Steve Tew, previously with the Hillary Commission in Wellington, sets out to recruit full-time professional coaches. The first signed up are Wayne Smith and Peter Sloane.

The next step is for everyone to decide where Canterbury teams need some assistance. So, in 1997, loose forward Scott Robertson moves from the Bay of Plenty, lock Steve Lancaster and prop Kevin Nepia arrive from Auckland, and Steve Surridge comes from Auckland via Cambridge University. There will be more recruiting. Three-quarter Caleb Ralph has a battle untangling contract ties with Auckland but eventually moves to Christchurch. Prop Greg Feek and utility back Darryl Lilley come from Taranaki.

There is a genuine effort to make players feel part of the scene. Ralph, who grew up in Rotorua, had never felt at ease in the Auckland environment but is apprehensive about moving to Christchurch with his young family. However, there are functions for wives and partners that make him feel more comfortable about going away for games and, far from being treated with suspicion, he finds himself 'welcomed with open arms.'

As Canterbury's successes mount, there are many in the rest of New Zealand who want to know the province's secret which, according to Robbie Deans, is that there isn't one, just a lot of small decisions and systems that add up to a potent whole.

There are certainly some important steps along the way, and one of the biggest is holding training camps before Super 12, something even the champions of the first two years, the Blues, have never done.

Here is where the spirit of Crusaders sides is forged. Look at 1998, where the squad sits under the stand at QE2 Park, venue for the 1974 Commonwealth Games, watching a rugby video that contains some great red and black rugby moments plus interviews with Don Hayes and Tane Norton, two unpretentious men who talk of sacrifice and team unity and helping your mate.

It's the way Smith and Sloane want the group to act and play, and a large part of that attitude draws on the character of captain Blackadder. Smith believes that a champion team requires that every player has to buy into something bigger than himself. Blackadder loves the whole set of values, the winning attitude and being part of something special.

His transparent sincerity allows him to use imagery with the team that is extremely powerful. Without his sincerity, one of the most potent moments of the 1998 Super 12 campaign could have been laughable instead of moving.

Small swords to wear on the lapels of their blazers have been made for the squad, to fit with the name Crusaders and the campaign slogan and song, 'The Search for the Holy Grail.' Before a key round-robin game in Durban which has to be won to give the Crusaders a home semifinal, there's not a sound in the room as Blackadder says, 'Draw your swords, boys, we've got a battle tomorrow.'

It takes unity to hold the Crusaders together in 1998. Before the round-robin games have even started, they've lost Afato So'oalo, a Samoan wing who has not been recruited but just turns up in 1997 looking for a run on the wing for Canterbury. Small but lightning fast, he was a try-scoring sensation during the 1997 NPC. But in a 1998 pre-season game with the Waratahs he ruptures an anterior cruciate ligament.

Also wanted, but gone, is Leon MacDonald, moved by decree of the New Zealand Rugby Union to play for the Chiefs. The Crusaders had planned to use him at fullback, but the All Black selectors demand that he is played at first five, which means, against his will, he is shifted to Hamilton.

He plays a blinder for the Chiefs in the first round of the competition, helping them to a 25–23 victory over the Crusaders at Albany, but in the fifth round of the competition he's injured and invalided home.

Added quickly to the list of the missing Crusaders is halfback Justin Marshall, who snaps his Achilles tendon in the last minute of the game against the Waratahs, won 33–12, as he hauls in a high pass from Daryl Gibson and hops over the try line. Poor Gibson will carry the team nickname 'The Black Widow' the rest of the year for his

Norm Maxwell played most of the 1998 Super 12 injured, but still had the energy to score a vital try in the final.

innocent role in the injury.

Marshall and So'oalo out with injury. MacDonald unavailable. Next up, a thrashing in Brisbane by the Reds, 35–9, and a 31–24 home loss to the Blues, made more embarrassing for the Crusaders by huge billboards erected in Christchurch by a team sponsor that mock the Auckland power crisis: 'What do you call three Aucklanders without power? The front row.'

It's now four games for three losses. Five rounds into the competition the Crusaders are at the bottom of the table, and the local rumour mill goes ballistic. Pub gossip goes public when a caller to a local radio station suggests that he's been told by Blackadder's mother that the Crusaders are now being coached by manager Deans in the wake of Smith's inability to get more victories.

When the man is tracked down by Blackadder's irate mother, he cries and admits he made it up. But what really kills the ugly suggestion is a run the Crusaders now make that takes them right to the final.

Hooker Matt Sexton snaps his Achilles in the game won against the Bulls at Lancaster Park, 31–20, but although the injury list keeps growing, so does the tally in the 'win' column.

It's the game with the Brumbies in Timaru that really marks the turning point. The culture that is growing in the team is rewarded with big games from Reuben Thorne and Norm Maxwell, both of whom play injured for most of the season. At training Graham Jack and Steve Lancaster do most of the scrummaging for Thorne and Maxwell, which allows the slightly damaged duo to be patched up on game day, jabbed with a painkiller and able to give 80 minutes of top footy on the field.

The Brumbies are beaten 38–26 and now the run is on. The Western Stormers fall 27–25, the Highlanders 40–24, the Hurricanes 39–17, and the Cats 34–25.

At this point the Crusaders face the Sharks. If the Crusaders win in Durban, the semifinal will be against the Sharks in Christchurch. If they lose, they'll have to stay in South Africa and play the Sharks again the following weekend.

Blackadder and Angus Gardiner room together in Durban, and Blackadder talks of how his son, Ethan, is having a birthday the following week.

On the afternoon of the game he suddenly starts rummaging through his clothes.

If the vibe was wrong in the All Blacks for Norm Berryman, it was perfect for him in the Crusaders.

He says to Gardiner, 'I have to get home. How can I miss Ethan's birthday? Bugger it, I'm packing my bags.' Gardiner thinks, 'What the hell, if it's good enough for him, it'll do me.' 'I'm with you, Toddy,' he says, and packs too. In the team talk Blackadder tells his men, 'Bugger this, we're not staying here another week.' A 32–20 win over the Sharks ensures that they fly home for the semi.

By now a special hero is a player from the draft, Norm Berryman, a man at the crossroads of his career. He'd been a teenage sensation for Northland and on the cusp of selection for the 1995 World Cup, but his star was fading when he came to Christchurch. He is regarded with suspicion by some coaches for his unique approach to life, and it's true that are times when he does seem to live on Planet Norm (population, one). Interviewed at Rugby Park for a television clip, he's asked if rugby was always the biggest sport in his life. Norm beams a massive smile and says, 'Aw, you know how it is, bro.'

In reality he's not as laid-back as he appears to the outside world. Before a pre-season game in Coolum, Berryman is so stressed that he throws up in the changing shed. Coach Smith has a private talk with him: 'Look, we don't want you feeling like this at all. Just make sure you don't get stuck with the serious guys during the build-up. You know Con [Barrell] from Northland, and you know Mehrts. Hang out with them before the game.'

Instructed to join the two most frivolous characters in the squad, Berryman soon thrives, reaching a point in home games where he and Mehrtens walk over to the bank at the newly named Jade Stadium so they can wave and trade quips with the fans.

It's not Berryman's size or strength that startles the Crusaders, but a level of skills that matches anybody else's in the side. Throughout the season he will be able to use those skills in the most pressured situations, and is often a match winner.

He'll make the All Blacks in 1998, but quickly detects 'no vibe' in the squad, on a horror run of five lost tests. When he leaves the All Blacks, he hitchhikes back to Northland, saying that he doesn't owe All Black coach, John Hart, any thanks 'because he only put me in because of public pressure.'

In the home semi of 1998 against the Sharks, Berryman gets the Crusaders away to an electrifying start. In the fourth minute his instincts put him in the line of a misdirected Sharks cross-kick and he races 60 metres for a try. Seven minutes later, fed the ball with two men to beat, he leaves them grasping at air and scores again.

Daryl Gibson runs into the line from fullback for another try, converted by Mehrtens, and after fifteen minutes the Crusaders are ahead by 20–0.

The Sharks, captained by the indefatigable No. 8 Gary Teichmann, fight back so well that they take the lead in the second half, but the Crusaders now have steel throughout the side and prevail by 36–32. They're not promising results any more; they're producing them.

On Friday 29 May, the day before the final, the Crusaders check in at the Centra Hotel in Albert Street, right in the heart of Auckland's central business district.

Coach Smith says to his captain, Blackadder, 'What are we going to do in the morning? We've got a long day, the boys are going to be hyped up, what'll we do?'

Blackadder looks out of the room's window. 'Well, why don't we have our lineout drills out in that car park there?' Smith agrees.

The squad wanders across the road in the morning, but by now the traffic is busy. Mehrtens, in Smith's recall, is so hyperactive that every time they do a move he sidesteps a couple of moving cars before he passes the ball. 'It was like taking out a bunch of kids who were bloody excited to be there but nervous at the same time.'

What gives Smith some confidence is the look he sees in Blackadder's eyes: 'When he gets that look you know the others are going to follow him, and it'll take a hell of a lot to beat you.'

The Blues, with a franchise that includes Counties-Manukau, field a team captained by Michael Jones, with Jonah Lomu and Joeli Vidiri on the wings, Carlos Spencer at first five, Robin Brooke and Royce Willis (a draft player that year from the Waikato) locking, and Olo Brown and Craig Dowd propping. Understandably they are the red-hot favourites to win a third successive title.

Although the Blues apply fierce pressure up front and the Crusaders lose Norm Berryman with a torn hamstring after 25 minutes, the visitors, to their own amazement, go to the break up 3–0 through a Mehrtens penalty.

In the shed at half-time Blackadder tries to ease the pressure by saying to his players,'We're playing like shit, and we still won the first half.'

The Crusaders defence is cracked just a minute after half-time when Lee Stensness, a fragile but gifted midfielder, slips through a gap to give new Blues hooker, James Christian, a try under the posts. A conversion and a 45 metre dropped goal by fullback Adrian Cashmore puts the Blues up 10–3 after 53 minutes.

The pivotal part of the game may have already passed. Straight after the Christian try, the Blues set a series of scrums at the Dominion Road end of the ground. One scrum screws and goes down, and every Crusader holds his breath in case referee Paddy O'Brien awards a penalty try. He doesn't, so the Crusaders survive and start to believe they can actually win the game.

With twenty minutes to go, the Crusaders strike back. Mark Mayhofler slams Carlos Spencer so hard in a tackle that the ball bounces free and is snapped up by Norm Maxwell.

'Maxi' is a special favourite of his Crusaders' team-mates. As one says, 'He starts a game playing like a maniac and then never stops for 80 minutes.' With the ball in his hands at Eden Park he dummies, stretches his long legs and flies twenty metres for a try, which Mehrtens converts to level the score at 10–10.

In the stand, Blues coach Graham Henry still believes his team is in control and makes no substitutions. Smith, by contrast, works the bench and the fresh legs provided by prop Greg Feek and flanker Angus Gardiner provide an obvious spark.

Adrian Cashmore and Andrew Mehrtens trade penalty goals and, with only a minute of regulation time to go and the score tied 13–13, Mehrtens is passed the ball some twenty metres from the Blues line.

He has no preconceived idea of what he will do, but through the white noise that is the roar of the local crowd he can just hear winger James Kerr yelling, 'Chip it, chip it!' He drops the ball to his right boot and lobs it just short of the goal-line.

Mehrtens watches the ball 'bobble around and take a horrible bounce' for the two Auckland defenders, Cashmore and Junior Tonu'u. Coach Smith says it was 'a very good option, very well executed by a player who had nailed every kick, and taken every right option for the previous eight games'.

Kerr flies to the ball, dives and scores the try. Back where he made his kick Mehrtens is stunned. 'I couldn't really believe we'd scored from it.' He regains his composure in time to kick a difficult conversion, and although the Blues attempt one last surge, the game is over with the score 20–13. The Crusaders are the new Super 12 champions.

Blackadder now has to make a victory speech. He quickly has a word with Gardiner, a schoolteacher with a double degree. 'Let me run this by you,' he says. Gardiner listens. 'Sounds bloody good to me. Go for it.'

Drenched in sweat, Blackadder steps up on the temporary stand in the middle of Eden Park. He thanks the red and black supporters for a 'tremendous year' and then has the presence of mind to thank and name, one by one, the six unions at the top of the South Island that join with Canterbury in the Crusaders.

That's grace under pressure personified, and there's a need for more coolness when their chartered flight reaches Christchurch. Condensation drips off the terminal ceiling and the players, wives and partners form a conga line to snake their way outside.

'We thought we had a good chance,' says Blackadder, 'and we had a bit of belief. But after being in the team in 1996, when the wheels were off the truck and bouncing along beside you down the road, to go to Eden Park and beat the guys who'd won it twice was amazing.'

The ultimate salute for the Crusaders comes the following Wednesday when a parade through the centre of the city draws well over 100,000 people, a crowd estimated by council traffic officials to be larger than the number of people drawn in for the annual Christmas parade. In 1998 in Canterbury the Crusaders are officially bigger than Santa Claus.

In New Zealand rugby the defence of the Crusaders will have an enormous influence on the game.

The team works on very tight, spread defences under Smith, a system of staying

Brothers in arms, Scott Robertson and Ron Cribb,
after the Crusaders third Super 12 title, in 2000 in Canberra.

inside a man, going forward, marking from the outside in, so he can only go round you and, if he cuts back inside, the body angle for the tackle is right.

'But if you don't believe in it,' warns Blackadder, 'or don't want to help your mate out, it won't work. You have to make your tackle, or I have to compromise my body position if your man cuts in. That year there was just wave after wave of red and black jerseys.'

After the euphoria of the Super 12 win, defending the NPC title with Mayerhofler, Mehrtens and Marshall away with the All Blacks for the first three games is always going to be tough, and so it proves.

There are flashes of form, a 50–17 whipping of Auckland and a superb 34–9 victory over Taranaki the most notable, but the games that really count are all lost, a Ranfurly Shield challenge against Waikato (29–23), a round-robin game against Counties-Manukau to get a home semifinal (49–42), and the semi in Hamilton against Waikato (32–13). Blackadder sums it up succinctly: 'By the end of the year we were buggered, with just no more legs.'

After the disappointments in the NPC, the TAB makes the Crusaders $9 outsiders to win 1999's Super 12, which also carries the hint that the 1998 title was a fluke.

They start like rockets, beating the Chiefs, the Blues and the Brumbies, and drawing with the Hurricanes, but there are mid-competition losses to the Reds, the Highlanders and the Stormers, before a crucial game with the Bulls in Pretoria. The Crusaders have now dropped to eighth on the table. Another loss and there won't be time to get back into the top four.

With seconds rather than minutes to go against the Bulls, Andrew Mehrtens kicks a famous 35 metre dropped goal, which he celebrates by giving a vigorous double-handed middle-finger salute to the crowd.

The lead-up to the dropped goal is probably as noteworthy as the aftermath. Justin Marshall holds the ball to feed a scrum being set straight in front of the Bulls' posts, and looks to Blackadder for advice. The sweat is pouring off the captain, his jersey is hanging out and he's sucking in air. In what he will later call 'a great piece of captaincy,' Blackadder says to Marshall, 'Just bloody do something!' then buries his head in the scrum.

Marshall calls to Mehrtens, '50,' the team's code for a dropped goal. Mehrtens calls back, 'No, no.' He later explains, 'I thought they'd all expect the drop kick, so I wanted Ron Cribb to run from No. 8. They'd follow him and then we'd sweep blind and catch them on the hop. In the end Justin didn't hear me, and I started moving to where I shouldn't have been. I had to go back to grab the ball. It turned out to be the best thing we could have done.'

Mehrtens drops the goal and the Crusaders sneak through, 30–28. It what he later calls something 'completely out of character,' Mehrtens then flips the bird at the vocal Pretoria crowd with both hands. Straight after the game he grabs coach Smith and asks, 'Can I come to the press conference?' The coach, who missed the gesture, doesn't know what he's talking about.

Mehrtens apologises at the conference, and Bulls captain Rueben Kreuger generously says he might have done the same thing in the circumstances. It takes a meeting for Mehrtens with the New Zealand Union in Wellington, more public apologies and a secret monetary penalty to put the controversy to rest.

Back home the Crusaders bounce back from a 31–6 deficit to beat the Cats in Nelson, 58–38, then the Sharks (34–29) and the Waratahs (38–22) are dispatched to ensure a semifinal against the Reds.

The Crusaders stay in Sydney to prepare for the game in Brisbane, and coaches Smith and Hansen pick the Reds tactics to the last detail. They expect a lot of kick and chase. So at Ballymore the Crusaders drop Mehrtens back to fullback when the Reds have the ball for scrums and lineouts. They kick, Mehrtens returns with interest and the Crusaders win 28–22.

The final in Dunedin against the Highlanders, who have to fly back from South Africa at the start of the week, is promoted as a 'Party at Tony Brown's Place,' a reference to a huge insurance campaign running on television: 'Party at Kelly Browne's Place.'

Justin Marshall, as so often during his illustrious career, is under some media

Aaron Mauger, part of a great Lyttleton rugby heritage that sees uncles, Graham and Steve Bachop, and brothers, Aaron and Nathan, all All Blacks.

pressure for the All Black spot, but on the day at Carisbrook he overwhelms the man the critics want in his place, Byron Kelleher.

Kelleher is fast and strong, but Marshall muscles him, bumps him, rattles him and leads the way to a 24–19 victory.

There are individual moments of sheer brilliance. The most notable comes from winger Afato So'oalo. Fed from a scrum on halfway by Steve Surridge, he beats his marker, fellow Manu Samoa wing Brian Lima, kicks in-field at the 22 and beats Lima and Jeff Wilson in a sprint to touch down the ball over the goal line. No wonder he's late for Monday's street parade, groaning as he clambers on the bed of a truck, 'Ah, too many rums last night.'

When the World Cup squad is announced, eight Cantabrians – Gibson, Mehrtens, Marshall, Scott Robertson, Reuben Thorne, Maxwell, Greg Feek and Mark Hammett – are included. All Black coach, John Hart, decides his cup squad players will not be involved in the NPC, so a radically different Canterbury team takes the field in 1999.

Coach Robbie Deans introduces three youngsters who will soon be All Blacks: fullback Ben Blair, five-eighths Aaron Mauger and lock Chris Jack.

Blair is a Coaster, born in Westport, whose father and grandfather both played for Buller. Ben has been talent spotted by St Andrew's College and given a sports scholarship. He plays in several positions in the First XV, and for a time is considered a potential top flight halfback, but his speed and ball skills make him a natural for wing or fullback.

Mauger, brother of future All Black Nathan Mauger, is also the nephew of All Blacks Graeme and Stephen Bachop, and remembers starting his rugby in Lyttleton as a four-year-old lock in Nathan's under-nine team. He moved to halfback then to the midfield while at Christchurch Boys' High.

He's just eighteen in 1999, with less than a dozen club games under his belt, when he signs a professional contract with Canterbury for the NPC, but as Robbie Deans points out, 'While he's not that old in years, he's very mature in life and on the rugby field.'

Chris Jack, 'reasonably tall' at primary school, was a soccer player until he was ten or eleven, then switched to rugby. He played at second five or centre, then at No. 8 in his early days at Shirley Boys' High School, but by the time he gets into the First XV it is as a lock, having shot up in height when he was fifteen or sixteen.

His coach, Glen Fyall, says that above everything at school Jack had the right mental attitude to succeed in rugby: 'I recall often the boys talking after the weekend about the party they'd had in the weekend, how much they'd drunk and so on. Chris often either wouldn't attend or, if he did, he wasn't a big drinker. He got on very well with the rest of the guys but he knew very well what he wanted to do with his rugby. He just wanted to get on with it.'

The NPC in 1999 is a training ground for Canterbury, and a good one, but with so many experienced men away on national call, it's never going to be won. The team finishes fifth and just misses the playoffs.

In the World Cup in Britain the All Blacks are knocked out in the semifinals by France and limply surrender in the play-off for third and fourth against South Africa. Coach John Hart resigns and his replacement is Wayne Smith. That opens the door at Super 12 level for Robbie Deans and he is appointed, with Steve Hansen, to run both the Crusaders and Canterbury in 2000.

There is more common ground, suggest men who have been coached by them both, between Smith and Deans than outsiders might believe. Both want to innovate, both want players to improve individual skills, both are committed to the idea of team before self. If the messages are similar, the delivery is probably a point of difference. Deans is more direct. 'In a nutshell,' says captain Blackadder, 'Smithy will ask you; Robbie will tell you. But if you don't agree with either, you're quite free to fight for your argument.'

There are two significant changes in the loose forwards. Angus Gardiner is gone, off to play for the Bath Club in England, and Steve Surridge is contracted to play out his career in Japan.

In the squad as a full-time member for the first time is No. 8, Ron Cribb, unwanted by the Blues. His career explodes with the Crusaders. Cribb comes from North Harbour, where the culture, Frank Bunce once explained, is so casual that 'if we dropped every guy who was late for training from the next game, you'd be lucky to have anyone on the field.'

So when Big Ron sashays into his first gym session with Crusaders trainer, Mike

Anthony, a fitness fanatic who regularly competes in the Coast to Coast endurance event and detests lateness, the local players wait for the fun. They're not disappointed. Cribb is verbally pinned to the wall and lashed with words until he's reeling. He's never late again and his season will end with All Black selection.

His combination with Scott Robertson and Reuben Thorne will be an X–factor for the Crusaders of 2003, who start by beating the Chiefs 27–24 on a bone-dry Rugby Park in Hamilton, then the Blues at Jade Stadium, 32–20.

The Reds rattle the Crusaders in Brisbane, ahead 16–3 at half-time and looking like winners until Justin Marshall intercepts an inside pass from Reds first five, Shane Drahm, and runs 80 metres for a try. 'For somebody like me,' says Marshall, 'who hasn't got the fastest set of legs in the team, knowing that you haven't got a lot of support is not a nice feeling.' Inspired by Marshall's effort, the Crusaders pull away to win 27–19.

The game against the Stormers in Nelson sees the Crusaders make it three from three, with a 47–31 victory, and Ron Cribb in such outstanding form he is already being tipped to become an All Black. One tackle on Percy Montgomery is so fierce that it's suggested a headstone should be erected where the Stormers fullback was buried.

Marika Vunibaka, the Fijian winger, is firing too. Vunibaka had been in outstanding form at the 1999 World Cup for Fiji, although he ran into judicial trouble after some push and shove in pool play.

The Highlanders are tough at Jade Stadium, although beaten 42–36, but the fifth game is lost to the Hurricanes, 28–22, Jonah Lomu's dynamic power exposing the problems Norm Berryman is having with injuries. It will be the last time Berryman is a frontline player for the Crusaders.

The annual visit to South Africa starts in Durban with a 32–24 win over the Sharks, followed by a game against a Cats team at Ellis Park, coached by Laurie Mains, that blitzes the visitors, 54–31. Back home there's a 75–27 romp over the Bulls and a 22–13 victory against the Waratahs.

The Crusaders now display some lateral thinking for their last round-robin game, against the Brumbies. Both teams are already guaranteed a home semifinal, but a win in the round-robin game will decide who might have a home final.

Amazingly, the Crusaders don't really focus on trying to beat them to ensure a home final. Robbie Deans says to his players, 'Let's go out there and smash them.' In the process, although the game is lost 17–12, the Crusaders have a happy changing shed. Big hits have been made, the Brumbies have been shaken and there's still plenty of petrol in the red and black tank. Not that the game doesn't have plenty of passion.

Four minutes from the end Justin Marshall is told by referee André Watson to clear the ball from a maul.

'It's still moving, André,' shouts Marshall.

'Clear it,' commands Watson, then blows for a scrum.

'Aw, ****, André,' yells Marshall.

Watson reaches for a yellow card in his pocket.

'I'll save you the bloody trouble,' says Marshall, and starts walking off.

He is some metres away when Blackadder joins the mêlée, fronting Watson, to

Justin Marshall's fierce passion for the game is rewarded with a try coming up, while on the ground Daryl Gibson smiles with delight.

ask what the hell's going on. Watson, one hand in his pocket, his eyes on Marshall's disappearing back, can't really explain. 'Get him back,' he says, pointing at Marshall.

By the time a fuming Marshall is recalled, Watson forgoes the card but awards a penalty against him.

Marshall is cited and told he'll be suspended from the semifinal with the Highlanders if he doesn't make a public apology. He grits his teeth, makes the apology on camera and then promptly tears a calf muscle at training, so can't play the semi anyway.

By a strange coincidence, Daryl Gibson, 'The Black Widow', is the man passing the ball to the halfback at Rugby Park when Marshall's calf tears.

So 21-year-old Ben Hurst, the son of 1970s All Black midfielder Ian Hurst, is called to the field of play for the semi and final, just as Aaron Flynn, the tough, irrepressible Sydenham halfback had been in 1998 when Marshall was injured.

Tension is so high before the semi against the Highlanders at Jade Stadium that the team manager, Darren Shand, is on the phone calling for another bus before the driver realises the reason he can't start his vehicle is that he's got it in drive, not neutral or park. Hurst, on the other hand, is not so stressed. 'It was such a shock and felt so unreal,' he says, 'that I was actually more nervous before the Christchurch Club final than the Super 12 games.'

Andrew Mehrtens kicks eight from eight shots at goal, and his tactical kicking means the Highlanders play most of the game in their own half, the Crusaders winning, 37–15.

Come the final in Canberra against the Brumbies, and Blackadder has his usual visionary moments about a Crusaders victory, while sleet and snow roll into Australia's capital city.

It's actually snowing when the final starts on Saturday night, 27 May 2000, and the Crusaders, $1.50 to $2.40 underdogs with the New Zealand TAB, are making tackle after tackle. By the end of the game Razor Robertson will have clocked up 32.

Eleven minutes after half-time Cribb scores the only try for the Crusaders. Mehrtens delays his pass, Cribb races into a half-gap, grubbers the ball ahead, regathers and scores.

But four minutes from the end the Brumbies have slugged back to be ahead 19–17. Mehrtens is asked to kick for goal from 42 metres, straight into the freezing wind. He's battling with cramp. 'I tend to get it in both legs. It's not too bad running around, it's when I tense up and extend my leg, so making a tackle seems to bring it on. Towards the end I can remember making a tackle, and then sitting beside the ruck, sticking out my legs in front of me, like a little kid at school.

'It's when I'm kicking that it really grips. I can kick but then, on my follow-through, it really grabs hold. I was worried that knowing I'd be in some sort of pain might make me hold back. So I really tried hard to give it everything, just whack it, and whatever happens won't matter if you've kicked the ball properly. It did come off nicely, and in the end I don't think I even cramped up.'

With the Crusaders ahead 20–19, it's the end of the Brumbies and a remarkable three-peat for the Crusaders. They stay awake all night to celebrate, then fly into Christchurch airport on a chilly Sunday afternoon, tired and nursing hangovers.

All the other passengers leave the plane, and then former All Black captain, Andy Dalton, now the president of the New Zealand Rugby Union, comes on board and reads out the new All Black squad, selected by new coach Wayne Smith, Tony Gilbert and Peter Thorburn.

There are eleven Crusaders named, and three of them – Leon MacDonald, centre Mark Robinson and prop Greg Somerville – are in the All Blacks for the first time. Blackadder is the new All Black captain.

Robinson, a former Taranaki player who has been away on a post-graduate course at Cambridge University, has overcome the social slip of saying, 'Good morning, chaps,' when he was first in the Canterbury squad to become well-liked for his thoughtful character and admired for the skills and vision he brings to centre. Injury will prevent him making a bigger impression at international level.

Tighthead prop Somerville, 'Yoda' to the team, is living proof, along with fellow Crusaders and future All Black prop, Dave Hewett, that coach Deans has flashes of extraordinary inspiration.

Here's how Somerville's provincial career begins with Canterbury in 1998. He cruises down to Rugby Park to hold the tackle bags for the NPC team, who are getting ready to fly to Hamilton to face Waikato in the semifinal. His own season with the Canterbury Colts has finished and his mind is on heading back home to Wairoa in Hawke's Bay.

He needs to find some labouring work to pick up a few bucks so he can return to Lincoln University the next year. His scarfie flat needs to be packed. Then he's drawn aside by the team management and told, 'We're going to give you a run this week.' He is caught completely off guard.

Unhappy with the way the scrum had gone in a losing game against Counties-Manukau the previous week, coaches Deans and Hansen have decided to omit veterans Stu Loe and Kevin Nepia. Con Barrell is injured, so they look to Somerville and then unknown Sydenham Club prop, Hewett.

Was it a surprise to the team as well as to Somerville? Hell yes. 'When they said Greg was coming into the team to play Waikato,' his captain Todd Blackadder says, 'I'd never even heard of him.'

Was it, at the time, a secret as well as a surprise? Hell yes. It's such a big secret that the other props' names are still on the flight tickets. Somerville flies to Hamilton under the name Mr C. Barrell. The game isn't won, but Hewett and Somerville are on the way.

Hewett, born in Christchurch, but brought up on a farm in Cheviot was just thirteen years old when his family's life took a big turn in 1985. His father was employed as a farm advisor by stock and station agents, Pyne Gould Guinness, which was commissioned to provide experts to direct state farms in Hungary. For three years the Hewetts lived in the middle of Hungary, in a place called Mezoflava, where Dave learnt to speak Hungarian but played no organised sport.

When the family returned to Canterbury in 1988, Dave went to Christchurch Boys' High for his sixth and seventh form years. In his last year at school he was in the Second XV, as a prop, and continued to progress quietly in rugby when he went to Lincoln University, where he completed a Bachelor of Commerce and Management degree, majoring in marketing.

When the Lincoln University senior team disbanded, he moved to Sydenham for the 1993 season. There he stayed, and in 1997 was seconded to play for South Canterbury in the NPC. The last eight games of the season were lost and the team was relegated to the third division.

Then 26, Hewett and his wife, Michelle, made a decision that will prove momentous for them both: 'I had always wanted to play for Canterbury and can remember at the start of the 1998 season sitting down and having a talk with Michelle and saying, "If I don't get into a decent team this year I'm going to pull the plug."' When he talked of a decent team, he was thinking of Canterbury B.

After the shock selection for the Waikato semi, both Hewett and Somerville are offered Super 12 contracts for the following year. The lifestyle for the average player in his early 20s changes dramatically when $65,000 a year is suddenly on the table, but it isn't so straightforward for Hewett. He is working for PDL as an international salesman, going to Chicago and also to Germany to deal with people looking after

PDL's products there, and there are trips to Asia on the horizon.

Hewett deals with switch gear, from basic light switches in a house up to industrial switches, three-stage power switches and waterproof versions. At the time he signs a Super 12 contract, he knows he has the chance in his work to quickly get a much higher salary than a Super 12 contract offers. He asks his wife whether he should pursue his rugby dream. She tells him, 'If you want to do it, go for it, give it as much as you can. If you reach a point where you feel you can't give it any more, and you want to stop, we'll just turn to what we want to do from there.'

In the NPC season of 2000 there will be more thrills, and very nearly the treble of the Super 12 and NPC titles, and the Ranfurly Shield.

It's decided by Deans and Hansen that Daryl Gibson will be the team's captain during the season to give Blackadder a break from his work as All Black captain.

The All Blacks drift back into the Canterbury fold at the behest of All Black coach Smith and the demands of their playing schedule but, after a 27–20 loss to Wellington in the first round of the NPC, there are wins over North Harbour, Counties-Manukau, Auckland, Taranaki and Southland before a 23 September challenge against Waikato in Hamilton, when all the Canterbury All Blacks are available.

Captain Gibson nearly doesn't make the kick off, suffering severe food poisoning two days before the challenge, but lasts 57 minutes before sheer exhaustion sees him replaced by Mark Mayerhofler.

It's the 69th minute before the game is sealed. With the score 19–13 to Canterbury, Caleb Ralph counterattacks from a Waikato kick, Mayerhofler and Mark Robinson carry the attack on, and Blackadder is there to time the final pass to Justin Marshall, who crosses for a try that is converted by Ben Blair, kicking for Mehrtens, who has a slight groin strain.

Waikato score again, but the shield is won, 26–18. It's defended against Otago, 29–26, in an absolute thriller, and then against Northland, 26–22, a game that's such a disappointment that the best Steve Hansen can say is that the display is 'pretty ugly'.

By now Canterbury are at the top of the division-one table so the semifinal against Taranaki, a game that coach Colin Cooper says pits his amateurs against Canterbury's professionals, is at Jade Stadium. The 'amateurs', who proudly boast five working farmers in the pack, give the professionals hell for 80 minutes, Canterbury finally winning, 31–23.

Wellington arrives for the final on the back of a 48–23 whipping of Auckland at Eden Park in the other semi, the team strong from the front row with bullnecked hooker Norm Hewitt, to fullback, where Christian Cullen, a huge star since he scored four tries in his 1996 All Black debut, wears the No. 15 jersey.

'We'll have to play better than we did against Taranaki to beat Wellington,' says coach Robbie Deans, and he's dead right.

There is a strange moment late in the game when, with Wellington ahead just 34–29, referee Paul Honiss, who has constantly sought reassurance from touch judge Paddy O'Brien throughout the game that he's doing a good job, sin-bins Wellington lock Dion Waller. What's weird is that Waller is binned for being offside when he knocks down an Andrew Mehrtens pass that would have certainly cleared the men outside for a try. But there's no penalty try awarded and, as Mehrtens says afterwards, 'from the Canterbury end we didn't have any argument with Wellington winning the title. The way Wellington played in the last three or four weeks of the NPC they deserved it.'

On the national stage Wayne Smith takes an All Black team to France and Italy, captained by Blackadder and including nine other Canterbury players: Gibson, Mehrtens, Marshall, Robertson, Thorne, Maxwell, Feek, Somerville and Hammett.

At the same time that the All Blacks are touring, a New Zealand A team is playing in Europe too, coached by Robbie Deans and Steve Hansen. It contains five Canterbury players: Blair, Ralph, Jack, Barrell and Hewett.

Many of the players, most notably Blackadder, return to New Zealand mentally and physically drained.

Adding to the woes for the Super 12 of 2001 is the fact that, to allow the players some recovery time, there are only three weeks of preparation, instead of the usual seven or eight, before the competition starts. The Crusaders are punished for the lack of lead-in, a problem compounded with the loss of Cribb back to the Blues and the appearances of players like Mehrtens, Hammett, Maxwell and Vunibaka limited through injury.

The team slides from first to tenth place, and on reflection the only real positive is the arrival of a big, tough, quiet man from the Brisbane Broncos, Brad Thorn, to bolster the pack.

Thorn was born in Mosgiel, but his family move to Brisbane when he's a kid, and by the time he's 21 he's a star in the Brisbane Broncos league team, playing in three NRL grand finals and eight tests for the Kangaroos. At the back of his mind lurks a desire to play rugby for his country of birth, so he takes a massive pay cut (reputed to be as much as $400,000 a year) and signs with Canterbury. A committed Christian, he shuns personal publicity but does allow that the change in climate from Brisbane to Christchurch shouldn't be a problem. 'I was brought up in Mosgiel, mate.'

For the 2001 NPC Steve Hansen is in charge, assisted by Aussie McLean, with Deans concentrating on Super 12 coaching. Hansen, a former policeman, appeared in 21 games for Canterbury, but his more remarkable claim to fame is that for every one of the fourteen years he plays senior football for Marist in the midfield he made the Canterbury B team.

He's part of a Hansen coaching dynasty, his father, Des, a championship-winning legend with Marist, and brother Kelly later coaching Marist-Albion. Steve considers himself 'very lucky to have as a father a great mentor in my early days as a coach. He sees things that many other coaches could miss.'

Some thought Hansen was aiming too high when he applied in 1996 for a position as assistant coach to Vance Stewart with Canterbury, but he got the job, selected ahead of, among others, Wayne Smith, who had just returned from Italy.

Hansen was the back coach under Stewart, but in 1997, when Deans took over as NPC coach, Hansen was assigned to the forwards. It raised eyebrows at the time, especially when one of the candidates for the NPC coaching position was Grizz Wyllie, just back from coaching in South Africa.

Hansen spent hundreds of hours studying the technical aspects of forward play,

Brad Thorn soars for the ball in a lineout, a skill he had never needed in his days with the Brisbane Broncos league team.

seeking information from experts like Don Hayes, former All Black hooker, John Mills, and the man who coached the forwards at the Old Boys Club when Hansen and he forged a championship team, Neville Duckmanton. The study paid off. Referee Paddy O'Brien went on the record as saying that he never really understood what was happening in the front row of a scrum until he heard a lecture by Hansen explaining the mechanics of a scrum.

In May it's announced that Hansen has accepted a coaching position with Wales, initially as an assistant to Graham Henry. (When Henry leaves, Hansen will become head coach and take Wales to the 2003 World Cup.)

In January the Canterbury Rugby Football Union had told the New Zealand Union they were keen to see Hansen's and Deans' contracts extended. No new contracts are struck. 'I was disappointed with New Zealand that they couldn't have got those contracts negotiated earlier,' says Canterbury chairman, Mike Eagle. 'They were slow in my opinion.'

Just turned 42, Hansen is exactly the sort of tried and proven coach New Zealand rugby should be fighting to keep. He proves that point in the NPC, where he welds together a team led by a revitalised Blackadder, who has taken a break after being dropped from the All Blacks and regained all his enthusiasm for the game while playing club rugby for Glenmark. A stock truck serves as the grandstand for two regional television commentators at one Glenmark game. 'We should all be glad they haven't been carting pigs in it,' grins one local.

There are brilliant newcomers in the Canterbury side too, not least openside flanker Richie McCaw, a young man born in Oamaru and educated at Otago Boys' High, who comes to Christchurch to study at Lincoln University. After an early NPC training session in 2001, Blackadder is in awe of the skills and attitude McCaw brings to the game. By the end of the year he will be in the All Blacks and wins the man of the match award in his first test, against Ireland.

The Canterbury team's form is strong right through the season, the only loss a fifth-round defeat by North Harbour in wet, slippery conditions at Albany.

Canterbury bounces back in the next game, thrashing Otago 62–19 in Dunedin, with McCaw scoring three tries. Counties-Manukau are disposed of, 42–17, and then it's time for a Ranfurly Shield challenge from Wellington on 29 September.

'They spook me,' Blackadder says privately during the week. 'The buggers can score a try against you from all over the field.'

So it proves, with Canterbury staring a seventeen point deficit in the face with twenty minutes to play. Two things bring Canterbury back into contention: one is the self-belief in the side; the other the problems Wellington faces with a penalty count by referee Steve Walsh that zooms out to 26–4 against the visitors, and the sin-binning of midfielder Jason O'Halloran. It's reported that one Wellington supporter seeks a legal opinion on whether he can sue Walsh on behalf of his team.

Three minutes into injury time Wellington still leads 29–24, but Canterbury have an attacking scrum in midfield. Marshall slips the ball to Aaron Mauger on the short side, and he runs enough to put doubt into the minds of the last Wellington defenders, Cullen and Jonah.

Flying onto Mauger's pass is fullback Ben Blair, who races over for a try as the crowd goes ballistic. With a calm that belies his youth, the 22-year-old converts his try from a wide angle and the Log is saved.

No such problems with the last three challenges: Taranaki dispatched 38–17, Auckland 38–10, and Waikato 52–19. Auckland and Waikato are not weak teams, finishing fourth and fifth on the round-robin table, but by now Canterbury is efficient in every area, from a bankable lineout to Leon MacDonald's play at fullback, where his tackling draws comparisons to the legendary Fergie McCormick.

With the shield locked away, Auckland gets another drubbing in the NPC semifinal, 53–22.

Two weeks earlier, in the shield challenge, Auckland had tried a patterned, controlled game, featuring a lot of kicking, and were thumped. Astutely coached by Wayne Pivac and the former masterly All Black first five, Grant Fox, in the semi they try the helter-skelter approach, but the final result is no better.

The NPC final marks the end of their playing days for Canterbury for both Blackadder, off to play for Edinburgh in Scotland for three years, and hooker Matt Sexton.

Sexton is living proof that front-rowers have a different view on life. In 1998 he

Ben Blair: born in Westport, his rugby skills are honed in Canterbury.

snapped an Achilles tendon. The medical experts looked at it and asked, 'Do you actually want to play again?' It was a reasonable question. At this point Sexton was 28 years old and the glittering career that beckoned when he was hooking for the New Zealand Colts back in 1990 and 1991 had stalled at national and even local level, where he was taking a back seat to Mark Hammett.

But he did want more, so had the operation. Six months later, at his first training session with the Canterbury NPC squad, he pushed himself so hard that the Achilles in his other leg snapped.

Looking for reassurance, he sought out cricket legend Sir Richard Hadlee: 'I knew that he'd needed an Achilles operation and made a full recovery from it. I went to him and he told me that if you did enough rehabilitation work, you could come back.'

There was one more blow to come. In 2000 Sexton wrecked his anterior cruciate ligament training with the Crusaders. Did he really, really want to keep playing? Yes he did. So it was back to the operating theatre, back to medical rehab, and, finally, back to the field and out with his team-mates in an absolute blaze of glory with the final against Otago.

Sexton jokes that his play for Canterbury in the last weeks of the 2001 NPC may have been 'a bit like an old lawnmower that goes flat out just before it finally runs out of gas.'

If gas levels are low, there's not a sign of it in the final where, despite a terrific early effort by Otago, leading 16–6 at half-time after playing with a stiff wind, Canterbury is too strong in the second half and, guided by a dominant Mehrtens, draw away for a 30–19 victory and another NPC title.

The next day an All Black touring team is announced at the Centra Hotel in Christchurch by new coach, John Mitchell. In an extraordinary turn of events, Wayne Smith had been the victim of his own honesty and has been dumped.

After a 2001 season under new captain, Anton Oliver, the All Blacks record was the same as it was in 2000: two wins and two losses. Although both tests with the Wallabies were lost, it took a last-minute try for Australia to win the second in Sydney, 29–26, so there were encouraging signs and it was generally recognised that Smith deserved to keep his job.

But at a review meeting with the NZRU in Wellington, just a couple of weeks after the gut-wrenching loss in Sydney, Smith, after a long day of presentation and questioning, said that he was not sure if he wanted to continue as All Black coach.

Just two days later, when NZRU chief executive David Rutherford reported to the Union's board, that uncertainty became 'Smith doesn't want the job.' A couple of days later this juicy morsel was on the front page of the *New Zealand Herald*.

The following week, at a press conference in the boardroom of the Canterbury Rugby Football Union, Smith confirmed that he said he 'wasn't sure' he wanted the job on that fateful Tuesday in Wellington, not that he definitely didn't want it. However, he said he can fully understand how the review panel would have thought he didn't want it.

Applications were sought for job by the NZRU, and, although Smith was now unequivocal about wanting to stay, he was sacked and Mitchell, who had coached the Chiefs to sixth place in the 2001 Super 12, was appointed with Robbie Deans as his assistant. Smith soon left New Zealand to coach in England.

The first task for Mitchell and Deans is to take the All Blacks to Ireland, Scotland and Argentina, and the squad named includes a record sixteen Canterbury players: Ben Blair, Leon MacDonald, Caleb Ralph, Nathan Mauger, Aaron Mauger, Andrew Mehrtens, Justin Marshall, Scott Robertson, Richie McCaw, Reuben Thorne, Chris Jack, Norm Maxwell, Brad Thorn, Greg Somerville, Greg Feek and Dave Hewett.

Marshall decides not to tour, but the real sensation is when Brad Thorn announces that he must withdraw because he can't guarantee that he'll be available for the All Blacks in the future. He's accused of just about everything from manipulating New Zealand rugby to ramp up his bargaining power for a return to the Broncos, to being big-headed, to being on the grassy knoll in Dallas in 1963. The reality, it will emerge with time, is that he is telling the truth in 2001.

Thorn's homesick, his family is in Brisbane and his strong personal beliefs meant his Brisbane girlfriend living with him in Christchurch is not an option. He wants time at the end of the 2001 NPC season to clear his head and decide whether his sporting quest will take precedence over his personal life. When he quietly returns to Christchurch in 2003, he's married, happy to be there, and will soon have another shot at being an All Black.

There are many great memories from 2002 for Canterbury fans but the most remarkable are from the best campaign ever in the short history of Super 12.

Now led by Reuben Thorne, the Crusaders are coached again by Robbie Deans but, with Steve Hansen in Wales, a new forward coach is drafted in from Taranaki: Colin Cooper, a former New Zealand Maori loose forward, who has a measured, modest manner that strikes a huge chord with the Crusaders players.

Thorne, by 2002 a specialist blindside flanker, was a promising loose forward when he first made the Canterbury team in 1997, but injuries forced him into a locking spot. He was tall enough but way too light: 'I would have been about 97 kilos, maybe 100 with a wet jersey on a good day, which is pretty small for a lock,' he says. 'We had all these other quality loose forwards like Angus Gardiner, Razor Robertson and Toddy Blackadder at No. 6, so I was initially consigned to being a reserve. Then the chance came up to be a lock. I jumped at it.'

It took no time for Thorne to be both well-respected and well-liked. He remained a throwback to the days when rugby players did the hard yards and then were happy to fade out of the public eye.

Andrew Mehrtens (whose sister, Kate, is married to Thorne) paints a vivid word picture of dinner at a family gathering. 'Reuben's the strong, silent type who's always the first in line when there's work to be done. At a dinner we over-run him in conversation. Everyone is just chipping, chipping, chipping, and then Reuben goes, "Yeah."'

Thorne's football career, which has never included national age group or school selection, took a quantum leap when he started playing for High School Old Boys while studying at Lincoln University. 'Steve Hansen was the guy who had the big influence. He was bloody good.'

A little quirk in the Crusaders began after the 1998 Super 12 final, when the team start a victory chant featuring the nickname of reserve No. 8, Clark McLeod, who was known in the team as Bungle Bear. When the Crusaders won at Eden Park, they moved on from 'Bungle Bear, Bungle Bear, Bungle Bear' to other players' nicknames. 'We were chanting names that fitted into that rhythm,' recalls Thorne, more than a little ruefully. 'My name was just one of them. But now those guys have gone, and there's only one name left that fits. It's mine. It'd be nice if another one came along.'

The breakthrough at national level in 1999 for Thorne was the result of a selfless act by his captain, Blackadder. Crusaders coaches, Deans and Hansen, decided to ask Blackadder if he would move to lock. The argument that Hansen advanced on a drive to Ashburton for a post-season promotion was that not only might Blackadder win an All Black jersey as a lock, but Thorne might become an All Black flanker.

Blackadder quickly agreed. 'It certainly wasn't easy to give your jersey up to someone else when it means so much to you. What made it easier for me was that with Reuben I knew the guy I'd be swapping with. It would have been a lot harder if I hadn't respected him so much.'

The plan didn't work immediately for Blackadder in '99, but by the end of the year Thorne was a fixture in the No. 6 jersey for the All Blacks at the World Cup.

Reuben Thorne (Left) started as a skinny lock, and developed into a World Cup All Black captain.

Early in the 2002 Super 12, Thorne pinpoints why there's a real spring in the Crusaders' step: 'The biggest thing is the enjoyment. After the 2001 Super 12, we went away to the Tri-Nations and when we got back to the NPC we had fun. There was a slightly different approach and that real group enjoyment was right back there. It's just flowed on from that. It got the enthusiasm back up and, although we didn't have much of a break, when we got together over summer that enthusiasm was still there.

'We wanted to keep growing that feeling and it's stayed there. Physically we're no better off that we were last year, the boys worked just as hard, but mentally we're better. I think it's the flow-on from last year's NPC.'

These words are soon proved to be far from hollow. Early in the competition the wins are narrow but well-earned. The Highlanders (30–28), the Chiefs (34–27), the Blues (30–11) and the Reds (34–27) are all disposed of before an Easter Sunday thriller at Jade Stadium against the Brumbies, won 33–32. With time almost up, the Crusaders shape to set up a dropped goal for Mehrtens. Instead the ball is flicked to Aaron Mauger by Marshall, and the second five snaps a dropped goal for victory.

The Bulls at Jade Stadium are beaten 49–15, and the Stormers 41–21, before the annual trek to South Africa, where there are two more wins, against the Sharks, 37–34, and the Cats, 37–30.

Just how good the form the Crusaders are running into is rubbed into the Hurricanes in Wellington. It's a measure of where the 2002 model of the Crusaders has got to that they're prepared to rest such key players as Leon MacDonald and Richie McCaw for the game.

The blazing start and the continued fierce will to attack are epitomised in the play of Marshall, who starts the ball rolling for a seven-try victory by seizing on a loose Hurricanes pass, belting the ball downfield for 25 metres, then clearing it to Sam Broomhall, who tips it on to Marika Vunibaka to score with exactly 33 seconds on the clock. After 80 minutes the score is 48–20.

Next is a game that may be the best attacking display ever by a Crusaders team. The Waratahs come to Jade Stadium lying second on the points table. They leave beaten 96–19, conceding fourteen tries, thirteen of them converted by Mehrtens.

It's true that the Waratahs have rested No. 8 David Lyons and wing Marc Stcherbina, but all their big-name players, from fullback Matt Burke to hooker Brendan Cannon, are there and, as *Sydney Morning Herald* rugby writer Greg Growden says in the press box, 'To be honest, the result would have been the same regardless of who we'd put on the field.'

The players and coach Deans are almost as stunned as the crowd and quick to point that this is the sort of performance that almost arrives out of the clear blue sky. They won't get carried away with it, says Deans, because they know that on a normal night every pass won't stick, as they did against the Waratahs.

Waratahs coach, Bob Dwyer, usually one of the most articulate and voluble men in the game, is dumbfounded and in fact is checked over at Christchurch Hospital for what is feared to be, but fortunately is not, a mild heart attack.

The semifinal is against the Highlanders and while the Crusaders are methodically working their way to a 34–23 win, with Chris Jack an increasingly dominant player, the shell-shocked Waratahs get another drubbing in their semi, lowered 52–10 in Sydney by the Brumbies.

For once the Crusaders are hot favourites going into the final of Super 12, and Jade Stadium is packed, fans queuing for tickets, the last of which sell out in less than two hours.

The game is really over by half-time, the Brumbies, with a strong wind at their backs, only able to scramble 30 per cent of the possession, down 11–3 and turning in deep trouble. There's a thrilling try in that first half, started by Leon MacDonald in his own half from a Brumbies kick, with the attack carried on by Mehrtens, Aaron Mauger (three times), Robertson (twice), Marshall and Thorne, who flicks the ball to Marika Vunibaka for a diagonal run to the corner.

Behind 24–13 into the last minute, the Brumbies desperately throw a wide ball that is intercepted by Caleb Ralph. He's 75 metres from the tryline, but halfway there he begins smiling as the speed he retains from his schoolboy sprinting days in the Bay of Plenty allows him to glide in untroubled for the try. Mehrtens converts, the game is won 31–13 and, although the Christchurch victory parade on Monday is the fourth in five years, the glow is still warm enough to draw 100,000 excited fans to the central city.

Aussie McLean becomes head coach for the NPC, assisted by Ian Mallard, a former Linwood player who has been working with the Canterbury Colts and the Crusaders Development teams.

Over the NPC, sixteen players will be in the All Blacks which, with the requirement to rest them when they are available for Canterbury, makes the semifinal of the NPC one bridge too far in 2002.

What does excite fans in the NPC are the first appearances of Daniel Carter, a 20-year-old five–eighths. Carter grew up in Southbridge, went to Ellesmere College and only moved to the city to attend and play for Christchurch Boys' High in his seventh form year.

It was quickly obvious that he had huge footballing abilities. He can step off both feet, has very good hands and is, as Leon MacDonald comments after Carter has fended off one East Coast tackler with his right hand and the next with his left, 'deceptively strong.'

Canterbury's All Blacks filter back slowly into the NPC team, and it's the fourth round, against Waikato in Hamilton, before all of them are available. By then Canterbury has lost to Wellington but beaten Bay of Plenty and defended the Ranfurly Shield against Southland, the last appearnace in red and black for Daryl Gibson, who is co-captain of Canterbury with Mark Hammett.

Gibson's All Black career started in 1999, when the All Black backline had fullbacks playing at centre, wings playing at fullback, and half the forward pack playing silly buggers. It wasn't a flash time for someone with some genuine skills to offer in the midfield. After starting the lead-up tests for the All Blacks in 1999, Gibson was shunted aside at the World Cup for the more crash-and-bash approach of Alama Ieremia at second five.

After the Southland game in 2002, Gibson is off to play for the Bristol Club in England. He takes with him the painful souvenir of a broken nose. A well-rounded person with two university degrees, Gibson had almost left Canterbury two years before. The professional era, he pointed out then, had led to an unusual situation: 'Coaches use tradition to build up loyalty to a union, but the reciprocal side is that administrators, because rugby's now a business, don't have the same loyalty.' He's not being judgmental, just stating an obvious fact. Rugby at the top level is now a business, and businesses can't afford to be sentimental.

The return of the All Blacks isn't the answer to every prayer, with Waikato dominating in the forwards and romping away to a 59–41 win in Hamilton. Now sixth on the NPC table Canterbury dig in, beating Northland, Auckland, North Harbour, Taranaki and Otago to keep the Ranfurly Shield and earn a home semifinal by finishing second to Waikato in the round robin.

But coach Aussie McLean knows that 'there's no petrol left in the tank' where, by comparison, Auckland arrives for the semi with two aces up the sleeve. One is second five Sam Tuitupou, a pint-sized player with such strength that he can break lines and make shattering tackles, even if his own velocity means that before he's 21, he's had two shoulder operations. The second is Graham Henry, back from coaching

Daniel Carter moved from Southbridge to Christchurch to the All Blacks, with a talent that was obvious from the time he first played in the NPC as a 20-year-old.

Wales and the Lions, who acts as a video expert analyst for Auckland, directing defensive patterns that have gone from sieve-like to rock-like in the time he's been involved.

The score at Jade Stadium in the semi, 29–23, looks close, but the reality is that Auckland never looked like being beaten.

Robbie Deans coaches the Crusaders again in 2003, with a new assistant, 1980s Ranfurly Shield captain Don Hayes replacing Colin Cooper, who takes over as head coach of the Hurricanes. They've actually coached together in the early 1990s with Canterbury Country, and Hayes has already been an advisor with the Crusaders.

As quietly as he arrived the first time, Brad Thorn reappears in Canterbury keen to play rugby again. Initially he's too late for squad selection and is placed in the draft. When he's not picked up by another franchise, Ben Blair's bad luck – not able to recover soon enough from an operation for a bad shoulder injury suffered playing for the All Blacks late in 2002 – becomes Thorn's good fortune. The tiny fullback is replaced by the huge lock.

An ugly loss is suffered in third game of Super 12, the Blues 39–5 winners at Albany, a result that quickly revises the Crusaders TAB $2.75 favouritism to win another title. Coach Deans and his players aren't as concerned as their fans. They know that the Super 12 is a long-distance contest, not a sprint, and that their fitness programmes are still at a building stage.

A 75th minute penalty goal by Daniel Carter squeaks the Crusaders to a 17–16 win over the Highlanders at Carisbrook, the first loss on the Brook for the home team in seventeen games. And though there are further losses to the Waratahs in Sydney, 34–31, and the Bulls in Pretoria, 32–31, they're close, and wins over the Cats, the Sharks, the Stormers and, most notably, the Brumbies in Canberra, secure a home semifinal with the Hurricanes.

The Hurricanes come to Jade Stadium with fire in the belly, expressed most notably by their captain, Tana Umaga who, after a high tackle that is bruising but looks legal, expresses his disgust to Australian referee Peter Marshall with an incredulous, 'We're not playing tiddlywinks here.'

Scott Robertson matches passion with passion in the forwards, Daniel Carter's kicking is again impeccable and the Crusaders make the final against the Blues with a 39–16 victory.

The Blues are the talk of the nation, playing a high-speed, high-risk game that has at its foundation the defensive patterns drilled into the players by Graham Henry.

Here's what the fans at Eden Park on 24 May 2003 expect. If the Blues win, it will be through tries; if the Crusaders win, it will be through kicking. The Blues have a lightning back three, with All Black Doug Howlett, who first played for Auckland in 1996 while still head boy at Auckland Grammar School; Mils Muliaina, lured to Auckland from Southland to board at Graham Henry's old school, Kelston Boys' High, who had won a Commonwealth Games gold medal with the 2002 New Zealand sevens team in Manchester; and a teenage sensation on the wing, Joe Rokocoko, who arrived with his family from Fiji when he was five and starred for St Kentigern's College in Auckland school rugby. He had been invited to the All Blacks pre-season fitness tests in 2003 and charmed everyone by describing himself as feeling 'like a kid in a candy store.'

But the final is a surprise for most. The Crusaders crank up the volume, and Mark Hammett, who later ditches plans to retire and plays in the World Cup, scores one try off a planned lineout move, and a second when Carlos Spencer drops the ball twenty metres from the Blues line. Eyes blazing and knees pumping, Hammett scythes past tacklers, is stopped at the line but slams the ball down for a second try. At half-time it's 10–6 to the Crusaders, two tries to nil.

Ironically, it's kicking that finally wins the game for the Blues, although Howlett scores his twelfth try of the Super 12 in 2003, and Daniel Braid picks up another after a drive from a lineout fifteen metres from the line.

Caleb Ralph scores after a quick tap four minutes from the end but, with Spencer kicking three penalties and a conversion to Mehrtens' sole conversion, goal kicks present the title to the Blues, 21–17.

Two days later John Mitchell names his first All Black squad of the year, which includes eleven Crusaders, a number that will grow to fourteen Canterbury players by the end of the year at the World Cup. Reuben Thorne is retained as All Black captain, a position he first assumed when Anton Oliver was unable to play the 2002 home tests because of a serious leg injury.

The NPC and Ranfurly Shield season is a very strange one for coach Aussie McLean, who now has former Canterbury and Marlborough captain, Rob Penney, as his coaching assistant.

Captaining the side is Ben Hurst, who had started his Super 12 career in such spectacular fashion in 2002 when he was called in to play the semi and final.

Canterbury's fourteen World Cup All Blacks appear in dribs and drabs in the earlier stages, their games varying from seven for Ben Blair to one for Mark Hammett and Cory Flynn.

Much like the appearance record of the All Blacks, the results for Canterbury are erratic. There are early-season Ranfurly Shield wins over North Otago, Hawke's Bay and Southland, and in the NPC the first games – against Northland, Bay of Plenty and Taranaki – are all won. The 31–26 victory over Bay of Plenty clocks up twenty defences of the Ranfurly Shield and confounds the challenger's main sponsor offering a $10,000 a man win bonus.

But Otago clean out Canterbury 32–16 at Carisbrook, and Southland also wins 32–26 at home. Reasonably enough there's deep concern over the Waikato challenge for the Log the next weekend, but 40 minutes of brilliance from Andrew Mehrtens sees Canterbury up 20–5 at half-time and, if a tweaked hamstring keeps him off the field in the second spell, it doesn't really matter. The Log is retained, 35–24.

A week later, against Wellington, Canterbury look odds-on to keep the shield, and pick up at least four NPC points. With thirteen minutes to go, Canterbury leads by 35–10. Then Wellington catches fire. In nine minutes they score three tries and the game is drawn 38–38. Aussie McLean stares in amazement, not knowing, he says, whether 'to laugh or to cry.'

The last game of 2003 is a Ranfurly Shield game with Auckland, in ominous form. Canterbury's defence leaks to the tune of 27 missed tackles and, although a restored Mehrtens is like a one-man band with his running, six penalties and two dropped goals, there is never going to be a revival. The Log, after 24 defences, just one fewer than the record of the 1982–85 side, goes to Auckland with a 40–31 victory. Razor Robertson farewells his fan club and Canterbury rugby. He'll go to France, he says, with some fantastic memories.

And somewhere in the crowd at Jade Stadium, you can bet, is a schoolkid who, when the next history of Canterbury rugby is written, will add to the line that runs from William Millton, captain of the first New Zealand team, through men like Pat Vincent, Fergie McCormick, Robbie Deans, Todd Blackadder, Andrew Mehrtens and Richie McCaw, all part of a great red and black heritage, with a future to match.

APPENDIX A

CANTERBURY

Versus	Date	Location	Result	Score For	Score Against	Ranfurly Shield (•)
Otago	1878	Dunedin	D	0	0	
Otago	1879	Christchurch	D	0	0	
Otago	1880	Dunedin	D	1	1	
Otago	1881	Christchurch	L	0	4	
Otago	1882	Dunedin	L	0	21	
Otago	1883	Christchurch	L	0	6	
Otago	1884	Dunedin	W	4	0	
Otago	1885	Christchurch	W	9	0	
Otago	1886	Dunedin	D	0	0	
Otago	1887	Christchurch	D	3	3	
Otago	1888	Dunedin	L	0	7	
Otago	1889	Christchurch	L	1	9	
Otago	1890	Dunedin	L	4	9	
Otago	1891	Christchurch	L	3	8	
Otago	1892	Dunedin	W	7	4	
Otago	1893	Christchurch	W	5	2	
Otago	1895	Dunedin	L	11	13	
Otago	1896	Christchurch	L	6	8	
Otago	1897	Dunedin	L	6	20	
Otago	1898	Christchurch	L	0	16	
Otago	1899	Dunedin	L	6	12	

Versus	Date	Location	Result	Score For	Score Against	Ranfurly Shield (•)
Otago	1900	Christchurch	L	0	8	
Otago	1901	Dunedin	W	3	0	
Otago	1902	Christchurch	D	3	3	
Otago	1903	Dunedin	L	3	20	
Otago	1904	Christchurch	L	9	20	
Otago	1905	Dunedin	L	4	11	
Otago	1906	Christchurch	L	8	12	
Otago	1907	Dunedin	W	14	0	
Otago	1908	Christchurch	D	8	8	
Otago	1909	Dunedin	L	9	3	
Otago	1910	Christchurch	D	6	6	
Otago	1911	Dunedin	L	0	8	
Otago	1912	Christchurch	W	11	3	
Otago	1913	Dunedin	W	6	3	
Otago	1914	Christchurch	W	31	8	
Otago	1915	Christchurch	W	32	9	
Otago	1915	Dunedin	L	3	30	
Otago	1918	Christchurch	W	11	8	
Otago	1919	Dunedin	W	13	3	
Otago	1920	Dunedin	W	9	0	
Otago	1921	Christchurch	W	19	14	
Otago	1922	Dunedin	L	9	15	
Otago	1923	Christchurch	W	15	13	
Otago	1924	Dunedin	W	25	14	
Otago	1925	Christchurch	W	17	14	
Otago	1926	Dunedin	W	26	13	
Otago	1927	Christchurch	L	13	6	
Otago	1928	Dunedin	L	9	31	
Otago	1929	Christchurch	W	21	10	
Otago	1930	Dunedin	L	3	11	
Otago	1931	Christchurch	W	17	6	
Otago	1932	Dunedin	L	9	24	
Otago	1933	Christchurch	W	8	5	

Otago	1934	Dunedin	L	12	16	
Otago	1935	Christchurch	L	6	15	
Otago	1936	Dunedin	L	0	16	
Otago	1937	Christchurch	L	7	16	
Otago	1938	Dunedin	L	7	16	
Otago	1939	Christchurch	L	3	10	
Otago	1941	Dunedin	W	11	10	
Otago	1941	Christchurch	D	0	0	
Otago	1942	Dunedin	W	9	6	
Otago	1942	Christchurch	W	16	15	
Otago	1943	Christchurch	W	19	15	
Otago	1943	Dunedin	W	11	10	
Otago	1944	Dunedin	L	8	15	
Otago	1944	Christchurch	W	18	9	
Otago	1945	Dunedin	L	0	34	
Otago	1945	Christchurch	W	20	10	
Otago	1946	Dunedin	L	11	25	
Otago	1947	Christchurch	W	15	9	
Otago	1948	Dunedin	L	0	31	
Otago	1949	Christchurch	L	12	16	
Otago	1950	Dunedin	W	18	6	
Otago	1951	Christchurch	W	18	6	
Otago	1952	Dunedin	D	6	6	
Otago	1953	Christchurch	W	11	8	
Otago	1954	Dunedin	L	6	16	
Otago	1954	Christchurch	D	9	9	
Otago	1955	Christchurch	W	15	8	
Otago	1956	Dunedin	L	3	8	
Otago	1957	Christchurch	W	27	8	
Otago	1959	Dunedin	W	17	9	
Otago	1960	Christchurch	W	30	9	
Otago	1960	Dunedin	L	25	26	
Otago	1961	Dunedin	W	16	11	
Otago	1961	Christchurch	W	30	0	
Otago	1962	Christchurch	W	17	3	

Versus	Date	Location	Result	Score For	Score Against	Ranfurly Shield (•)
Otago	1962	Dunedin	L	0	6	
Otago	1963	Dunedin	L	8	17	
Otago	1963	Christchurch	W	8	5	
Otago	1964	Dunedin	L	3	11	
Otago	1964	Christchurch	W	17	11	
Otago	1965	Dunedin	W	17	14	
Otago	1965	Christchurch	W	17	6	
Otago	1966	Dunedin	L	6	16	
Otago	1966	Christchurch	D	6	6	
Otago	1967	Dunedin	W	12	10	
Otago	1967	Christchurch	W	11	8	
Otago	1968	Dunedin	L	9	11	
Otago	1968	Christchurch	W	9	6	
Otago	1969	Dunedin	L	9	17	
Otago	1969	Christchurch	L	17	20	
Otago	1970	Dunedin	L	3	9	
Otago	1970	Christchurch	W	16	12	
Otago	1971	Dunedin	L	6	11	
Otago	1971	Christchurch	W	10	9	
Otago	1972	Dunedin	W	4	3	
Otago	1972	Christchurch	W	26	9	
Otago	1973	Dunedin	W	17	11	
Otago	1973	Christchurch	W	20	9	
Otago	1974	Dunedin	D	9	9	
Otago	1974	Christchurch	W	7	6	
Otago	1975	Christchurch	W	13	10	
Otago	1975	Dunedin	L	14	15	
Otago	1976	Christchurch	W	34	12	
Otago	1977	Dunedin	W	14	9	
Otago	1978	Dunedin	W	13	7	
Otago	1978	Christchurch	L	15	21	
Otago	1979	Christchurch	W	14	12	
Otago	1979	Dunedin	W	32	20	

Otago	1980	Christchurch	W	23	3	
Otago	1981	Dunedin	W	24	13	
Otago	1982	Christchurch	W	25	18	
Otago	1983	Dunedin	W	24	9	
Otago	1984	Christchurch	W	44	3	•
Otago	1985	Dunedin	W	26	9	
Otago	1986	Christchurch	W	38	18	
Otago	1987	Dunedin	L	12	15	
Otago	1988	Christchurch	L	16	18	
Otago	1989	Dunedin	W	25	23	
Otago	1990	Christchurch	L	18	25	
Otago	1991	Christchurch	L	31	42	
Otago	1991	Dunedin	L	15	44	
Otago	1992	Dunedin	L	20	23	
Otago	1992	Christchurch	L	15	27	
Otago	1993	Christchurch	W	35	26	
Otago	1993	Dunedin	L	16	46	
Otago	1994	Dunedin	L	25	56	
Otago	1994	Christchurch	W	22	20	•
Otago	1995	Christchurch	L	6	27	
Otago	1995	Dunedin	W	28	26	
Otago	1996	Dunedin	W	24	6	
Otago	1996	Christchurch	W	43	22	
Otago	1997	Dunedin	L	13	35	
Otago	1998	Christchurch	L	23	41	
Otago	1999	Dunedin	W	35	16	
Otago	2000	Christchurch	W	29	26	•
Otago	2001	Dunedin	W	62	19	
Otago	2001	Christchurch	W	30	19	
Otago	2002	Christchurch	W	16	13	•
Otago	2003	Dunedin	L	16	32	
KingCountry	1933	Christchurch	W	36	0	
KingCountry	1958	Christchurch	W	8	6	
KingCountry	1970	Te Kuiti	W	17	0	

Versus	Date	Location	Result	Score For	Score Against	Ranfurly Shield (•)
KingCountry	1985	Christchurch	W	33	0	•
KingCountry	1992	Christchurch	L	20	24	
KingCountry	1993	Te Kuiti	W	34	23	
KingCountry	1994	Christchurch	W	44	31	
KingCountry	1995	Te Kuiti	L	28	48	
KingCountry	1996	Christchurch	W	38	27	
Thames Valley	1955	Christchurch	W	24	11	
Thames Valley	1964	Christchurch	W	22	6	
Thames Valley	1966	Paeroa	W	25	14	
Wellington	1876	Wellington	W	19	1	
Wellington	1879	Christchurch	L	1	3	
Wellington	1883	Wellington	L	0	1	
Wellington	1885	Christchurch	W	1	0	
Wellington	1887	Wellington	L	3	4	
Wellington	1891	Christchurch	W	16	1	
Wellington	1892	Wellington	L	4	12	
Wellington	1895	Christchurch	W	6	4	
Wellington	1896	Wellington	L	3	12	
Wellington	1897	Christchurch	L	0	4	
Wellington	1898	Wellington	D	6	6	
Wellington	1899	Christchurch	W	6	5	
Wellington	1900	Wellington	L	6	16	
Wellington	1901	Christchurch	W	12	3	
Wellington	1902	Wellington	W	9	3	
Wellington	1903	Christchurch	W	8	5	
Wellington	1904	Wellington	L	3	6	
Wellington	1905	Christchurch	W	6	3	
Wellington	1906	Wellington	L	0	34	
Wellington	1907	Christchurch	W	9	6	
Wellington	1908	Wellington	L	5	11	
Wellington	1909	Christchurch	L	6	11	

Wellington	1910	Wellington	L	9	26	
Wellington	1911	Christchurch	L	9	26	
Wellington	1912	Wellington	L	9	16	
Wellington	1913	Christchurch	L	3	6	
Wellington	1914	Wellington	W	11	9	
Wellington	1918	Christchurch	L	0	9	
Wellington	1918	Wellington	L	8	18	
Wellington	1919	Wellington	L	9	23	
Wellington	1919	Christchurch	L	8	21	
Wellington	1920	Wellington	L	3	15	
Wellington	1920	Christchurch	L	13	16	
Wellington	1921	Wellington	L	11	27	
Wellington	1922	Christchurch	L	9	25	
Wellington	1923	Wellington	W	8	6	
Wellington	1924	Christchurch	W	32	6	
Wellington	1925	Wellington	L	6	8	
Wellington	1926	Christchurch	W	41	14	
Wellington	1927	Wellington	L	17	20	
Wellington	1928	Christchurch	L	7	14	
Wellington	1929	Wellington	L	6	34	
Wellington	1930	Christchurch	L	3	11	
Wellington	1931	Wellington	W	8	6	
Wellington	1932	Christchurch	W	9	6	
Wellington	1933	Wellington	L	6	14	
Wellington	1934	Christchurch	L	17	25	
Wellington	1935	Wellington	L	8	11	
Wellington	1936	Christchurch	W	19	17	
Wellington	1937	Wellington	W	19	17	
Wellington	1938	Christchurch	L	8	14	
Wellington	1939	Wellington	L	9	14	
Wellington	1940	Christchurch	L	11	14	
Wellington	1941	Wellington	L	12	17	
Wellington	1941	Christchurch	L	8	14	
Wellington	1943	Christchurch	D	8	8	
Wellington	1943	Wellington	L	6	16	

Versus	Date	Location	Result	Score For	Score Against	Ranfurly Shield (•)
Wellington	1944	Christchurch	W	29	6	
Wellington	1944	Wellington	L	10	11	
Wellington	1945	Wellington	L	6	11	
Wellington	1945	Christchurch	L	6	23	
Wellington	1946	Christchurch	L	7	11	
Wellington	1946	Wellington	L	9	21	
Wellington	1947	Christchurch	L	8	9	
Wellington	1947	Wellington	W	8	3	
Wellington	1948	Christchurch	L	20	39	
Wellington	1948	Wellington	D	14	14	
Wellington	1949	Christchurch	L	13	18	
Wellington	1949	Wellington	W	13	11	
Wellington	1950	Christchurch	W	6	3	
Wellington	1950	Wellington	L	8	25	
Wellington	1951	Christchurch	W	6	3	
Wellington	1951	Wellington	W	3	0	
Wellington	1952	Christchurch	L	11	25	
Wellington	1952	Wellington	W	22	15	
Wellington	1953	Christchurch	W	9	8	
Wellington	1953	Wellington	W	24	3	
Wellington	1955	Wellington	W	9	3	
Wellington	1955	Christchurch	W	30	11	
Wellington	1956	Christchurch	L	0	8	
Wellington	1957	Wellington	D	8	8	
Wellington	1958	Christchurch	W	32	19	
Wellington	1959	Wellington	L	17	20	
Wellington	1960	Christchurch	W	14	6	
Wellington	1960	Wellington	D	15	15	
Wellington	1961	Christchurch	W	9	3	
Wellington	1961	Wellington	W	19	9	
Wellington	1962	Christchurch	L	11	14	
Wellington	1962	Wellington	W	10	3	
Wellington	1963	Christchurch	W	6	0	

Wellington	1963	Wellington	W	14	9	
Wellington	1964	Wellington	L	14	24	
Wellington	1964	Christchurch	D	14	14	
Wellington	1965	Christchurch	L	12	14	
Wellington	1965	Wellington	L	3	19	
Wellington	1966	Christchurch	W	11	3	
Wellington	1966	Wellington	L	6	14	
Wellington	1967	Christchurch	D	11	11	
Wellington	1967	Wellington	L	17	19	
Wellington	1968	Christchurch	W	25	9	
Wellington	1968	Wellington	L	12	16	
Wellington	1969	Wellington	L	11	12	
Wellington	1969	Christchurch	W	23	3	
Wellington	1970	Wellington	W	24	3	
Wellington	1970	Christchurch	D	3	3	
Wellington	1971	Wellington	W	16	6	
Wellington	1971	Christchurch	L	17	24	
Wellington	1972	Christchurch	L	13	18	
Wellington	1972	Wellington	W	29	16	
Wellington	1973	Wellington	L	37	10	
Wellington	1973	Christchurch	W	32	19	
Wellington	1974	Wellington	W	14	6	
Wellington	1974	Christchurch	L	4	16	
Wellington	1975	Christchurch	W	36	6	
Wellington	1975	Wellington	W	27	18	
Wellington	1976	Wellington	W	15	14	
Wellington	1977	Christchurch	W	17	0	
Wellington	1978	Wellington	L	7	29	
Wellington	1979	Christchurch	L	7	18	
Wellington	1980	Wellington	L	16	26	
Wellington	1981	Christchurch	L	6	31	
Wellington	1982	Wellington	W	16	12	•
Wellington	1983	Christchurch	W	20	16	•
Wellington	1984	Wellington	W	25	18	
Wellington	1985	Christchurch	D	10	10	

Versus	Date	Location	Result	Score For	Score Against	Ranfurly Shield (•)
Wellington	1986	Christchurch	W	19	9	
Wellington	1986	Wellington	L	16	22	
Wellington	1987	Wellington	W	31	16	
Wellington	1987	Christchurch	L	9	27	
Wellington	1988	Christchurch	L	15	21	
Wellington	1988	Wellington	L	10	26	
Wellington	1989	Wellington	L	28	31	
Wellington	1989	Christchurch	W	48	11	
Wellington	1990	Christchurch	W	30	21	
Wellington	1990	Wellington	L	11	48	
Wellington	1991	Christchurch	W	25	12	
Wellington	1992	Christchurch	W	31	20	
Wellington	1992	Wellington	L	30	34	
Wellington	1993	Wellington	W	28	25	
Wellington	1993	Christchurch	W	15	12	
Wellington	1994	Christchurch	W	31	20	
Wellington	1994	Wellington	L	28	37	
Wellington	1995	Christchurch	W	66	17	•
Wellington	1996	Christchurch	L	16	25	
Wellington	1996	Wellington	L	28	29	
Wellington	1997	Christchurch	W	73	7	
Wellington	1998	Wellington	W	40	28	
Wellington	1999	Christchurch	L	6	27	
Wellington	2000	Wellington	L	20	27	
Wellington	2000	Christchurch	L	29	34	
Wellington	2001	Christchurch	W	31	29	•
Wellington	2002	Wellington	L	24	33	
Wellington	2003	Christchurch	D	38	38	•
West Coast	1907	Greymouth	L	0	11	
West Coast	1912	Christchurch	L	14	17	
West Coast	1913	Greymouth	W	20	5	
West Coast	1923	Greymouth	L	6	17	

West Coast	1926	Christchurch	W	37	7	
West Coast	1927	Hokitika	W	11	6	
West Coast	1929	Greymouth	W	27	12	
West Coast	1932	Christchurch	W	5	3	
West Coast	1932	Christchurch	D	6	6	
West Coast	1933	Christchurch	W	23	14	
West Coast	1933	Greymouth	L	8	9	
West Coast	1934	Greymouth	D	6	6	
West Coast	1934	Christchurch	W	25	21	
West Coast	1935	Greymouth	W	16	12	
West Coast	1935	Christchurch	W	16	11	
West Coast	1936	Greymouth	L	13	15	
West Coast	1937	Greymouth	L	14	23	
West Coast	1937	Greymouth	W	14	11	
West Coast	1938	Christchurch	W	13	8	
West Coast	1938	Greymouth	D	5	5	
West Coast	1939	Christchurch	W	24	6	
West Coast	1939	Greymouth	D	6	6	
West Coast	1940	Christchurch	W	27	16	
West Coast	1940	Greymouth	L	11	13	
West Coast	1941	Greymouth	W	16	14	
West Coast	1941	Christchurch	L	5	13	
West Coast	1942	Greymouth	W	6	4	
West Coast	1942	Christchurch	W	31	16	
West Coast	1943	Greymouth	W	26	5	
West Coast	1943	Christchurch	W	17	16	
West Coast	1944	Greymouth	W	11	5	
West Coast	1944	Christchurch	W	17	3	
West Coast	1945	Greymouth	L	8	17	
West Coast	1945	Christchurch	W	11	3	
West Coast	1946	Greymouth	L	9	11	
West Coast	1946	Christchurch	W	24	13	
West Coast	1947	Greymouth	L	3	16	
West Coast	1947	Christchurch	W	6	3	
West Coast	1948	Greymouth	W	22	3	

Versus	Date	Location	Result	Score For	Score Against	Ranfurly Shield (•)
West Coast	1948	Christchurch	W	32	14	
West Coast	1949	Greymouth	W	21	14	
West Coast	1949	Christchurch	W	15	11	
West Coast	1950	Greymouth	W	22	6	
West Coast	1950	Christchurch	W	17	12	
West Coast	1951	Greymouth	L	14	18	
West Coast	1951	Christchurch	W	37	11	
West Coast	1952	Greymouth	W	16	3	
West Coast	1952	Christchurch	W	21	19	
West Coast	1953	Greymouth	W	26	6	
West Coast	1953	Christchurch	W	11	3	
West Coast	1954	Greymouth	L	0	3	
West Coast	1954	Christchurch	W	8	0	
West Coast	1955	Greymouth	W	17	0	
West Coast	1955	Christchurch	W	20	11	
West Coast	1956	Greymouth	L	8	12	
West Coast	1956	Christchurch	W	19	6	
West Coast	1957	Greymouth	W	9	8	
West Coast	1957	Christchurch	W	37	18	
West Coast	1958	Greymouth	W	6	0	
West Coast	1958	Christchurch	W	45	3	
West Coast	1959	Greymouth	W	40	6	
West Coast	1959	Christchurch	W	27	3	
West Coast	1960	Christchurch	W	40	9	
West Coast	1960	Greymouth	W	3	0	
West Coast	1961	Greymouth	W	14	9	
West Coast	1961	Christchurch	W	14	8	
West Coast	1962	Greymouth	D	6	6	
West Coast	1962	Christchurch	W	24	6	
West Coast	1963	Greymouth	W	25	3	
West Coast	1963	Christchurch	W	30	9	
West Coast	1964	Greymouth	W	19	6	
West Coast	1966	Greymouth	W	41	0	

West Coast	1967	Greymouth	W	30	6	
West Coast	1968	Greymouth	W	21	16	
West Coast	1969	Greymouth	W	44	0	
West Coast	1970	Greymouth	W	58	3	
West Coast	1971	Greymouth	W	32	5	
West Coast	1971	Christchurch	W	35	0	
West Coast	1972	Greymouth	W	39	11	
West Coast	1972	Christchurch	W	47	3	
West Coast	1973	Greymouth	W	17	7	
West Coast	1973	Greymouth	W	29	10	
West Coast	1974	Christchurch	W	80	3	
West Coast	1974	Greymouth	W	50	4	
West Coast	1975	Greymouth	W	36	13	
West Coast	1976					
West Coast	1977	Greymouth	W	33	13	
West Coast	1978	Greymouth	W	40	4	
West Coast	1979	Greymouth	W	37	7	
West Coast	1980	Greymouth	W	20	3	
West Coast	1981	Greymouth	D	9	9	
West Coast	1982	Greymouth	W	38	7	
West Coast	1983	Greymouth	W	23	9	
West Coast	1984	Christchurch	W	68	3	•
West Coast	1985	Greymouth	W	48	9	
West Coast	1987	Greymouth	W	68	0	
West Coast	1988	Greymouth	W	52	0	
West Coast	1989	Greymouth	W	75	3	
West Coast	1991	Greymouth	W	86	0	
West Coast	1992	Greymouth	W	128	0	
West Coast	1994	Hokitika	W	98	0	
North Auckland	1936	Christchurch	W	43	9	
North Auckland	1953	Whangarei	W	16	9	
North Auckland	1955	Christchurch	W	39	11	
North Auckland	1960	Whangarei	L	6	11	
North Auckland	1968	Christchurch	W	5	3	

Versus	Date	Location	Result	Score For	Score Against	Ranfurly Shield (•)
North Auckland	1972	Whangarei	W	19	14	
North Auckland	1975	Christchurch	L	6	9	
North Auckland	1976	Whangarei	W	21	13	
North Auckland	1978	Whangarei	W	24	13	
North Auckland	1979	Christchurch	W	18	0	
North Auckland	1980	Whangarei	L	6	14	
North Auckland	1981	Christchurch	L	3	6	
North Auckland	1982	Whangarei	W	12	3	
North Auckland	1983	Christchurch	W	39	9	•
North Auckland	1984	Whangarei	W	27	9	
North Auckland	1985	Christchurch	W	29	3	•
North Auckland	1986	Whangarei	W	21	7	
North Auckland	1987	Christchurch	L	7	27	
North Auckland	1988	Whangarei	L	3	29	
North Auckland	1989	Christchurch	W	35	21	
North Auckland	1990	Whangarei	W	21	19	
North Auckland	1991	Christchurch	W	21	16	
North Auckland	1992	Whangarei	L	16	24	
Counties	1960	Papakura	W	20	15	
Counties	1961	Christchurch	W	26	18	
Counties	1973	Christchurch	W	38	6	
Counties	1976	Christchurch	L	6	11	
Counties	1977	Pukekohe	W	9	4	
Counties	1978	Christchurch	L	6	21	
Counties	1979	Pukekohe	L	0	7	
Counties	1980	Christchurch	L	15	21	
Counties	1981	Pukekohe	L	9	35	
Counties	1982	Christchurch	D	15	15	•
Counties	1983	Pukekohe	W	37	3	
Counties	1984	Christchurch	W	27	19	•
Counties	1985	Pukekohe	W	19	15	
Counties	1986	Christchurch	W	32	7	

Counties	1987	Pukekohe	W	32	17	
Counties	1988	Christchurch	L	18	19	
Counties	1989	Pukekohe	W	35	3	
Counties	1990	Christchurch	W	14	3	
Counties	1991	Pukekohe	W	31	15	
Counties	1994	Christchurch	W	42	16	•
Counties	1995	Pukekohe	L	39	41	
Counties	1996	Christchurch	L	11	24	
Counties	1996		L	33	46	
Counties	1997	Pukekohe	W	33	18	
Counties	1997	Christchurch	W	44	13	
Counties	1998	Christchurch	L	42	49	
Counties	1999	Pukekohe	W	82	22	
Counties	2000	Christchurch	W	30	16	
Counties	2001	Pukekohe	W	42	17	
Mid-Canterbury	1939	Christchurch	W	40	9	
Mid-Canterbury	1940	Ashburton	L	14	21	
Mid-Canterbury	1942	Christchurch	W	26	9	
Mid-Canterbury	1942	Ashburton	L	6	14	
Mid-Canterbury	1943	Christchurch	L	12	19	
Mid-Canterbury	1943	Ashburton	L	8	12	
Mid-Canterbury	1944	Ashburton	W	17	16	
Mid-Canterbury	1945	Christchurch	W	26	11	
Mid-Canterbury	1945	Ashburton	L	3	10	
Mid-Canterbury	1946	Christchurch	L	0	6	
Mid-Canterbury	1946	Ashburton	W	6	0	
Mid-Canterbury	1947	Christchurch	W	15	6	
Mid-Canterbury	1948	Christchurch	L	8	14	
Mid-Canterbury	1948	Ashburton	L	16	17	
Mid-Canterbury	1949	Christchurch	W	21	19	
Mid-Canterbury	1949	Ashburton	W	12	9	
Mid-Canterbury	1951	Christchurch	W	18	8	
Mid-Canterbury	1951	Ashburton	L	6	13	
Mid-Canterbury	1952	Christchurch	W	21	15	

Versus	Date	Location	Result	Score For	Score Against	Ranfurly Shield (•)
Mid-Canterbury	1952	Ashburton	W	8	3	
Mid-Canterbury	1953	Christchurch	W	9	6	
Mid-Canterbury	1953	Ashburton	L	14	23	
Mid-Canterbury	1954	Christchurch	W	9	6	
Mid-Canterbury	1954	Ashburton	L	14	26	
Mid-Canterbury	1955	Christchurch	W	24	6	
Mid-Canterbury	1955	Ashburton	W	28	6	
Mid-Canterbury	1956	Christchurch	W	14	6	
Mid-Canterbury	1957	Ashburton	W	14	5	
Mid-Canterbury	1958	Ashburton	W	23	9	
Mid-Canterbury	1959	Ashburton	L	19	21	
Mid-Canterbury	1960	Christchurch	W	11	3	
Mid-Canterbury	1960	Ashburton	W	27	16	
Mid-Canterbury	1961	Ashburton	W	11	0	
Mid-Canterbury	1962	Ashburton	W	22	13	
Mid-Canterbury	1963	Christchurch	W	17	8	
Mid-Canterbury	1963	Ashburton	W	11	8	
Mid-Canterbury	1964	Ashburton	W	17	14	
Mid-Canterbury	1965	Ashburton	W	26	18	
Mid-Canterbury	1966	Ashburton	W	28	15	
Mid-Canterbury	1967	Ashburton	W	11	9	
Mid-Canterbury	1967	Christchurch	W	21	0	
Mid-Canterbury	1968	Ashburton	W	8	6	
Mid-Canterbury	1969	Ashburton	W	23	15	
Mid-Canterbury	1970	Ashburton	W	53	0	
Mid-Canterbury	1970	Christchurch	W	28	8	
Mid-Canterbury	1971	Ashburton	W	25	11	
Mid-Canterbury	1972	Ashburton	W	27	3	
Mid-Canterbury	1973	Ashburton	W	17	4	
Mid-Canterbury	1974	Ashburton	W	14	9	
Mid-Canterbury	1975	Ashburton	W	41	12	
Mid-Canterbury	1976	Ashburton	L	17	21	
Mid-Canterbury	1977	Ashburton	W	37	6	

Mid-Canterbury	1978	Ashburton	W	38	4	
Mid-Canterbury	1979	Ashburton	L	7	10	
Mid-Canterbury	1980	Ashburton	L	3	17	
Mid-Canterbury	1981	Ashburton	D	15	15	
Mid-Canterbury	1982	Ashburton	L	6	13	
Mid-Canterbury	1983	Christchurch	W	28	0	•
Mid-Canterbury	1984	Ashburton	W	31	19	
Mid-Canterbury	1985	Christchurch	W	17	7	•
Mid-Canterbury	1986	Ashburton	W	48	7	
Mid-Canterbury	1987	Ashburton	W	19	6	
Mid-Canterbury	1988	Ashburton	W	57	7	
Mid-Canterbury	1989	Ashburton	W	39	9	
Mid-Canterbury	1990	Ashburton	W	55	4	
Mid-Canterbury	1991	Ashburton	W	44	3	
Mid-Canterbury	1992	Ashburton	W	34	22	
Mid-Canterbury	1993	Ashburton	W	90	6	
Mid-Canterbury	1994	Christchurch	W	73	3	
Mid-Canterbury	1995	Ashburton	W	64	19	•
Mid-Canterbury	2002	Ashburton	W	78	10	•
Taranaki	1892	Hawera	L	6	10	
Taranaki	1894	Christchurch	L	3	17	
Taranaki	1899	Christchurch	L	3	5	
Taranaki	1902	New Plymouth	D	10	10	
Taranaki	1906	Christchurch	L	0	6	
Taranaki	1911	Christchurch	L	3	24	
Taranaki	1912	Stratford	L	0	21	
Taranaki	1914	New Plymouth	L	5	6	
Taranaki	1921	Hawera	W	14	5	
Taranaki	1922	Christchurch	W	17	13	
Taranaki	1923	New Plymouth	W	15	8	
Taranaki	1927	Christchurch	W	17	8	
Taranaki	1929	Stratford	W	10	9	
Taranaki	1933	Christchurch	D	15	15	
Taranaki	1935	Christchurch	L	8	21	

Versus	Date	Location	Result	Score For	Score Against	Ranfurly Shield (•)
Taranaki	1937	Stratford	W	16	9	
Taranaki	1951	New Plymouth	W	32	6	
Taranaki	1954	Christchurch	W	11	6	
Taranaki	1955	New Plymouth	W	26	22	
Taranaki	1958	Christchurch	W	9	6	
Taranaki	1960	New Plymouth	W	8	6	
Taranaki	1962	Christchurch	L	6	8	
Taranaki	1964	New Plymouth	L	9	12	•
Taranaki	1966	Christchurch	W	22	6	
Taranaki	1968	New Plymouth	W	19	3	
Taranaki	1970	Christchurch	W	13	3	
Taranaki	1972	New Plymouth	W	14	9	
Taranaki	1974	Christchurch	W	36	3	
Taranaki	1975	Christchurch	W	35	9	
Taranaki	1977	Christchurch	W	22	3	
Taranaki	1978	New Plymouth	L	10	26	
Taranaki	1979	Christchurch	W	12	7	
Taranaki	1985	Christchurch	W	27	3	•
Taranaki	1986	Christchurch	W	18	9	
Taranaki	1987	New Plymouth	W	17	16	
Taranaki	1988	Christchurch	W	19	10	
Taranaki	1989	New Plymouth	W	24	14	
Taranaki	1990	Christchurch	W	42	12	
Taranaki	1991	New Plymouth	W	25	12	
Taranaki	1993	Christchurch	W	48	31	
Taranaki	1994	New Plymouth	W	23	18	
Taranaki	1996	New Plymouth	W	38	21	
Taranaki	1997	Christchurch	W	40	21	
Taranaki	1998	New Plymouth	W	34	6	
Taranaki	1999	Christchurch	W	34	16	
Taranaki	2000	New Plymouth	W	43	9	
Taranaki	2000	Christchurch	W	31	23	
Taranaki	2001	Christchurch	W	38	17	•

Taranaki	2002	New Plymouth	W	46	15	
Taranaki	2003	Christchurch	W	32	27	•
Waikato	1929	Hamilton	L	17	21	
Waikato	1932	Christchurch	W	17	6	
Waikato	1953	Hamilton	L	9	11	
Waikato	1954	Christchurch	D	6	6	
Waikato	1957	Hamilton	L	8	22	
Waikato	1958	Christchurch	L	6	8	
Waikato	1960	Hamilton	W	17	15	
Waikato	1962	Christchurch	W	16	8	
Waikato	1964	Hamilton	L	3	16	
Waikato	1966	Christchurch	W	17	0	
Waikato	1968	Hamilton	W	31	12	
Waikato	1970	Christchurch	W	14	9	
Waikato	1972	Hamilton	L	8	13	
Waikato	1974	Christchurch	W	30	0	
Waikato	1981	Hamilton	L	7	14	•
Waikato	1982	Christchurch	W	27	16	
Waikato	1983	Hamilton	W	22	14	
Waikato	1984	Christchurch	W	16	10	•
Waikato	1985	Hamilton	W	18	13	
Waikato	1987	Christchurch	W	30	4	
Waikato	1988	Hamilton	W	27	21	
Waikato	1989	Christchurch	W	23	22	
Waikato	1990	Hamilton	L	6	31	
Waikato	1991	Christchurch	W	47	18	
Waikato	1992	Hamilton	L	17	22	
Waikato	1993	Christchurch	L	9	18	
Waikato	1994	Hamilton	W	29	26	•
Waikato	1995	Christchurch	W	58	30	•
Waikato	1996	Hamilton	W	29	20	
Waikato	1997	Christchurch	L	18	24	
Waikato	1998	Hamilton	L	23	29	
Waikato	1998	Hamilton	L	13	32	

Versus	Date	Location	Result	Score For	Score Against	Ranfurly Shield (•)
Waikato	1999	Christchurch	L	6	20	
Waikato	2000	Hamilton	W	26	18	•
Waikato	2001	Christchurch	W	52	19	•
Waikato	2002	Hamilton	L	41	59	
Waikato	2003	Christchurch	W	35	24	•
Auckland	1875	Christchurch	W	9 1/2	0	
Auckland	1876	Auckland	L	3	7	
Auckland	1883	Christchurch	L	1	4	
Auckland	1887	Auckland	D	3	3	
Auckland	1889	Christchurch	W	1	0	
Auckland	1892	Auckland	W	25	0	
Auckland	1895	Christchurch	W	10	0	
Auckland	1898	Auckland	L	3	24	
Auckland	1899	Christchurch	D	3	3	
Auckland	1902	Auckland	L	3	19	
Auckland	1903	Christchurch	L	0	11	
Auckland	1906	Auckland	L	6	29	
Auckland	1907	Christchurch	L	0	3	
Auckland	1910	Auckland	L	4	6	
Auckland	1911	Christchurch	L	3	6	
Auckland	1914	Auckland	L	3	11	
Auckland	1922	Christchurch	W	31	15	
Auckland	1925	Auckland	L	8	35	
Auckland	1928	Christchurch	L	10	12	
Auckland	1929	Auckland	L	6	17	
Auckland	1932	Christchurch	W	14	0	
Auckland	1935	Auckland	W	16	13	
Auckland	1936	Christchurch	W	24	15	
Auckland	1939	Auckland	W	6	3	
Auckland	1947	Christchurch	L	15	21	
Auckland	1949	Auckland	L	3	21	
Auckland	1951	Christchurch	D	11	11	

Auckland	1952	Auckland	D	11	11	
Auckland	1953	Auckland	W	15	12	
Auckland	1955	Christchurch	W	12	6	
Auckland	1957	Auckland	L	6	16	
Auckland	1959	Christchurch	W	27	14	
Auckland	1960	Auckland	L	18	19	•
Auckland	1961	Christchurch	W	16	13	
Auckland	1962	Auckland	L	6	15	•
Auckland	1963	Christchurch	L	8	16	
Auckland	1964	Auckland	W	23	20	
Auckland	1965	Christchurch	L	11	14	
Auckland	1966	Auckland	D	11	11	
Auckland	1967	Christchurch	W	11	6	
Auckland	1968	Auckland	L	14	18	
Auckland	1969	Christchurch	W	19	5	
Auckland	1970	Auckland	L	8	14	
Auckland	1971	Christchurch	L	16	20	
Auckland	1972	Auckland	W	12	6	
Auckland	1973	Christchurch	W	42	3	
Auckland	1974	Auckland	L	16	24	
Auckland	1975	Christchurch	L	7	8	
Auckland	1976	Auckland	L	9	19	
Auckland	1977	Christchurch	W	37	18	
Auckland	1978	Auckland	W	13	7	
Auckland	1979	Christchurch	W	16	9	
Auckland	1980	Auckland	W	12	10	
Auckland	1981	Christchurch	W	13	7	
Auckland	1982	Auckland	W	19	15	
Auckland	1983	Christchurch	W	31	9	•
Auckland	1984	Auckland	L	3	32	
Auckland	1985	Christchurch	L	23	28	•
Auckland	1986	Christchurch	W	16	9	
Auckland	1986	Auckland	L	15	28	
Auckland	1987	Auckland	W	21	16	
Auckland	1987	Christchurch	L	15	24	

Versus	Date	Location	Result	Score For	Score Against	Ranfurly Shield (•)
Auckland	1988	Christchurch	L	15	26	
Auckland	1988	Auckland	L	10	31	•
Auckland	1989	Auckland	L	15	33	
Auckland	1989	Christchurch	L	6	15	
Auckland	1990	Christchurch	L	12	36	
Auckland	1990	Auckland	L	30	33	•
Auckland	1991	Auckland	L	14	42	
Auckland	1992	Christchurch	L	10	22	
Auckland	1992	Auckland	L	38	47	
Auckland	1993	Christchurch	L	13	39	
Auckland	1994	Auckland	L	17	30	
Auckland	1995	Auckland	L	22	27	
Auckland	1995	Christchurch	L	0	35	•
Auckland	1996	Auckland	L	10	30	
Auckland	1997	Christchurch	W	20	9	
Auckland	1997	Christchurch	W	21	15	
Auckland	1998	Auckland	L	18	26	
Auckland	1998	Auckland	W	50	17	
Auckland	1999	Christchurch	W	12	10	
Auckland	2000	Auckland	W	29	26	
Auckland	2001	Christchurch	W	38	10	•
Auckland	2001	Christchurch	W	53	22	
Auckland	2002	Auckland	W	18	11	
Auckland	2002	Christchurch	L	23	29	
Auckland	2003	Christchurch	L	31	40	•
Hawkes Bay	1887	Napier	L	1	5	
Hawkes Bay	1889	Christchurch	L	1	3	
Hawkes Bay	1892	Napier	W	11	2	
Hawkes Bay	1898	Napier	W	15	1	
Hawkes Bay	1901	Christchurch	W	34	0	
Hawkes Bay	1902	Napier	W	24	3	
Hawkes Bay	1903	Christchurch	L	9	13	

Hawkes Bay	1922	Christchurch	L	3	29	
Hawkes Bay	1923	Hastings	L	8	9	
Hawkes Bay	1925	Napier	L	18	24	
Hawkes Bay	1926	Christchurch	L	15	17	
Hawkes Bay	1927	Napier	L	8	11	
Hawkes Bay	1930	Christchurch	W	12	3	
Hawkes Bay	1931	Hastings	L	14	17	
Hawkes Bay	1934	Christchurch	L	0	9	
Hawkes Bay	1935	Hastings	L	5	24	
Hawkes Bay	1938	Christchurch	L	6	15	
Hawkes Bay	1939	Napier	L	3	11	
Hawkes Bay	1948	Christchurch	W	9	6	
Hawkes Bay	1949	Napier	W	11	8	
Hawkes Bay	1952	Christchurch	W	39	16	
Hawkes Bay	1953	Napier	W	29	11	
Hawkes Bay	1956	Christchurch	W	21	9	
Hawkes Bay	1957	Napier	L	9	13	
Hawkes Bay	1958	Napier	W	21	6	
Hawkes Bay	1960	Christchurch	W	18	13	
Hawkes Bay	1962	Napier	L	6	9	
Hawkes Bay	1964	Christchurch	L	6	20	
Hawkes Bay	1966	Hastings	D	12	12	
Hawkes Bay	1968	Christchurch	L	3	8	
Hawkes Bay	1969	Napier	W	18	11	
Hawkes Bay	1970	Napier	L	3	17	
Hawkes Bay	1972	Christchurch	W	27	3	
Hawkes Bay	1974	Hastings	L	11	13	
Hawkes Bay	1976	Christchurch	W	13	6	
Hawkes Bay	1977	Hastings	W	32	19	
Hawkes Bay	1978	Christchurch	W	23	0	
Hawkes Bay	1980	Napier	L	19	28	
Hawkes Bay	1981	Christchurch	W	30	9	
Hawkes Bay	1982	Hastings	L	13	21	
Hawkes Bay	1983	Christchurch	W	32	3	•
Hawkes Bay	1984	Hastings	W	15	3	

Versus	Date	Location	Result	Score For	Score Against	Ranfurly Shield (•)
Hawkes Bay	1989	Christchurch	W	40	19	
Hawkes Bay	1991	Christchurch	D	31	31	
Hawkes Bay	1992	Christchurch	W	34	9	
Hawkes Bay	1993	Napier	W	30	22	
Hawkes Bay	2003	Christchurch	W	76	14	•
Manawatu	1896	Palmerston Nth	W	8	3	
Manawatu	1905	Christchurch	W	6	3	
Manawatu	1923	Christchurch	W	31	16	
Manawatu	1933	Palmerston Nth	L	8	11	
Manawatu	1934	Christchurch	W	22	3	
Manawatu	1936	Christchurch	W	22	9	
Manawatu	1949	Christchurch	L	11	14	
Manawatu	1951	Palmerston Nth	W	11	8	
Manawatu	1953	Christchurch	W	20	0	
Manawatu	1957	Palmerston Nth	W	23	5	
Manawatu	1958	Palmerston Nth	L	13	20	
Manawatu	1961	Christchurch	W	11	3	
Manawatu	1962	Palmerston Nth	W	31	3	
Manawatu	1965	Christchurch	W	25	0	
Manawatu	1966	Palmerston Nth	W	19	8	
Manawatu	1969	Christchurch	W	10	5	
Manawatu	1970	Palmerston Nth	L	8	14	
Manawatu	1973	Christchurch	W	32	9	
Manawatu	1974	Palmerston Nth	W	14	9	
Manawatu	1976	Palmerston Nth	L	10	15	
Manawatu	1977	Christchurch	W	4	3	
Manawatu	1978	Palmerston Nth	W	14	4	
Manawatu	1979	Christchurch	W	19	8	
Manawatu	1980	Palmerston Nth	L	10	19	
Manawatu	1981	Christchurch	L	9	18	
Manawatu	1982	Palmerston Nth	L	13	26	
Manawatu	1983	Christchurch	W	28	15	•

Manawatu	1984	Palmerston Nth	D	15	15	
Manawatu	1985	Christchurch	W	29	6	
Manawatu	1986	Palmerston Nth	D	18	18	
Manawatu	1987	Christchurch	W	40	16	
Manawatu	1988	Palmerston Nth	W	22	6	
Nelson	1876	Nelson	W	12	0	
Nelson	1898	Nelson	W	9	3	
Nelson	1899	Christchurch	W	17	0	
Nelson	1901	Christchurch	W	27	0	
Nelson	1902	Nelson	W	25	7	
Nelson	1923	Nelson	W	7	6	
Nelson	1934	Christchurch	W	31	12	
Nelson	1947	Nelson	D	9	9	
Nelson	1982	Christchurch	W	18	12	
Nelson	1984	Christchurch	W	34	10	•
Nelson	1991	Nelson	W	75	9	
Nelson	1995	Christchurch	W	43	17	•
Nelson	2001	Christchurch	W	67	10	•
Manawhenua	1927	Palmerston Nth	W	17	6	
Manawhenua	1928	Christchurch	W	25	19	
Wanganui	1898	Wanganui	W	14	6	
Wanganui	1904	Christchurch	L	0	5	
Wanganui	1906	Wanganui	W	16	8	
Wanganui	1911	Christchurch	W	19	8	
Wanganui	1912	Wanganui	W	8	0	
Wanganui	1914	Wanganui	W	6	3	
Wanganui	1920	Christchurch	W	19	11	
Wanganui	1921	Wanganui	W	21	0	
Wanganui	1925	Christchurch	W	27	11	
Wanganui	1930	Christchurch				
Wanganui	1931	Wanganui	W	20	6	
Wanganui	1935	Christchurch	W	15	11	

Versus	Date	Location	Result	Score For	Score Against	Ranfurly Shield (•)
Wanganui	1937	Wanganui	W	12	3	
Wanganui	1948	Christchurch	L	8	22	
Wanganui	1951	Wanganui	W	32	13	
Wanganui	1952	Christchurch	W	21	11	
Wanganui	1954	Christchurch	W	17	13	
Wanganui	1955	Wanganui	W	11	6	
Wanganui	1956	Christchurch	W	20	9	
Wanganui	1960	Christchurch	W	35	8	
Wanganui	1964	Wanganui	W	13	9	
Wanganui	1965	Christchurch	W	53	3	
Wanganui	1968	Wanganui	W	19	3	
Wanganui	1973	Christchurch	W	65	16	
Wanganui	1987	Wanganui	W	47	7	
Buller	1907	Westport	W	28	9	
Buller	1913	Westport	L	5	8	
Buller	1923	Westport	W	25	6	
Buller	1929	Westport	W	22	9	
Buller	1932	Christchurch	W	13	0	
Buller	1933	Christchurch	W	13	3	
Buller	1937	Westport	W	15	11	
Buller	1938	Christchurch	W	23	9	
Buller	1938	Westport	D	13	13	
Buller	1939	Christchurch	W	12	4	
Buller	1943	Westport	W	13	5	
Buller	1943	Christchurch	W	20	10	
Buller	1945	Westport	L	8	20	
Buller	1945	Christchurch	L	14	16	
Buller	1946	Westport	W	29	6	
Buller	1946	Christchurch	W	20	19	
Buller	1947	Westport	W	22	13	
Buller	1947	Christchurch	L	6	7	
Buller	1948	Westport	L	8	11	

Buller	1949	Christchurch	W	13	3	
Buller	1950	Christchurch	W	20	9	
Buller	1951	Westport	W	30	3	
Buller	1952	Westport	W	11	6	
Buller	1953	Westport	W	46	8	
Buller	1953	Christchurch	W	19	3	
Buller	1954	Westport	W	13	5	
Buller	1954	Christchurch	W	22	0	
Buller	1955	Westport	L	6	11	
Buller	1957	Westport	W	20	15	
Buller	1957	Christchurch	W	22	3	
Buller	1958	Westport	W	6	0	
Buller	1958	Christchurch	W	35	14	
Buller	1959	Westport	W	19	0	
Buller	1959	Christchurch	W	63	11	
Buller	1960	Christchurch	W	12	3	
Buller	1960	Westport	W	8	0	
Buller	1961	Westport	W	31	6	
Buller	1962	Westport	W	19	0	
Buller	1962	Christchurch	W	11	0	
Buller	1963	Christchurch	W	26	3	
Buller	1964	Westport	W	32	5	
Buller	1965	Westport	W	20	3	
Buller	1966	Westport	W	34	5	
Buller	1967	Westport	W	14	3	
Buller	1968	Westport	W	34	3	
Buller	1969	Westport	W	27	6	
Buller	1970	Christchurch	W	14	5	
Buller	1984	Christchurch	W	57	13	•
Buller	1985	Westport	W	28	4	
Buller	2001	Westport	W	69	3	•
South Canterbury	1899	Christchurch	W	14	0	
South Canterbury	1890	Timaru	W	15	6	
South Canterbury	1891	Christchurch	W	17	2	

Versus	Date	Location	Result	Score For	Score Against	Ranfurly Shield (•)
South Canterbury	1892	Timaru	W	44	0	
South Canterbury	1894	Timaru	W	29	0	
South Canterbury	1895	Timaru	W	12	3	
South Canterbury	1896	Christchurch	W	39	0	
South Canterbury	1898	Christchurch	W	18	3	
South Canterbury	1898	Temuka	L	10	19	
South Canterbury	1899	Christchurch	W	26	3	
South Canterbury	1900	Christchurch	W	39	0	
South Canterbury	1900	Temuka	W	13	6	
South Canterbury	1902	Christchurch	W	29	5	
South Canterbury	1902	Temuka	L	5	11	
South Canterbury	1903	Christchurch	W	13	3	
South Canterbury	1903	Timaru	W	9	6	
South Canterbury	1904	Temuka	W	18	8	
South Canterbury	1904	Christchurch	W	25	3	
South Canterbury	1905	Timaru	W	37	0	
South Canterbury	1906	Christchurch	W	11	0	
South Canterbury	1907	Temuka	W	9	3	
South Canterbury	1909	Timaru	L	3	9	
South Canterbury	1910	Christchurch	W	20	9	
South Canterbury	1911	Timaru	L	3	19	
South Canterbury	1912	Christchurch	W	17	8	
South Canterbury	1913	Timaru	L	3	21	
South Canterbury	1914	Christchurch	W	12	6	
South Canterbury	1920	Timaru	W	16	6	
South Canterbury	1921	Christchurch	W	14	8	
South Canterbury	1922	Timaru	W	15	11	
South Canterbury	1923	Christchurch	L	3	11	
South Canterbury	1924	Timaru	L	18	21	
South Canterbury	1925	Christchurch	W	44	9	
South Canterbury	1926	Timaru	L	15	18	
South Canterbury	1927	Christchurch	W	47	7	
South Canterbury	1928	Christchurch	W	29	9	

South Canterbury	1928	Timaru	W	21	16	
South Canterbury	1929	Christchurch	W	37	14	
South Canterbury	1930	Timaru	W	25	13	
South Canterbury	1931	Christchurch	L	9	21	
South Canterbury	1932	Timaru	L	3	18	
South Canterbury	1932	Christchurch	W	11	5	
South Canterbury	1933	Christchurch	W	6	3	
South Canterbury	1934	Timaru	L	13	25	
South Canterbury	1935	Christchurch	W	12	11	
South Canterbury	1936	Timaru	L	8	16	
South Canterbury	1937	Christchurch	W	30	22	
South Canterbury	1938	Timaru	W	9	3	
South Canterbury	1939	Christchurch	W	19	12	
South Canterbury	1940	Timaru	L	8	22	
South Canterbury	1941	Christchurch	W	21	7	
South Canterbury	1945	Timaru	L	0	8	
South Canterbury	1946	Christchurch	W	23	20	
South Canterbury	1947	Timaru	W	29	18	
South Canterbury	1948	Christchurch	W	15	3	
South Canterbury	1949	Timaru	W	16	13	
South Canterbury	1950	Timaru	W	9	0	
South Canterbury	1950	Christchurch	D	9	9	
South Canterbury	1951	Timaru	W	20	6	
South Canterbury	1951	Christchurch	W	37	11	
South Canterbury	1952	Timaru	W	32	9	
South Canterbury	1952	Christchurch	W	33	0	
South Canterbury	1953	Timaru	L	9	18	
South Canterbury	1953	Christchurch	L	6	15	
South Canterbury	1954	Timaru	W	3	0	
South Canterbury	1954	Christchurch	W	24	11	
South Canterbury	1955	Timaru	L	8	12	
South Canterbury	1955	Christchurch	W	19	6	
South Canterbury	1956	Timaru	L	0	20	
South Canterbury	1956	Christchurch	W	32	17	
South Canterbury	1957	Timaru	L	8	9	

Versus	Date	Location	Result	Score For	Score Against	Ranfurly Shield (•)
South Canterbury	1957	Christchurch	W	22	17	
South Canterbury	1958	Timaru	W	24	18	
South Canterbury	1958	Christchurch	W	31	8	
South Canterbury	1959	Timaru	L	8	17	
South Canterbury	1959	Christchurch	W	24	6	
South Canterbury	1960	Timaru	D	8	8	
South Canterbury	1961	Timaru	W	11	8	
South Canterbury	1962	Timaru	W	17	11	
South Canterbury	1963	Timaru	W	9	3	
South Canterbury	1964	Timaru	W	9	6	
South Canterbury	1964	Christchurch	W	37	3	
South Canterbury	1965	Timaru	W	27	11	
South Canterbury	1965	Timaru	W	9	6	
South Canterbury	1966	Timaru	W	25	8	
South Canterbury	1967	Timaru	W	46	8	
South Canterbury	1968	Timaru	W	30	3	
South Canterbury	1969	Timaru	W	26	3	
South Canterbury	1970	Timaru	W	28	3	
South Canterbury	1970	Christchurch	W	19	8	
South Canterbury	1972	Timaru	L	10	20	
South Canterbury	1973	Timaru	L	6	13	
South Canterbury	1973	Christchurch	W	43	9	
South Canterbury	1974	Timaru	W	17	3	
South Canterbury	1975	Timaru	W	12	7	
South Canterbury	1976	Timaru	W	11	0	
South Canterbury	1977	Timaru	W	23	6	
South Canterbury	1978	Christchurch	W	18	7	
South Canterbury	1979	Christchurch	W	28	0	
South Canterbury	1979	Timaru	W	10	9	
South Canterbury	1980	Christchurch	W	26	6	
South Canterbury	1980	Timaru	W	29	0	
South Canterbury	1981	Timaru	W	20	9	
South Canterbury	1982	Timaru	W	20	3	

South Canterbury	1983	Christchurch	W	50	12	•
South Canterbury	1984	Timaru	W	19	3	
South Canterbury	1985	Timaru	W	45	3	
South Canterbury	1986	Timaru	W	30	9	
South Canterbury	1987	Christchurch	W	42	12	
South Canterbury	1987	Timaru	W	67	4	
South Canterbury	1988	Timaru	W	30	14	
South Canterbury	1990	Timaru	W	23	6	
South Canterbury	1991	Timaru	W	51	9	
South Canterbury	1992	Timaru	W	54	10	
South Canterbury	1993	Timaru	W	67	20	
South Canterbury	1994	Timaru	W	37	28	
South Canterbury	1995	Christchurch	W	72	27	•
South Canterbury	1996	Timaru	W	45	17	
South Canterbury	2001	Timaru	W	103	0	•
Bay Of Plenty	1938	Christchurch	D	8	8	
Bay Of Plenty	1969	Christchurch	W	11	6	
Bay Of Plenty	1974	Rotorua	W	10	9	
Bay Of Plenty	1975	Christchurch	L	10	16	
Bay Of Plenty	1976	Tauranga	L	6	12	
Bay Of Plenty	1977	Christchurch	W	30	12	
Bay Of Plenty	1979	Whakatane	L	8	20	
Bay Of Plenty	1980	Christchurch	W	28	19	
Bay Of Plenty	1981	Rotorua	W	20	18	
Bay Of Plenty	1982	Christchurch	W	28	0	
Bay Of Plenty	1983	Whakatane	W	26	24	
Bay Of Plenty	1984	Christchurch	W	18	13	•
Bay Of Plenty	1985	Tauranga	W	24	12	
Bay Of Plenty	1986	Christchurch	W	52	14	
Bay Of Plenty	1987	Rotorua	L	19	21	
Bay Of Plenty	1988	Christchurch	W	33	21	
Bay Of Plenty	1989	Rotorua	D	19	19	
Bay Of Plenty	1990	Christchurch	W	38	21	
Bay Of Plenty	1991	Rotorua	L	13	28	

Versus	Date	Location	Result	Score For	Score Against	Ranfurly Shield (•)
Bay Of Plenty	1996	Whakatane	L	18	21	
Bay Of Plenty	1997	Christchurch	W	42	22	
Bay Of Plenty	2001	Christchurch	W	72	3	•
Bay Of Plenty	2002	Rotorua	W	35	30	
Bay Of Plenty	2003	Christchurch	W	31	26	•
Bush Unions	1939	Christchurch	W	16	0	
Ashburton	1927	Ashburton	W	19	3	
Ashburton	1927	Christchurch	W	21	12	
Ashburton	1929	Ashburton	L	3	15	
Ashburton	1930	Ashburton	L	9	22	
Ashburton	1931	Ashburton	W	14	6	
Ashburton	1932	Christchurch	W	11	6	
Ashburton	1933	Christchurch	W	31	7	
Ashburton	1939	Christchurch	W	40	9	
North Otago	1929	Christchurch	L	14	17	
North Otago	1930	Oamaru	W	28	19	
North Otago	1937	Christchurch	W	34	13	
North Otago	1971	Christchurch	W	14	0	
North Otago	1983	Christchurch	W	88	0	•
North Otago	2003	Christchurch	W	85	24	•
Marlborough	1923	Blenheim	W	10	8	
Marlborough	1924	Christchurch	W	26	11	
Marlborough	1963	Christchurch	W	33	0	
Marlborough	1967	Christchurch	L	17	20	
Marlborough	1973	Christchurch	L	6	13	
Marlborough	1975	Blenheim	L	17	41	
Marlborough	1976	Christchurch	W	23	9	
Marlborough	1977	Blenheim	W	12	3	
Marlborough	1979	Blenheim	W	14	6	

Marlborough	1980	Christchurch	W	11	3	
Marlborough	1981	Blenheim	W	34	9	
Marlborough	1982	Christchurch	W	30	6	
Marlborough	1983	Blenheim	W	16	10	
Marlborough	1984	Blenheim	W	20	12	
Marlborough	1985	Christchurch	W	42	4	•
Marlborough	1986	Blenheim	W	30	15	
Marlborough	1987	Blenheim	W	42	3	
Marlborough	1988	Blenheim	W	31	22	
Marlborough	1989	Blenheim	W	60	12	
Marlborough	1990	Blenheim	W	69	9	
Marlborough	1992	Blenheim	W	98	16	
Marlborough	1995	Christchurch	W	79	0	•
Marlborough	2002	Blenheim	W	57	7	•
Southland	1890	Dunedin	W	6	4	
Southland	1893	Christchurch	W	9	5	
Southland	1895	Invercargill	W	10	4	
Southland	1896	Christchurch	D	3	3	
Southland	1897	Invercargill	L	3	13	
Southland	1898	Christchurch	W	4	0	
Southland	1899	Invercargill	W	6	3	
Southland	1900	Christchurch	W	3	0	
Southland	1901	Invercargill	W	12	3	
Southland	1902	Christchurch	W	21	6	
Southland	1903	Invercargill	L	6	16	
Southland	1904	Christchurch	W	8	5	
Southland	1905	Invercargill	W	4	0	
Southland	1906	Christchurch	W	14	3	
Southland	1907	Invercargill	W	14	3	
Southland	1908	Christchurch	W	22	5	
Southland	1909	Invercargill	W	6	5	
Southland	1910	Christchurch	W	37	0	
Southland	1911	Invercargill	W	12	9	
Southland	1912	Christchurch	W	20	3	

Versus	Date	Location	Result	Score For	Score Against	Ranfurly Shield (•)
Southland	1913	Invercargill	W	9	8	
Southland	1914	Christchurch	W	31	10	
Southland	1920	Invercargill	L	9	15	
Southland	1921	Christchurch	L	3	12	
Southland	1922	Invercargill	L	11	33	
Southland	1923	Christchurch	W	29	10	
Southland	1924	Invercargill	L	8	12	
Southland	1925	Christchurch	W	13	11	
Southland	1926	Invercargill	W	8	0	
Southland	1927	Christchurch	W	11	0	
Southland	1928	Invercargill	L	17	25	
Southland	1929	Christchurch	W	21	3	
Southland	1930	Invercargill	L	12	24	
Southland	1931	Christchurch	W	24	21	
Southland	1932	Invercargill	L	5	28	
Southland	1933	Christchurch	W	21	3	
Southland	1934	Invercargill	L	12	20	
Southland	1935	Christchurch	W	8	3	
Southland	1936	Invercargill	L	14	32	
Southland	1937	Christchurch	W	19	7	
Southland	1938	Invercargill	L	0	9	
Southland	1939	Christchurch	L	8	10	
Southland	1946	Invercargill	L	3	11	
Southland	1947	Christchurch	L	9	17	
Southland	1948	Invercargill	L	16	17	
Southland	1949	Christchurch	W	21	11	
Southland	1950	Invercargill	L	8	25	
Southland	1951	Christchurch	W	20	6	
Southland	1952	Invercargill	L	14	25	
Southland	1954	Christchurch	W	18	10	
Southland	1956	Invercargill	L	16	26	
Southland	1956	Christchurch	W	17	3	
Southland	1959	Invercargill	L	0	5	

Southland	1960	Christchurch	W	30	9	
Southland	1961	Invercargill	W	9	6	
Southland	1962	Christchurch	W	22	3	
Southland	1963	Invercargill	W	16	6	
Southland	1964	Christchurch	W	19	14	
Southland	1965	Invercargill	L	9	11	
Southland	1966	Christchurch	W	14	3	
Southland	1967	Invercargill	W	24	9	
Southland	1968	Christchurch	W	24	6	
Southland	1969	Invercargill	W	15	8	
Southland	1970	Christchurch	W	20	9	
Southland	1971	Invercargill	D	11	11	
Southland	1972	Christchurch	W	32	7	
Southland	1973	Invercargill	W	14	9	
Southland	1974	Christchurch	D	12	12	
Southland	1975	Invercargill	L	10	13	
Southland	1976	Christchurch	W	16	7	
Southland	1977	Invercargill	W	13	10	
Southland	1978	Christchurch	W	21	16	
Southland	1979	Invercargill	W	24	17	
Southland	1980	Christchurch	L	10	15	
Southland	1981	Invercargill	L	7	14	
Southland	1983	Christchurch	W	28	10	•
Southland	1985	Christchurch	W	53	0	•
Southland	1986	Invercargill	W	41	23	
Southland	1988	Invercargill	W	18	16	
Southland	1989	Invercargill	W	27	16	
Southland	1990	Invercargill	W	10	0	
Southland	1992	Invercargill	W	20	17	
Southland	1993	Christchurch	W	88	12	
Southland	1994	Invercargill	W	52	14	
Southland	1995	Christchurch	W	27	22	•
Southland	1996	Invercargill	W	77	3	
Southland	1997	Invercargill	W	42	20	
Southland	1998	Christchurch	W	52	12	

Versus	Date	Location	Result	Score For	Score Against	Ranfurly Shield (•)
Southland	1999	Invercargill	W	34	5	
Southland	2000	Christchurch	W	71	8	
Southland	2001	Invercargill	W	37	12	
Southland	2002	Christchurch	W	48	27	•
Southland	2003	Invercargill	L	26	32	
Wairarapa	1887	Masterton	W	1	0	
Wairarapa	1895	Christchurch	W	12	0	
Wairarapa	1898	Masterton	W	13	4	
Wairarapa	1900	Christchurch	L	0	4	
Wairarapa	1902	Carterton	W	24	3	
Wairarapa	1903	Christchurch	W	28	0	
Wairarapa	1906	Masterton	W	15	9	
Wairarapa	1908	Christchurch	W	15	5	
Wairarapa	1910	Carterton	L	3	19	
Wairarapa	1913	Christchurch	W	8	3	
Wairarapa	1914	Masterton	W	22	0	
Wairarapa	1920	Christchurch	W	9	5	
Wairarapa	1921	Masterton	W	8	5	
Wairarapa	1923	Christchurch	W	15	0	
Wairarapa	1925	Masterton	L	12	14	
Wairarapa	1928	Christchurch	L	7	8	
Wairarapa	1929	Masterton	L	12	17	
Wairarapa	1931	Christchurch	W	28	17	
Wairarapa	1933	Carterton	L	9	11	
Wairarapa	1934	Christchurch	W	28	23	
Wairarapa	1935	Christchurch	W	27	16	
Wairarapa	1937	Masterton	W	13	8	
Wairarapa	1946	Christchurch	W	14	11	
Wairarapa	1949	Masterton	W	24	12	
Wairarapa	1950	Christchurch	L	0	3	
Wairarapa	1954	Christchurch	W	16	3	
Wairarapa	1955	Masterton	W	23	11	

Wairarapa	1958	Masterton	W	14	8	
Wairarapa	1967	Christchurch	W	25	3	
Wairarapa Bush	1972	Christchurch	W	16	3	
Wairarapa Bush	1982	Christchurch	W	51	6	•
Wairarapa Bush	1983	Masterton	W	36	7	
Wairarapa Bush	1984	Christchurch	W	24	6	•
Wairarapa Bush	1985	Masterton	L	9	13	
Wairarapa Bush	1986	Christchurch	W	31	7	
Wairarapa Bush	1987	Masterton	W	20	16	
East Coast	1957		W	12	11	
East Coast	2002	Christchurch	W	51	6	•
Poverty Bay	1948		W	12	3	
Poverty Bay	1957		W	11	9	
North Harbour	1988	Christchurch	W	22	16	
North Harbour	1989	Takapuna	W	32	21	
North Harbour	1990	Christchurch	W	17	13	
North Harbour	1991	Takapuna	W	30	23	
North Harbour	1992	Christchurch	W	27	11	
North Harbour	1993	Takapuna	L	23	45	
North Harbour	1994	Christchurch	W	25	16	
North Harbour	1994	Takapuna	L	27	59	
North Harbour	1995	Takapuna	D	13	13	
North Harbour	1996	Christchurch	W	43	20	
North Harbour	1997	Albany	W	20	3	
North Harbour	1998	Christchurch	W	31	29	
North Harbour	1999	Albany	L	11	19	
North Harbour	2000	Christchurch	W	31	3	
North Harbour	2001	Albany	L	9	20	
North Harbour	2002	Christchurch	W	65	10	•
North Harbour	2003	Albany	W	18	10	

Versus	Date	Location	Result	Score For	Score Against	Ranfurly Shield (•)
Buller / West Coast	1990	Christchurch	W	74	0	
Buller / West Coast	1993	Greymouth	W	57	11	
Northland	1998	Christchurch	W	40	17	
Northland	1999	Whangarei	L	20	27	
Northland	2000	Christchurch	W	28	22	•
Northland	2001	Whangarei	W	26	18	
Northland	2002	Christchurch	W	44	17	•
Northland	2003	Whangarei	W	30	26	
N.Z. Universities	1939	Christchurch	L	5	24	
N.Z. Universities	1947	Christchurch	L	0	21	
N.Z. Universities	1952	Christchurch	L	18	32	
N.Z. Universities	1957	Christchurch	W	8	3	
N.Z. Universities	1960	Christchurch	W	17	8	
N.Z. Universities	1962	Christchurch	D	10	10	
N.Z. Universities	1983	Christchurch	W	37	6	
Cantabrians	1958	Christchurch	L	19	21	
Cantabrians	1960	Christchurch	W	44	14	
South Island Varsities	1941	Christchurch	W	24	8	
Army	1941	Christchurch	W	16	12	
N.Z. Combined Services	1941	Christchurch	L	9	11	
N.Z. Combined Services	1959	Christchurch	W	57	16	
New Zealand Maoris	1947	Christchurch	W	14	11	
New Zealand Maoris	1982	Christchurch	L	12	27	
New Zealand Maoris	1985	Temuka	W	41	13	
N.Z. Wasps	1984	Rotorua	W	31	20	

N.Z. Div. XV	1996	Timaru	L	27	33	
Crusaders XV	1996	Christchurch	W	35	17	
Invitation XV	1995	Christchurch	W	67	24	
Australia	1905	Christchurch	W	8	3	
Australia	1931	Christchurch	W	16	13	
Australia	1936	Christchurch	W	19	18	
Australia	1946	Christchurch	W	20	11	
Australia	1949	Christchurch	L	12	16	
Australia	1955	Christchurch	L	8	19	
Australia	1962	Christchurch	W	5	3	
Australia	1986	Christchurch	W	30	10	
South Africa	1921	Christchurch	W	6	4	
South Africa	1937	Christchurch	L	8	23	
South Africa	1956	Christchurch	W	9	6	
South Africa	1965	Christchurch	L	5	6	
South Africa	1994	Christchurch	L	11	21	
New South Wales	1882	Christchurch	L	2	7	
New South Wales	1886	Christchurch	W	6	0	
New South Wales	1886	Christchurch	W	17	0	
New South Wales	1894	Christchurch	W	11	3	
New South Wales	1901	Christchurch	W	11	5	
New South Wales	1925	Christchurch	W	22	13	
New South Wales	1980	Christchurch	W	22	20	
New South Wales	1986	Sydney	L	15	16	
New South Wales	1987	Christchurch	L	24	25	
New South Wales	1988	Sydney	L	16	36	
New South Wales	1989	Christchurch	L	24	25	
New South Wales	1990	Sydney	L	21	23	
New South Wales	1992	Christchurch	L	14	35	
New South Wales	1994	Christchurch	W	33	3	

Versus	Date	Location	Result	Score For	Score Against	Ranfurly Shield (•)
British Isles	1888	Christchurch	L	6	14	
British Isles	1888	Christchurch	L	0	4	
British Isles	1888	Christchurch	L	0	8	
British Isles	1908	Christchurch	W	13	8	
British Isles	1930	Christchurch	W	14	8	
British Isles	1950	Christchurch	L	5	16	
British Isles	1959	Christchurch	W	20	14	
British Isles	1966	Christchurch	L	6	8	
British Isles	1971	Christchurch	L	3	14	
British Isles	1977	Christchurch	L	13	14	
British Isles	1983	Christchurch	W	22	20	
British Lions	1993	Christchurch	L	10	28	
Scotland	1981	Christchurch	L	12	23	
Scotland	1990	Christchurch	L	12	21	
American Universities	1910	Christchurch	W	19	0	
Fiji	1951	Christchurch	W	24	22	
Fiji	1957	Christchurch	W	22	16	
Fiji	1980	Christchurch	W	10	4	
Fiji	1986	Suva	W	20	13	
Fiji	1987	Christchurch	W	23	19	
Fiji	1988	Suva	W	13	3	
Fiji	1989	Christchurch	L	19	23	
Fiji	1990	Suva	L	7	20	
Fiji	1991	Christchurch	W	47	24	
Fiji	1992	Suva	L	17	38	
Fiji	2003	Christchurch	L	38	41	
Tonga	1995	Christchurch	W	75	5	

New Zealand	1905	Christchurch	L	0	3	
New Zealand	1957	Christchurch	W	11	9	
Queensland A	1896	Christchurch	W	13	8	
Queensland A	1896	Christchurch	W	16	14	
Queensland A	1976	Ballymore	L	10	16	
Queensland A	1977	Christchurch	L	15	19	
Queensland A	1978	Ballymore	W	25	0	
Queensland A	1979	Christchurch	L	6	19	
Queensland A	1981	Brisbane	L	20	22	
Queensland A	1982	Christchurch	W	21	9	
Queensland A	1983	Brisbane	L	12	17	
Queensland A	1984	Christchurch	W	33	9	
Queensland	1985	Brisbane	L	7	21	
Queensland	1986	Christchurch	W	23	9	
Queensland	1987	Brisbane	W	22	16	
Queensland	1988	Christchurch	W	27	21	
Queensland	1989	Brisbane	L	6	16	
Queensland	1990	Christchurch	L	16	31	
Queensland	1991	Christchurch	W	20	16	
Queensland	1991	Brisbane	L	24	48	
Queensland	1992	Brisbane	L	12	32	
Queensland	1992	Christchurch	L	10	26	
Queensland	1993	Brisbane	W	29	23	
Queensland	1994	Christchurch	W	18	16	
Queensland	1995	Brisbane	L	6	24	
Queensland B	1981	Maroochydore	L	12	17	
Sydney	1981	Sydney	W	25	17	
Ireland	1992	Christchurch	W	38	13	
W. Province	1993	Christchurch	W	54	31	

Versus	Date	Location	Result	Score For	Score Against	Ranfurly Shield (•)
Eastern Prov.	1994	Christchurch	W	30	11	
Orange F.S.	1995	Christchurch	L	35	42	
Russia	1991	Christchurch	W	73	15	
Argentina	1989	Christchurch	W	33	16	
Buenos Aires	1996	Buenos Aires	L	25	36	
Cordoba	1996	Cordoba	W	47	22	
Salta	1996	Salta	W	41	17	
Tucuman	1996	Tucuman	W	36	16	
Bridgend	1994	Bridgend	W	54	13	
Bedford	1994	Bedford	W	32	14	
Cornwell	1994	Camborne	W	67	5	
West Hartlepool	1994	W. Hartlepool	W	56	5	
Moseley	1994	W. Hartlepool	W	39	0	
Coventry	1994	Coundon Rd	W	53	13	
Gloucester	1994	Gloucester	W	70	7	
Bristol	1994	Bristol	W	27	16	
Treorchy	1994	Treorchy	W	44	20	

APPENDIX B

CRUSADERS

Versus	Date	Location	Result	Score For	Score Against
Waikato Chiefs	1996	Hamilton	L	26	27
Waikato Chiefs	1997	Timaru	W	24	15
Waikato Chiefs	1998	Albany	L	23	25
Waikato Chiefs	1999	Christchurch	W	48	3
Waikato Chiefs	2000	Hamilton	W	27	24
Waikato Chiefs	2001	Christchurch	W	40	11
Waikato Chiefs	2002	Hamilton	W	34	27
Waikato Chiefs	2003	Christchurch	W	36	29
Auckland Blues	1996	Christchurch	L	18	49
Auckland Blues	1997	Pukekohe	L	28	29
Auckland Blues	1998	Christchurch	L	24	31
Auckland Blues	1998	Auckland	W	20	12
Auckland Blues	1999	Auckland	W	22	16
Auckland Blues	2000	Christchurch	W	32	20
Auckland Blues	2001	Auckland	L	12	17
Auckland Blues	2002	Christchurch	W	30	11
Auckland Blues	2003	Albany	L	5	39
Auckland Blues	2003	Auckland	L	17	21
Queensland Reds	1996	Christchurch	L	16	52

Versus	Date	Location	Result	Score For	Score Against
Queensland Reds	1997	Christchurch	W	48	3
Queensland Reds	1998	Ballymore	L	9	35
Queensland Reds	1999	Christchurch	L	23	36
Queensland Reds	1999	Brisbane	W	28	22
Queensland Reds	2000	Brisbane	W	27	19
Queensland Reds	2001	Christchurch	W	32	26
Queensland Reds	2002	Brisbane	W	34	27
Queensland Reds	2003	Christchurch	W	34	6
West Province Stormers	1996	Christchurch	D	16	16
West Province Stormers	1998	Christchurch	W	37	25
West Province Stormers	1999	Capetown	L	19	28
West Province Stormers	2000	Nelson	W	47	31
West Province Stormers	2001	Capetown	L	28	42
West Province Stormers	2002	Christchurch	W	41	21
West Province Stormers	2003	Newlands	W	51	13
New South Wales Waratahs	1996	Christchurch	W	21	16
New South Wales Waratahs	1997	Sydney	L	8	25
New South Wales Waratahs	1998	Christchurch	W	33	12
New South Wales Waratahs	1999	Sydney	W	38	22
New South Wales Waratahs	2000	Christchurch	W	22	13
New South Wales Waratahs	2001	Sydney	L	22	25
New South Wales Waratahs	2002	Christchurch	W	96	19
New South Wales Waratahs	2003	Sydney	L	31	34
Nth Transvaal Bulls	1996	Christchurch	L	18	34
Nth Transvaal Bulls	1997	Pretoria	L	22	23
Nth Transvaal Bulls	1998	Christchurch	W	31	20
Nth Transvaal Bulls	1999	Pretoria	W	30	28
Nth Transvaal Bulls	2000	Christchurch	W	75	27
Nth Transvaal Bulls	2001	Pretoria	W	42	29
Nth Transvaal Bulls	2002	Christchurch	W	49	15

Nth Transvaal Bulls	2003	Pretoria	L	31	32
A.C.T. Brumbies	1996	Christchurch	L	7	29
A.C.T. Brumbies	1997	Canberra	L	29	49
A.C.T. Brumbies	1998	Timaru	W	38	26
A.C.T. Brumbies	1999	Canberra	W	28	21
A.C.T. Brumbies	2000	Christchurch	L	12	17
A.C.T. Brumbies	2000	Canberra	W	20	19
A.C.T. Brumbies	2001	Canberra	L	16	51
A.C.T. Brumbies	2002	Christchurch	W	33	32
A.C.T. Brumbies	2002	Christchurch	W	31	13
A.C.T. Brumbies	2003	Canberra	W	28	21
Wellington Hurricanes	1996	New Plymouth	W	36	13
Wellington Hurricanes	1997	Christchurch	W	19	17
Wellington Hurricanes	1998	Napier	W	39	17
Wellington Hurricanes	1999	Christchurch	D	18	18
Wellington Hurricanes	2000	Wellington	L	22	28
Wellington Hurricanes	2001	Christchurch	L	29	41
Wellington Hurricanes	2002	Wellington	W	48	20
Wellington Hurricanes	2003	Christchurch	W	37	12
Wellington Hurricanes	2003	Christchurch	W	39	16
Transvaal	1996	Johannesberg	L	23	55
Gauteng Lions	1997	Christchurch	W	23	0
Golden Cats	1998	Bloemfontein	W	34	25
Cats	1999	Nelson	W	58	38
Cats	2000	Johannesberg	L	31	54
Cats	2001	Nelson	L	31	32
Cats	2002	Johannesberg	W	37	30
Cats	2003	Christchurch	W	65	34
Natal Sharks	1996	Durban	L	26	58
Natal Sharks	1997	Christchurch	D	26	26
Natal Sharks	1998	Durban	W	32	20

Versus	Date	Location	Result	Score For	Score Against
Natal Sharks	1998	Christchurch	W	36	32
Natal Sharks	1999	Christchurch	W	34	29
Natal Sharks	2000	Durban	W	32	24
Natal Sharks	2001	Christchurch	W	34	22
Natal Sharks	2002	Durban	W	37	34
Natal Sharks	2003	Christchurch	W	23	18
Otago Highlanders	1996	Christchurch	L	27	29
Otago Highlanders	1997	Dunedin	L	29	39
Otago Highlanders	1998	Christchurch	W	40	24
Otago Highlanders	1999	Dunedin	L	6	23
Otago Highlanders	1999	Dunedin	W	24	19
Otago Highlanders	2000	Christchurch	W	42	36
Otago Highlanders	2000	Christchurch	W	37	15
Otago Highlanders	2001	Dunedin	L	21	26
Otago Highlanders	2002	Christchurch	W	30	28
Otago Highlanders	2002	Christchurch	W	34	23
Otago Highlanders	2003	Dunedin	W	17	16
Free State Cheetahs	1997	Bloemfontein	W	16	11

INDEX

THE PASSION

THE STORIES BEHIND
125 YEARS OF CANTERBURY RUGBY